Cambridge Medieval Textbooks

MEDIEVAL WALES

Cambridge Medieval Textbooks

This is a series of specially commissioned textbooks for teachers and students, designed to complement the monograph series Cambridge Studies in Medieval Life and Thought by providing introductions to a range of topics in medieval history. This series combines both chronological and thematic approaches, and will deal with British and European topics. All volumes in the series will be published in hard covers and in paperback.

For a list of titles in the series, see end of book.

MEDIEVAL WALES

DAVID WALKER

Formerly Senior Lecturer in Medieval History,
University College, Swansea

CAMBRIDGE
UNIVERSITY PRESS

Published by the Press Syndicate of the University of Cambridge
The Pitt Building, Trumpington Street, Cambridge CB2 1RP
40 West 20th Street, New York, NY 10011–4211, USA
10 Stamford Road, Oakleigh, Melbourne 3166, Australia

First published 1990
Reprinted 1991, 1994

Printed in Great Britain by Athenaeum Press Limited,
Newcastle upon Tyne

British Library cataloguing in publication data
Walker, David
Medieval Wales – (Cambridge medieval textbooks)
1. Wales, history
I. Title
942.9

Library of Congress cataloguing in publication data
Walker, David, 1923–
Medieval Wales/David Walker.
p.   cm. – (Cambridge medieval textbooks)
Includes bibliographical references.
ISBN 0-521-32317-7 – ISBN 0-521-31153 5 (pbk)
1. Wales – History – To 1536. I. Title. II. Series.
DA715.W25 1990
942 – dc20   89-37174
CIP

ISBN 0 521 32317 7 hardback
ISBN 0 521 31153 5 paperback

CONTENTS

FIGURES

MAPS

vii

PREFACE

For many years my concern has been with the history of the border shires and the Welsh marches, and more remotely with their Welsh neighbours. In this book I have tried to provide an introduction to Welsh medieval history which, I hope, may tempt readers to a closer study of a people and an area too often written off as matters of marginal interest. It is true that people turn away from Welsh history because of the unfamiliar personal names and place-names, though they are no more difficult than the German and middle-European names which any serious medieval historian can take for granted. With rare exceptions, I have used Welsh forms of personal names. With place-names I have adopted a familiar compromise, using anglicised forms for many names, especially for such places as Cardiff, Carmarthen and Llandovery, and using some Welsh forms, now in common use, for such places as Conwy, Caernarfon and Cricieth.

I have concentrated on political developments, on the interplay of personal and political ambitions, and on the clash of race and culture which is so characteristic of Wales. The survival of independent princely power in Gwynedd and its eventual overthrow give the thirteenth century a place of special importance, and the war with Edward I and the settlement which followed in 1284 demand close attention. So, too, do the attempts of isolated Welsh leaders to reverse the harsh decisions of the 1280s. By contrast, the decline of Wales in the fifteenth century has been given less prominence. I have not ventured into the field of Welsh literary culture where the first-hand guidance of Welsh scholars is essential, nor into the field of the Welsh economy where the skills of the linguist and the anthropologist are both needed in equal measure.

I have incurred many debts. I owe much to discussion over the years with my friends and colleagues at the University College of Swansea and elsewhere in the University of Wales, with Celtic scholars at the University of Cambridge and with regular habitués of the Battle conferences on Anglo-Norman studies. To Professor Glanmor Williams and Professor R. R. Davies, I am grateful for reading this book in typescript and for saving me from a number of errors. The maps, based on the work of William Rees, were produced by Guy Lewis, senior cartographer in the Department of Geography at the University College of Swansea. The staff of Cambridge University Press have been very helpful. In terms of discussion and practical assistance, I owe a great debt to my wife, Margaret, and my last and greatest word of thanks must be to her.

David Walker

I

WALES IN THE DARK AGES

The transition from Roman Wales to medieval Wales shows some remarkable elements of continuity. Tribal chiefs, familiar to Roman military commanders, were the precursors of Welsh kings and princes, many of whom displayed the same qualities of courage and ruthlessness. The great estates of the Roman period are clearly to be discerned in the agrarian organisation of Wales in the dark ages, with their heavy dependence upon bondmen, slave labour and even with a physical structure not unlike the great *latifundia* of the empire. Historians concentrating on the period from the sixth century to the eleventh century have shown a curious lack of confidence in recent decades: they can explore technical problems to great advantage, but they are generally less willing to venture on a broad survey. In the universities of Wales, and notably of Cambridge, linguistic and literary studies are producing valuable reassessments of early sources and are achieving a sustained attack on critical problems. Perhaps because of the uncertainties which these studies have made apparent, and perhaps because this process of re-exploration is still far from complete, it is much more difficult to produce a detailed and authoritative survey of early medieval Welsh history. The broad sweep which Sir John Lloyd produced in 1911, a study which has been reissued four times in the last eighty years, is probably still the most widely read and influential book on the early history of Wales. Wendy Davies, writing in 1982, began her survey of early medieval Wales with the uncompromising claim: 'It is not possible to write a history of early Medieval Wales that will stand up to the requirements of modern scholarship.' With the tenth and eleventh centuries, greater assurance is possible, and from about 1100 a general survey can be written without frequent qualification and without the mental reservations which inadequate source materials inevitably impose upon a scholar.

Yet, without at least a framework of what happened in the dark ages, the course of Welsh history from about 1000 to about 1500 may not be intelligible. Three questions, in particular, need to be asked, and some attempt at reasonable answers, however brief, is essential. The first concerns kings and kingship. The second concerns the church. The third concerns the interaction between Welsh and English through the centuries.

Wales, like England in the dark ages, was a land of multiple kingship. The rugged terrain, with impenetrable mountain massifs and inhospitable upland ranges, broken by river valleys, did not make for a unified control or a unified development. The boundary with England was not marked by natural defences, and productive lowland areas as well as profitable upland pastures were open to frequent attacks. Not until Offa of Mercia built his dyke in the second half of the eighth century was there a linear frontier, and then that was designed to deter Welsh attacks and to control trade across the frontier. Small local communities acknowledged a ruler whose principal function might seem at times to wage war on his neighbours and to plunder their lands. In general, war made them defensive. The Welsh were the remnants of the British population which had been conquered by the Romans and, after their departure, by Germanic peoples emigrating from northern Europe into Britain. Anglo-Saxon codes of law and place-names suggest the survival of 'British' or 'Welsh' communities in the English kingdoms. Those who remained free from English control did so by seeking refuge in the west and finding it in Wales; by maintaining constant vigil against English encroachments, they defended a distinctive language and culture. The racial antipathy between English and Welsh goes far back into the past.

The principal divisions of Wales were the four major kingdoms, or principalities. Gwynedd was based on the Snowdonia massif and on Anglesey. Powys stretched from the borders of Mercia into central Wales. Dyfed, in the south-west, has been thought to represent the survival of very early traditions, some pre-Roman, some linked with the settlement of those who spoke the Goedelic form of Celtic. Deheubarth was a general name for the whole of south Wales, but in later centuries, certainly by the eleventh century, it was a recognisable kingdom extending from Ceredigion on the west coast to Brycheiniog on the English border. As Dyfed declined, so Deheubarth absorbed parts of south-west Wales. In the eleventh and twelfth centuries, under pressure of Norman attacks and settlement, that part of Deheubarth which remained independent grew smaller; the name implies a different range of territory in different periods.

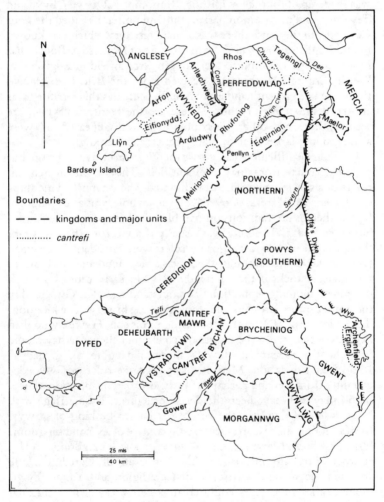

Map 1   The main divisions of Wales

Medieval Wales

An early kingdom of Glywysing broke up into smaller units, the kingdom of Morgannwg, the *cantref* of Gwynllŵg, and the divisions of Gwent Uwchcoed (Upper Gwent) and Gwent Iscoed (Nether Gwent). Brycheiniog was an independent kingdom during the dark ages, though it came within the orbit of the later kingdom of Deheubarth. Two areas were disputed territory. In the north there was the land known as the Perfeddwlad, or the Middle Country, which was considered as the land between Gwynedd and Powys. It was made up of four *cantrefi*, Rhos, Rhufoniog, Dyffryn Clwyd and Tegeingl, and in common parlance it could often be called the Four Cantreds. In the south there was a small territory which was known in Old English as *Ircingafeld*; from the time of Domesday Book it has produced forms leading to the modern Archenfield in English – in Welsh, Erging. All these are derived from the British *Ariconium*. From the late eleventh and early twelfth centuries this territory was absorbed into Herefordshire. These are the territories which are secure; there are other kingdoms which disappeared or were absorbed into larger units, notably Buellt and Ceredigion.

It would be difficult to categorise the Welsh princes as a group, but certain characteristics may be identified. They were, in general, rulers of a single kingdom. An individual who established his authority over several areas, or over Wales as a whole, was an exceptional figure: there is no tradition comparable with Irish *ruiri* or the Anglo-Saxon *bretwalda*. The king was usually drawn from the royal kin, though some of the most vigorous rulers were intruders. Even when these are taken into account, there was a clear tendency to return to the ancient stock of the ruling dynasty. In early centuries much depended upon the reputation of an outstanding ruler. Gwynedd in the ninth century presents an interesting case history. The kingdom descended through Rhodri Molwynog to his son, Hywel, who died in 825. Gwriad, said to be a northern chieftain, believed to have come from Scotland, married Hywel's niece, a daughter of Cynan ap Rhodri, and their son, Merfyn Frych, became ruler of Gwynedd, certainly from 825 and perhaps as early as 816. The injection of new blood may well have been the decisive element. By marriage with Nest, sister of Cyngen, the last of his line to be king of Powys, Merfyn found the opportunity to gain control of a second kingdom. His son, Rhodri Mawr (the Great), inherited both kingdoms, and by another fortunate marriage with Angharad of Ceredigion, he acquired the western territories of Ceredigion and Ystrad Tywi. None of these marriages could create a hereditary claim, and each was probably valuable because it established the conditions in which a successful bid for power could be made. Until his death in 878, Rhodri was acknowledged as ruler of more than half of Wales, and that more by diplomacy than by conquest. In his last years his power was challenged: in 877 Viking attacks made it necessary for him to seek refuge in Ireland, and a year later he was killed fighting a Saxon force. Scandinavian attacks and influence would remain a feature of Welsh history until the eleventh century; generally they were a scourge – the 'black gentiles' of the *Annales Cambriae*, a compilation of the earliest Welsh historical annals – but at times they could be allies. They gave their names to a number of places along the Welsh coasts and must have settled in some places long enough for them and their place-names to be taken for granted. Under Rhodri and his successors, a dynasty of kings of more than average distinction brought a semblance of unity to Wales and contributed a great deal to the historical traditions which would mould the Wales of a distant future.

For four generations Gwynedd remained with Rhodri and his direct heirs. His son, Anarawd, was succeeded by his son, Idwal Foel, and grandson, Iago, who was followed by his nephew, Hywel ab Idwal. When Hywel died in 985, he was succeeded by his brother, Cadwallon. From that point there is apparent confusion, but it

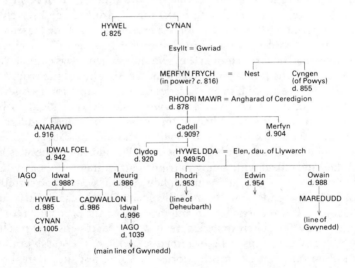

Figure 1 The ruling dynasty of Gwynedd from the ninth to the early eleventh centuries
Note: kings of Gwynedd are indicated in capitals.

seems that direct succession had given way to a more complex pattern, known technically as segmentation, in which cousins claimed the right to inherit as alternate branches of the family assumed power in succeeding generations. Something of the same pattern may be discerned in the southern territory of Glywysing. The greater the number of those who could claim an interest in the succession, the greater the fear of violence as a means of clearing the way and settling problems of power. Early entries in the Welsh *Annales* are brief in the extreme, but there are hints of ugly deeds. In 814, Griffri ap Cyngen was slain by the treachery of his brother; in 904, Merfyn ap Rhodri of Gwynedd was killed by his own men; in 969, Ieuaf ab Idwal of Gwynedd was seized by his brother Iago, and imprisoned; in 974, Meurig ab Idwal was blinded. These are pointers to what was happening and to what would happen in the future. Rivals were eliminated: they were to be blinded, so that they could not be effective leaders in peace or commanders in war; they were castrated so that they could not sire rival candidates for power. As the sources become more informative, so the number of recorded acts of violence increases. It looks as if the first half of the twelfth century saw this violence reach its peak, but by then it was an established part of Welsh life. Walter Map, a man of the marches, wrote a satirical book, his *Courtiers' Trifles*, for the amusement of Henry II and his court, and, seeking to make fun of Gruffydd ap Llywelyn (the outstanding Welsh ruler of the eleventh century), he presented a picture of violence and a justification for it. One of Llywelyn's nephews had fled from him in fear, and later, when it was completely safe, he met the prince who asked him why he should run from his court, and promised him any sureties he might name for his safety. 'Then', said the boy, 'I name Hywel, whom you caused to be smothered in secret when he was on a mission for you; Rhydderch, whom you left-handedly received with a kiss and embrace and killed with a knife in your left hand; Tewdws (Theodosius], whom as he walked and talked with you, you tripped up with your foot and cast down the sheer rocks; and your nephew Meilin, whom you secretly captured by guile and let him die loaded with chains in your dungeon.' It was stirring stuff, and there may have been much truth in the story. The interesting feature of Walter Map's gossip is that he preserves what seems to be an authentic saying of the Welsh prince: 'I kill no one, but I blunt the horns of Wales, lest they hurt their mother.' When it came to blood-letting, Gruffydd ap Llywelyn was not alone. Perhaps Gerald of Wales had the answer. The habit in his day, he wrote, was to put sons out to fosterage, and the boys grew up with strong ties of affection and loyalty to their foster-father and his sons. They had little contact with or affection for their siblings. It was an ancient practice.

It is unavoidable that for medieval chroniclers and modern historians interest should centre on those rulers who extended their power over much of Wales. They foreshadowed the attempts by the princes of Gwynedd in the thirteenth century to create a unified Welsh 'state', and they matched contemporary developments in England, and similar but later developments in Scotland. So, Rhodri Mawr (844–78) is presented as one who set a pattern for the future. He either ruled or, by his personal qualities, dominated much of Wales. His grandson, Hywel Dda (*c.* 909–49/50), had the good fortune to be ruler of three principalities with all the wider influence which that could give him. In the eleventh century, Gruffydd ap Llywelyn (1039–63) battled his way to a position of supremacy in Wales. Historians search for 'national' heroes. In the dark ages, Wales produced only heroes of Gwynedd, or Dyfed, of Deheubarth or Morgannwg.

The codification of Welsh law has been traditionally associated with Hywel Dda (the Good), who shared with his brother lands in Ceredigion and Ystrad Tywi after the death of their father, Cadell, about 909. He united their inheritance in 920, and acquired Gwynedd after the death of Idwal Foel in 942. He married Elen, daughter of Llywarch of Dyfed, and on Llywarch's death in 904 he took over the southern kingdom. In the perspective of the dark ages he was a powerful prince, and it may be that later generations borrowed his personal authority to buttress their own power. The law was Hywel's law, *cyfraith Hywel*; his name gave to the law an authority comparable with that given to the laws of Mercia by King Offa or the laws of Wessex (and a larger area of England) by King Alfred. From the twelfth century there seems to have been a cult of Hywel Dda, and increasingly Welsh medieval historians are moving to the view that he was regarded as a valuable focus for the reform and reorganisation of Welsh customary law, even though the period of active reform was probably the twelfth century.

The major problem is that, rich though the resources of the thirteenth century are, there is no pattern of development in Welsh law comparable to that which can be discerned in Anglo-Saxon law from the earliest codes of Wessex in the seventh century to the extensive code of Cnut in the eleventh century. A small number of later rulers were said to have added to or amended the laws of Hywel. Bleddyn ap Cynfyn, ruler of Gwynedd (1063–75), was said to have amended the laws of his kingdom. Rhys ap Gruffydd of Deheubarth (1155–97) was credited with amending the law relating to property, and Dafydd ap Llywelyn of Gwynedd (1240–6) was said to have abolished the payment of *galanas*, that is blood-price or compensation for homicide. It is now believed that there was in circulation in the twelfth century a series of short tractates on law which may have been codified before 1197, and that these lie behind the major codifications of the thirteenth century. But it is also clear that customary law had been in the making for some centuries, and that it was administered and transmitted by practitioners who had used and respected a long oral tradition. It should be regarded as the product of a semi-professional group of lawmen: to see it as the work of any one legislator or ruler might be misleading. To ascribe the early codification to Hywel Dda had, and retains, considerable merit. He was a contemporary of Edward the Elder and Athelstan in England at a time when the extension of codified law was recognised as part of the function of kingship. He had the opportunity, rare before the eleventh century, to control Gwynedd (and, by assumption, Powys), the border territory of Ceredigion, and the kingdom of Dyfed. If it were possible to disentangle thirteenth-century practice from the custom and practice of earlier centuries, the links between the surviving codes of law and the distant past might be clarified. Hywel Dda's name added a venerable quality to medieval Welsh law. His contribution to the process of codification still eludes definition.

The roots of Christianity in Wales are to be found in Roman times, but the epoch which has marked the physical pattern and the emotional colouring of the church in Wales was the age of the saints. Missionaries, working in a hostile environment in the sixth and seventh centuries, sought to convert local chieftains to Christianity. Part of their strength lay in the rigours of self-discipline under which they lived, part lay in their undoubted courage, and part, perhaps much, lay in the devoted groups of disciples whom they inspired. Their cults attest to the range of country within which they and their followers worked. The pattern demonstrated in the range of ancient dedications is essentially one of local activity and local influence. In north Wales the cult of St Beuno was centred on Clynnog Fawr and spread widely along the northern coastal lands and into Anglesey; he, or those who owed much to his teachings, took the faith to Deeside and to isolated pockets in eastern Wales. Deiniol, for whose cult the evidence is more limited, was associated with important monastic churches at Bangor-in-Arfon and at Bangor-on-Dee (Bangor-is-coed), south-east of Wrexham, with its chapels at Marchwiel and Worthenbury. In the eastern parts of Powys the dominant cult was that of St Tysilio whose principal church was Meifod. In mid-Wales the cult of St Padarn spread from his church at Llanbadarn Fawr eastwards into Brycheiniog. South Wales demonstrates the extent to which cults could be intermingled. St Dyfrig's base was at Hentland, near Ross-on-Wye, and almost all the early Dyfrig dedications occur in a narrow and limited area of local settlement. St Illtud was associated especially with Llanilltud Fawr – the modern form is Llantwit Major – in another heavily Romanised area, southern Glamorgan. Dedications to St Illtud, and to St Cadog of Llancarfan, follow the network of Roman roads and Roman sites. Further west, the cult of St Teilo spread from his church of Llandeilo Fawr. But in south Wales the remarkable feature is the number of ancient dedications to St David – Dewi Sant – spreading from St David's itself. That suggests his own pre-eminence, and it points clearly to the devotion which his successors had for his memory.

These missionaries proved the value of a community living under discipline. Much of the material bearing upon them was produced in the eleventh and twelfth centuries. The *Life* of St Cadog written by Lifris probably between 1070 and 1090 (and certainly before 1104), and the *Life* of St David written by Rhigyfarch about 1095, may contain memories and traditions preserved in their communities, but it is widely recognised that the monastic style of life which they describe and the virtues they admire reflect conditions in the writers' own day rather than in the age of the saints. Occasionally it is possible to go behind the evidence of the *Vitae* to earlier material. The *Life* of St Samson of Dol, which was probably written early in the seventh century, has much to say about Wales; St Dyfrig, St Illtud and the community at Llantwit Major all feature in the narrative. St David was named in an Irish martyrology produced about 800, and in a list of saints, again from Ireland, drawn up in the ninth or tenth centuries. In the *Life* of the Breton saint, Paul of Léon, written in 884, David was described as *aquaticus*, the waterman, the first indication of the asceticism which marked his life. Early in the tenth century, Asser mentioned the monastery and church of Dewi Sant, and in the tenth century the saint figured in an early prophetic poem, *Armes Prydein*, the *Prophecy of Britain*. At the very least, there is some justification for assuming that memories of St David's life survived, but not until the 1090s was anything of substance preserved in the written record.

To limit the discussion to the leading cults would be to over-simplify. There are churches dedicated to figures from the distant past, some historical, some legendary. Gwynedd place-names and dedications reflect the descendants of Cunedda, the early folk hero of north Wales, whose standing as a historical figure is a matter of controversy; to cite only two examples, Meirion links with Meirionydd, and with Llanfeirian; Edern with Edeirnion and the churches of Edern and Bodedern. All but one of Cunedda's eight sons were claimed as saints; at a much later date a ninth son was added to the family tree, presumably to meet current political needs, and it is difficult to determine how far the presence of the other names in the family tree is the product of imagination or wishful thinking. In the southern half of Wales, the Brychan whose name is preserved in, or derived from, Brycheiniog was placed in a dynasty which produced many saints. They form an interesting group, for they represent Irish settlers in Brycheiniog in the fifth century who, over two or three generations, were much concerned with the spread of Christianity in parts of south and mid-Wales. Firm claims about any single individual in the dynasty would be hard to establish, but that the family represents a genuine movement of settlement and missionary activity can scarcely be doubted. Irish Christians travelling into Wales left their mark on the church, introducing their own cults. St Ffraid, of Welsh place-names and dedications, is the Irish saint, Brigid, whose cult became very popular in Wales. The familiar Welsh name, Madog, conceals Mo-aid-og, one form of the name of the Irish saint, Aidan of Ferns. St Illtud's church seems at first sight to be divorced from the place-name *Llantwyt*, but the church was given the Goedelic (Irish) form of his name, *Llaniltwyt*, and the connection between the saint and the settlement is obvious.

One cult which demonstrates the nature of the problems to be solved is that of the Scottish missionary, Kentigern (Cyndeyrn), who died in 612. His cult was actively fostered in the twelfth century when two *Lives* were written, one of them by Jocelyn of Furness. Kentigern was said to have been driven from Strathclyde and to have found refuge in north Wales where he founded the church and bishopric of Llanelwy. When he returned to Scotland he was succeeded by Asa (Asaph), who gives the modern place-name. Later, Kentigern was active in north-east Scotland where early dedications point to foundations made by, or in honour of, him and his companions, and among them are dedications to St Nidan and St Ffinan. All this could be legend, rather than fact. Kentigern's name is associated with the medieval churches dedicated to St Asaph, but no ancient dedication has been claimed for him. On the other hand, two churches in Anglesey, lying close together, are dedicated to St Nidan and St Ffinan, while Asaph was honoured not only at the cathedral which bears his name but at Llanasa and at a holy well in the area. So much for orthodoxy, depending heavily on twelfth-century material. The early genealogies identify Nidan and Asaph as men who, like Kentigern, come from the north; Ffinan may possibly be Irish or of local provenance. There is a case to argue that the cult of Kentigern was brought to Llanelwy much later, between 872 and 878, by immigrants from Strathclyde, and if that should be the explanation of his cult, the traditional reconstruction of the foundation of the church at Llanelwy is thrown open to question.

Sadly, the Welsh church developed in isolation. In 597 St Augustine and his companions arrived in Kent and began the conversion of the southern English. He was anxious to contact Christians in Wales, even though it meant entering a war-zone. Their discussions were hampered by suspicion; Augustine was not yet sufficiently secure to yield precedence or courtesy. The critical battle between continental and Celtic Christianity took place in Northumbria in 663 when the synod of Whitby recorded a victory for Roman ways. It is a mark of Welsh conservatism, and hostility to the English, that they delayed their decision for more than a century. The Irish church accepted the decision in 703; Iona, the centre of Celtic Christianity in the north, accepted it as inevitable in 716. The Welsh Christians waited until 768 before they finally gave way.

In a more settled age, after the missionary work had borne fruit, Christian life in Wales was organised largely through the *clas* church. The *clas* was a community made up of *claswyr* who shared the responsibility for worship and pastoral work. They also shared part of the economic benefits accruing to the church. Marriage was accepted as a norm, and a member of the *clas* could pass on to an heir his share of the church and its revenues. Llanbadarn Fawr and Llancarfan were essentially family churches with a clear succession, while St David's retained this quality long after it had been transformed into a cathedral chapter. The standing of these greater Welsh churches was defined in early Welsh law. The head of the community was an abbot, but his community was made up of seculars (*canonwyr*). They had the ultimate power of deciding any disputes arising within the community. In function the *clas* was a mother church and could have a number of subsidiary chapels attached to it. In some cases the area for which a particular *clas* church was responsible could be identified easily. Many were associated with a single

commote: Aberdaron with Cymydmaen, Clynnog Fawr with
Uwchgwyrfai, Llangollen with Nanheudwy, and Bangor-on-Dee
and its chapels with the northern commotes of Maelor. Some were
linked with the larger unit of a *cantref*: Llanbadarn Fawr with
Penweddig, Towyn with Meirionydd. Meifod, with its dependent
chapels, covered a wide range of southern Powys. Elsewhere there
must be some doubt as to what territory the *clas* church might cover.
Was there a clean division between Llangyfelach, in the northern
section of the commote of Gower, and Bishopston (Llandeilofer-
wallt) in the south? How was influence in Rhos shared between
Abergele and Llanelwy (St Asaph)?

There were obvious factors which marked out a small number of
these churches. Llangadwaladr, in Anglesey, was built close to the
llys, the court of the prince of Gwynedd at Aberffraw; its foundation
is attributed to Cadwaladr ap Cadwallon, who died in 664 and whose
name the church bears. Meifod, with its impressive *llan*, was the
burial place of rulers of Powys Fadog in the twelfth century, a late
survival of its long-standing importance. Its decline can be linked
with the foundation of the Cistercian houses of Strata Marcella in
1170 and its daughter house at Valle Crucis in 1201. Bangor-in-
Arfon became the cathedral church of the diocese covering
Gwynedd, as St David's became the cathedral for the diocese covering south-west Wales. Llanbadarn Fawr and Llandeilo Fawr were
both claimed as centres from which a bishop exercised his authority.
So, too, was Llanelwy (St Asaph), though the continuous history of
a bishopric there belongs to the twelfth century. All this derives from
the fact that in a small number of major churches, the head of the
community was a bishop-abbot. There was also a persisting tradition that the sphere of episcopal authority and the area of territorial
princely power should remain closely linked.

With the exception of St David's and Llandaff there is remarkably
little evidence for the early history of the Welsh dioceses. Historical
annals produced at St David's in the middle of the tenth century
include references to the foundations of Bangor and St Asaph, and by
doing so imply that both bishoprics existed and were recognised
c. 955. For Bangor, knowledge of the foundation of the church by St
Deiniol was supplemented by references to the death in 809 of
Elfodd, archbishop of Gwynedd, who is assumed to have worked
from Bangor, and of Morlais, bishop of Bangor in 944. These references may be extended by claims voiced by the canons of St David's
at a much later date that Joseph, bishop of St David's, had consecrated Morlais and his successor, Duvan, as bishops of Bangor, and

that Bishop Sulien had consecrated Revedun for that see. With such rare exceptions, the names of the bishops of Bangor before 1092 have not survived, but there is nothing to suggest that the appointment of Hervé to Bangor in 1092 represented a revival of the diocese; it looks much more like a normal vacancy and appointment in a long sequence of episcopal succession. For St Asaph, the record is much slighter: it was said that Bleuddydd, bishop of St David's, had consecrated a certain Melanus for St Asaph before 1073, and there are one or two further names which might possibly be associated with the diocese in earlier years. There is a clear statement that in the mid-1120s a bishopric existed between the dioceses of Chester and Bangor, but that there was no bishop there at that stage. The first appointment made under Norman influence was that of Bishop Richard in 1143.

At St David's enough material survived in the later twelfth century for Gerald of Wales to draw up a list of forty-four bishops, first of the diocese of Mynyw and then, after the cult of St David had developed, of St David's. The earliest record in local annals is the death of Bishop Sadynfyw in 831, and there are references to the accession or death of six bishops between 840 and 999. Then, scattered references give way to more regular, though not complete, notices of the bishops. On the eve of the Norman incursions into south Wales, Bleuddydd was appointed as bishop of St David's, to be succeeded by Sulien, himself a scholarly figure and the father of scholars, who held the see from 1073 to 1078 and again from 1080 to 1085. It may be that he was too gentle a man for the hard conditions of his day. Even so, the influence which he and his sons, Rhigyfarch, Arthen, Daniel and John, exercised in Wales in the last decades of the eleventh century is, to say the least, quite remarkable. They sustained traditions of Welsh culture and memories of the Welsh past at a critical time and ensured that both would have an influence on the development of the diocese during the twelfth century. For his contemporaries in England, Sulien was a 'married' bishop with a family, an example of the type of churchman much out of favour with the reformers of the eleventh century, but to dismiss him in those terms was, and is, to understate his significance in the story of the Welsh church. Sulien's successor was Wilfrid, who was consecrated in 1085 and who ruled the diocese until 1115. They were difficult and momentous years, for he had to face the full force of Norman incursions, to work amicably with the invaders and with the civil and ecclesiastical authorities in England, while his sympathies were manifestly with the Welsh leaders fighting to resist the Norman advance. A change of bishop during these critical years might have been the cause of great weakness for the diocese, but St David's was able to reap the benefit of his long episcopate. The speed with which his successor, Bishop Bernard, was able to launch into constructive work, owes a considerable debt to the stability which Wilfrid had managed to maintain.

The diocese in south-east Wales is the most richly documented, but it presents difficult problems. In this part of Wales the Welsh church was most open to English influence, and the concept of a territorial diocese was established at a comparatively early date. A succession of bishops followed Dyfrig in Erging in the second half of the sixth century. At the same time, another bishop was working in Gwynllŵg. These two separate areas of episcopal authority were apparently combined early in the seventh century. From about 630 to about 700 the names of the bishops in this area have been lost, but from that time a continuous sequence can be drawn up. Where they worked, and which church they used as a base, remain obscure problems, but until the end of the tenth century it would be quite feasible to suggest the existence of a 'kingdom-bishopric' for Gwynllŵg. The association of Llandaff with this bishopric is a later development; so too, as it seems, was the extension of episcopal authority westwards into Morgannwg. Wendy Davies sees the episcopate of Bishop Joseph (1022–45) as a critical period in the development of this diocese. The whole question is bound up so closely with the policies of Bishop Urban (1107–34) that it ought to be discussed in that context. Joseph's successor was Herewald, consecrated by Joseph, bishop of St David's, in 1056, who held the diocese for half a century. His name suggests English affiliations, and the list of churches which he consecrated shows a heavy concentration in Erging, the most English area under his jurisdiction. At his best, he was an active and forward-looking diocesan. He was served by two archdeacons, one clearly based at Llandaff, the other, named in Domesday Book as a cleric of wealth and influence, had interests in Gwent. Herewald was aware of current development in the European church and was bringing new ideas on episcopal organisation into his Welsh diocese. He faced the first attacks of the Normans in Gwent, and he ensured that churches should be consecrated and endowed within his jurisdiction. When, in the 1090s a second wave of Norman incursions carried the invaders into Morgannwg, the bishop's problems increased, perhaps beyond the point where he could tackle them successfully. He had some twenty years ahead of him still, and the diocese suffered from the fact that his powers were failing. What strength remained was due to the oversight and energy of his archdeacons. His son, Lifris (in its English form, Leofric), served him as archdeacon; so, too, did Urban who was to succeed him as bishop. By the standards of the European church, Herewald was a difficult person to assess; as another married cleric, with a family, he represented an old tradition much disliked by monastic reformers, yet his ideas on diocesan administration were modern rather than archaic.

From an early period the Welsh chieftains had to live with pressure from English neighbours. Until the end of the ninth century, the English, like the Welsh, accepted the fact of multiple kingship, with a number of local, petty kings, one of whom might establish a dominant role. For the most part, the neighbours with whom the Welsh had direct contact were the rulers of the midland kingdom of Mercia. Attacks and plundering raids could be made from both sides of a frontier which was not clearly defined. The *Annales Cambriae* record a battle between Welsh and English near Hereford in 760, and a damaging raid into Dyfed by Offa of Mercia in 778. At some stage after 784 or 785, Offa built the dyke which marked the boundary; it checked Welsh incursions, and it served as a base-line for English attacks on Wales. In 818, King Cenwulf harried Dyfed, and three years later, apparently on another attack, he died at Basingwerk on the coast of north Wales some 15 miles from Chester. Such brief entries suggest an aggressive policy by no means limited to one particular part of Wales, and indicate a degree of mobility which could be dangerous for a number of Welsh kings. Throughout the ninth century, English pressure was sustained: Egbert of Wessex, having taken control of Mercia, raided Welsh territory in 830; so, too, did Aethelwulf in 853. A quarter of a century later, the death of Rhodri Mawr (the Great) in 878 was attributed to English forces, and a few years later Welshmen from Gwynedd sought vengeance for his death. Early in the tenth century the pattern of offence and retribution was reversed. A Mercian abbot was killed by Welshmen and in retaliation in 916, Aethelflaeda, the lady of the Mercians, sent an expedition into Wales which advanced as far as Brycheiniog and captured the wife of the ruling king from his *llys* – his residence – near Llangors lake. Two years later, her brother, Edward the Elder, ransomed Cyfeiliog, bishop in south-east Wales, who had been captured by a Scandinavian force.

Such episodes, minor in themselves, signalled two changes. In the tenth century, the kings of Wessex extended their direct authority over Mercia and the north, and became kings of the English: the old concept of multiple kingship was replaced by the concept of a single kingship for an enlarged kingdom which was united politically, however diverse it remained in racial terms. With this there went an increasing intervention in Welsh affairs, and the gradual recognition of the English king as overlord of Welsh territory. As far back as 878, five Welsh princes, Hyfaidd ap Bleddri of Dyfed, Elise ap Tewdwr of Brycheiniog, Hywel ap Rhys of Glywysing and Brochwel and Ffernfael ap Meurig of Gwynllŵg, had found it useful to seek Alfred's protection. Edward the Elder was acknowledged as overlord in the western half of Wales, and his successor, Athelstan, received a substantial tribute from a number of Welsh princes. Some of them, including Hywel Dda, were honoured guests at his court and attested his charters. For the English king, one obvious advantage was to acquire military reinforcements from Wales. When the English invaded Strathclyde in the 940s they had the support of Welsh forces from Dyfed. The reality of English overlordship was emphasised in the reign of Edgar when six kings submitted to him at Chester in 973 – the rulers of the Scots, the Cumbrians and the islands. In the twelfth century a Worcester chronicler gave the names of three Welsh kings who made up their number, but only one, Iago ab Idwal of Gwynedd, can be identified with any security. Overlordship may have been loosely defined; it was certainly personal rather than constitutional in nature. It would remain a permanent feature of Anglo-Welsh relations from the tenth century until 1282–3.

For Welsh princes along the border, the immediate 'English' problem remained the problem of Mercia, ruled by vigorous earls. In 1012, Eadric Streona was made responsible for the western midlands, and he launched one extensive raid into south Wales. When Leofwine emerged as Cnut's earl in Mercia, he and his family, and especially his brother, Edwin, were engaged in sporadic border conflicts. In 1034 the *Annales* record a battle between the sons of Edwin and the sons of Rhydderch, and the following year it was noted that the English had slain Caradog ap Rhydderch. Behind the local conflicts there lay the full power of the old English state. From the tenth century onwards, and increasingly during the period 1039–66, the issue basic to so much of the history of Wales in the central middle ages was being defined: how could a Welsh ruler handle the problem of a powerful neighbour with rich resources? That would become one major test of the gifts, as well as of the success, of any Welsh prince. Whatever he might achieve at home, always in the background would be that critical question.

These features emerge in sharp focus in the reign of Gruffydd ap Llywelyn (1039–63). He was an unexpected contender for power. By 1039 he was probably established in Powys, and in that year Iago ab Idwal of Gwynedd was murdered by his own men, perhaps with Gruffydd as an accomplice, and he emerged as the claimant for the northern kingdom. He was totally ruthless, his hands stained with the blood of rivals and opponents, but in retrospect his reign was seen as a period of outstanding achievement. For fifteen years he fought a hard struggle to make himself ruler of the southern kingdoms of Wales, but he was thwarted by two determined kings, and not until 1055 could he claim to dominate the whole of Wales. His first target was Deheubarth, and in 1039 he drove Hywel ab Edwin in flight from the kingdom. He underestimated both Hywel's strength and his resilience. Five years were to pass before Hywel was killed and the way appeared to be open for Gruffydd to control the south. Almost at once he found himself checked by the leading prince in south-east Wales, Gruffydd ap Rhydderch, who, like Hywel, displayed surprising strength. He was able to control Deheubarth for a short period and so to prevent the king of Gwynedd from taking that kingdom. Until his death in 1055, Gruffydd ap Rhydderch remained secure. He was an aggressive neighbour, and he explored and exposed the weakness of the English frontier, raiding and plundering, especially in Herefordshire. Early experiments in the use of castles and a cavalry force on the border were one response; Edward the Confessor's nephew, Ralph, was made earl of Hereford, and he used a Norman-type motte and bailey castle as his base. When Gruffydd ap Llywelyn took over south Wales he also assumed a similar aggressive policy. In 1055, Aelfgar, son of the earl of Mercia, was the victim of a political attack, and an attempt was made to have him exiled. He found Gruffydd ap Llywelyn a valuable ally, and supported by a Scandinavian force, he was reinstated. A Welsh attack on Herefordshire and the total defeat of Earl Ralph's forces contributed much to his success. That defeat caused Harold, earl of Wessex, to intervene directly, mustering a large army and arranging a settlement. Harold did not at that stage produce any permanent defence for the frontier; instead a number of different expedients were used over the next few years. A new bishop of Hereford was appointed, Leofgar, one of Harold's priests, a chaplain with a strong taste for military matters. He attempted a surprise attack in Wales which went disastrously wrong, and which Gruffydd ap Llywelyn repulsed, leaving the English army with heavy losses. To re-establish peace on the frontier was no easy task,

and defence was entrusted for the time being to Aldred, bishop of
Worcester, a more diplomatic and less pugnacious churchman. In
1058, the personal conflict between Earl Harold and Aelfgar, who
had by then succeeded as earl of Mercia, was renewed, and the
pattern of 1055 was repeated, but Aelfgar could not be removed
from the scene. Slowly events moved to crisis point. Harold
assumed responsibility for the earldom of Hereford and for the problems of border defence, and by the winter of 1062–3 he was ready to
strike. A swift attack launched in mid-winter was made on Rhuddlan
where Gruffydd had a *llys*, a substantial residence. Surprised by the
land force, he managed to escape by sea. In the summer of 1063 a
second attack was made, with a fleet supporting the army. This time
Gruffydd could not escape by sea, and he had to move into central
Wales, and there he was killed by his enemies. He paid a heavy price
for his alliance with the Mercian dynasty, an alliance which always
promised more for Earl Aelfgar than it could promise for the Welsh
prince.

Gruffydd ap Llywelyn was undoubtedly the outstanding Welsh
ruler of the eleventh century and the most distinguished prince to
emerge since the days of Hywel Dda. After his death the Welsh kingdoms were given to capable but lesser men who could be identified
as client-kings of Edward the Confessor. Under them, Bleddyn in
Gwynedd and Rhiwallon in Powys, the north was quiescent. In the
south there was some readjustment of power. The temporary control which Gruffydd ap Rhydderch had secured over Deheubarth
was broken and the kingdom was restored to its old dynasty with
Hywel ab Edwin's nephew, Maredudd ab Owain ab Edwin, assuming control. In the south-east, Caradog ap Gruffydd ap Rhydderch
was restricted to Gwynllŵg, and his power was further limited by
Earl Harold who carried out a military sweep in the southern parts of
Gwent. Harold had no gift for settlement, but his assessment of the
extent to which he believed Gwent had been subdued is indicated by
the fact that he built a hunting lodge at Portskewett, 3 miles west of
the Wye. Before it could be used, Caradog had destroyed it.

In the perspective of 1063–5, all this should be assessed in terms of
the changes in political balance in Wales, and between England and
Wales. It can be assessed in terms of the political changes which contemporaries could foresee with the death of the ageing King Edward
clearly not far away. It is much more difficult to gauge the interest
which Duke William of Normandy would show in the succession to
the English throne. The defeat and death of Gruffydd ap Llywelyn
were a disaster for Gwynedd and for Wales, and it might be expected

that ten or fifteen years would pass before the damage had been contained, and before the next leading figure among the Welsh princes could be identified. That the Normans would land in England, and that an entirely new factor would be introduced into Welsh history, could not be foreseen; nor could the unhappy fact that the death and eclipse of Gruffydd ap Llywelyn in 1063 had left Wales weak and fragmented only a few years before this new and very dangerous enemy appeared on the scene.

2

THE NORMANS IN WALES

———— • ————

Norman invasion and settlement in Wales added a new and permanent element to the history of Wales. The extent of Norman settlement and influence might vary, but it was never removed, and from the 1060s it affected Welsh society and Welsh politics very profoundly. For different reasons, it has also affected the study of Welsh history. English historical sources are very rich. The records of the central administration, even when they are far from complete, are a major asset. There is a wide range of narrative sources. English and Norman religious houses acquired lands in Wales, and they maintained elaborate archives; although much has been lost, much has survived. As a result, it is possible to get to know the French settlers in Wales in some depth; their interests, their family links, their religious affiliations and benefactions, their impact on the places where they settled and, for later centuries, their business management, can be examined in detail. By contrast, their Welsh contemporaries are less well recorded and seem often to be shadowy figures. It is dangerously easy to see Wales in the eleventh and twelfth centuries through Anglo-Norman eyes, and so to see only a distorted image of Welsh society.

There is another feature which deserves attention. The spread of the Normans and of Norman influence in Europe in the eleventh and twelfth centuries is a major phenomenon. They conquered England; they settled in southern Italy and Sicily, and there they created new political units. From Sicily, they were a commercial and political threat to Byzantium. They were influential in the crusades, and one of the new crusading states in the Holy Land was set up by a Norman leader. In that European setting, what the Normans did in Wales (or in Scotland or Ireland) is part of a large-scale movement, and it can easily be treated as a chapter in the history of Norman expansion, with little regard for Wales itself. The Welsh aspects of the story may be given scant treatment. Much of the history of these Celtic areas has been reassessed and rewritten in the last few decades in an attempt to redress the balance. Without very subtle treatment, the pendulum may swing too far and the balance easily be distorted.

The Norman invasion of England in the autumn of 1066 was fraught with danger for Wales. The English kingdom collapsed and yielded very quickly, and certainly within four years, by 1070, southern and midland England were subdued, and the north was being brought to heel by harsh and brutal methods. William the Conqueror came to England as a rightful claimant to the throne, and in the early years of his reign he was concerned to gain his kingdom and to provide for its defence. That meant, primarily, the defence of the channel coast which he himself had so successfully invaded. At a very early stage he was also concerned for the defence of the border with Wales. The Normans were aware of the recurrent danger which Welsh attacks on England had presented during the Confessor's reign. The Conqueror was also aware of the threat to his own authority posed by an alliance between the princes of north Wales and surviving English magnates in the west midlands. A strong presence along the frontier was an answer to both problems. A third factor may have influenced the king: that William was aware of the key role played by Earl Harold on the Welsh frontier before 1066, and that he was anxious to see that role continued in other hands. By 1067, he had entrusted to his close friend, William fitz Osbern, wide powers along the southernmost stretch of the frontier, with Hereford as the focal point. Fitz Osbern was dead by February 1071, but in that short interval he had introduced major changes.

He had built up a military following which included close relatives, powerful magnates, reliable lieutenants and a strong force of fighting men. His brother-in-law, Ralph de Tosny, was given the castle at Clifford and was active on the frontier. Walter de Lacy, representative of a family which became especially prominent in southern Shropshire, received land from him in Herefordshire and Gloucestershire. Turstin son of Rolf, Hugh the Ass and Gilbert son of Turold were among his tenants; Ralph de Limésy, Ralph de Bernay, and Roger de Pîtres and his brother, Durand, served him as administrators. Roger and Durand came from a Norman estate which William had acquired from the Tosnys when he married into the family; one of his military tenants, Ansfrid de Cormeilles, came from the vill where William founded a monastery. These were not men to remain supine, or to stand on the defensive; nor was William himself. He established castles and garrisons at Monmouth, Clifford, Ewyas Lacy and Wigmore, and refortified Ewyas Harold, at times moving into Welsh territory to find the site for a stronghold. He acquired a string of manors along the west bank of the Severn, from Awre to Tidenham, with the Wye as the western boundary of his Gloucestershire estates. At the mouth of the Wye he established his most splendid castle, Strigoil (Chepstow), planned as a great stone *donjon* with outer defences. It was a forward post, built on the Welsh bank of the Wye, and it rapidly became the springboard for offensive action and the centre of a lordship beyond the English border. From Chepstow the Normans moved westwards, settling the area described in Domesday Book as the castlery of Strigoil. They were working in territory where Earl Harold had once campaigned, but the Gloucestershire Domesday gives no grounds for supposing that it had been exposed to English settlement or exploitation. The western limits of this expansion formed a second castlery, Caerleon, held in 1086 by Turstin son of Rolf, which controlled the southern reaches of the Usk and incorporated land on the western side of that river. In 1086, Chepstow was the focal point of Norman settlement and expansion, and money due from Caerleon was paid at Chepstow.

By that time a number of tenurial changes had taken place. Fitz Osbern's older son took the family's Norman lands while his younger son, Roger de Breteuil, inherited the earldom of Hereford and his English lands, but was not given his father's wide powers. In particular, the sheriffs who had worked under fitz Osbern's control were not answerable to the new earl. Roger put everything in hazard by rebelling against the king in 1075; when that failed he lost his lands and his earldom, his sons were disinherited, and he himself was imprisoned for the rest of his life. The king made fresh arrangements for the southern frontier. Those who had worked with, or served under, Earl William emerged with enhanced responsibilities and standing. Ralph de Tosny and Walter de Lacy were more prominent; Walter had, in fact, played a notable part in defeating the rebellion of 1075. The local administrators were now, unmistakably, royal officers. Those who were the earl's tenants appear in Domesday Book as tenants-in-chief. In Chepstow there was also change and some confusion. Roger d'Ivry, Roger de Lacy and the bishop of

Coutances were prominent magnates holding land in the castlery; Alfred d'Epaignes, Roger de Berkeley, Walter the Crossbowman, Joscelin the Breton and Girard were lesser figures who, at some stage, had acquired lands there. Durand the sheriff was much in evidence, and a number of the king's reeves were mentioned – one, Ouus, by name. Turstin son of Rolf was well established, holding seventeen ploughlands within the castlery; his title to eleven and a half of them was secure, but the king's reeves disputed his right to the remaining five and a half and eventually made good their claim. He also held six ploughlands beyond the Usk. A number of Welsh reeves had control of lands organised by Welsh custom – *maenorau* made up of a number of contributory vills – for which they rendered payments in kind. The principal change which had taken place since 1075 was that William d'Eu had replaced Ralph de Limésy as a major holder in the castlery; but he was much aggrieved that he had gained possession of only thirty-two of the fifty ploughlands which Ralph had once held, and he also wanted a larger share than he had been given of the revenues of Chepstow itself. It was a complex society in which no one had a position of absolute dominance. By chance, Caerleon was included in the Domesday account of Herefordshire, and there Turstin son of Rolf was said to hold that territory of a tenant-in-chief, William d'Ecouis. Conflicting and inconsistent claims are not unusual in Domesday Book, and there need be no surprise that they are to be found in the account of the castleries of Strigoil and Caerleon. They allow different interpretations of the evidence, but the sequence seems to be clear; fitz Osbern's initiative was the key to early settlement and there were changes in and after 1075. Turstin son of Rolf's close connections with Earl William and his strength in the west are both patently obvious and his role can best be explained as part of the earl's dispositions in Gwent. William d'Eu appears as the leading figure introduced into the castlery after 1075, and he had difficulty in establishing his claims as a new man coming into the lordship. By 1086, the king's direct influence had been reasserted, his officers were active, his reeves at work, and the land was included in the Domesday survey as territory which produced revenues for the crown.

These advances in south Wales were restricted in scale. From the Norman positions on the Usk, the kingdom of Morgannwg was open to attack, and from Clifford the way was open into Brycheiniog. Orderic Vitalis believed that William fitz Osbern was responsible for the early Norman infiltration into Brycheiniog, though there is nothing to substantiate his claim. But it was not an

improbable step for the Normans to have taken. From their castle at
Ewyas, the Lacys were able to make limited advances into Wales.
But the magnates of the southern frontier were held in check.
Perhaps that owed something to the absence of strong Norman
leaders (a factor which was changed by royal policy in the reign of
William Rufus). It certainly owed a great deal to the emergence of a
strong leader in south Wales, Rhys ap Tewdwr, and to a major shift
in the Conqueror's policy in this region. The two rulers reached
accord, made manifest when William travelled through south Wales
to St David's in 1081, and the suspension of hostilities in the south
was maintained until the Conqueror's death.

King William turned to another close friend and adviser, Roger of
Montgomery, to control the middle range of the frontier, and he
built up a strong feudal enclave centred on his new castle of
Shrewsbury. He consolidated his hold on land which was technically
within England but not firmly under English control. He moved
into territory which was unmistakably Welsh and which passed into
the hands of his military tenants. Picot de Say was established at
Clun; the family of Tournai at Kinnersley; Reginald de Bailleul had
his principal castle at Maesbury, and his lands became the lordship of
Oswestry. The Corbets were masters of Caus, east and south of
Shrewsbury. The symbol of advance into Wales was the castle which
Earl Roger built at Montgomery, a typical motte and bailey, of
which the earthworks still survive. To distinguish it from the later
stone castle built at Montgomery by Hubert de Burgh, it came to be
known as Hen Domen – the old mound. It was a key point in the
natural communications into mid-Wales, and beyond that westwards to Ceredigion. From Montgomery, Ceri, Cydewain and
Arwystli were threatened and attacked. The threat from Oswestry
was directed at Cynllaith, Edeirnion, Nanheudwy and Iâl. The gains
which Earl Roger and his commanders made were compact and,
with the exception of Arwystli, did not drive deeply into Wales, but
they extended over a long stretch of the frontier; from the most
southerly point of Arwystli to the northern edge of Iâl would cover
some 60 miles. Iâl was a commote which extended deep into territory claimed by the earls of Chester. Roger of Montgomery, like
William fitz Osbern, was too useful an adviser to leave in isolation on
a frontier zone, and Orderic Vitalis suggests how he discharged his
duties in his earldom as well as at court. He appointed Warin the Bald
as his sheriff, and gave him a niece in marriage, and used him 'to
crush the Welsh and other opponents and to pacify the whole
province placed under his rule'. When Warin died, his office and his

wife passed to Reginald de Bailleul, lord of Oswestry. At an early date, in 1073, Earl Roger's men carried out a bold sweep which pointed to future developments in west Wales. They advanced into Ceredigion where Din Geraint, later to be known as Cardigan, would be their principal castle, and into Dyfed where they would establish their strategic and administrative centre at Pembroke.

Further north, Chester was the strategic centre for action in Wales and on the English side of the border. King William first appointed a Fleming, Gherbod, to deal with this sensitive area, but that proved unsuccessful. In his place the king appointed Hugh d'Avranches, hereditary vicomte of the Avranchin, the marchland between Normandy and Brittany. As earl of Chester, Hugh gathered around himself a number of tenants from Normandy, most of them holding land in shires at a distance from Chester. In Wales he relied heavily on his cousin, Robert de Tilleul, better known as Robert of Rhuddlan, whose bravery and savagery left their mark on the story of the Norman advance into north Wales. On the Welsh side of the Dee lay the *cantref* of Tegeingl, border territory which had frequently changed hands. Beyond that lay the *cantrefi* of Rhos, Rhufoniog and Dyffryn Clwyd which, with Tegeingl, made up the Middle Country, the Perfeddwlad, territory over which Welsh and Norman fought for control and which was to be disputed from the end of the eleventh century to the end of the thirteenth. Until his death in 1093, Robert was especially associated with this territory. On the coast, in the northern part of Rhos, he established the castle at Rhuddlan from which he took his name. The site had a long history, as an Anglo-Saxon *burh*, and as a place where Gruffydd ap Llywelyn had a residence. By 1086, a borough had been established near the castle; Earl Hugh and Robert of Rhuddlan shared the profits which accrued from it, and gave it the customs of Hereford (derived from those of Breteuil) which were especially favourable to immigrant settlers. For the Normans, operating from Chester, Rhuddlan was always an outpost; Earl Hugh was dependent upon the castles of Hawarden and Ewloe, and perhaps Basingwerk, to protect his lines of communication. Rhuddlan was also a difficult place from which to control Rhos and Rhufoniog but it was clearly beyond the resources of the earldom to subdue the whole of that area and to establish a more central point for its administration. In fact, Hugh and Robert looked elsewhere for expansion and conquest. Robert established a second and more advanced outpost at Degannwy, on the Conwy estuary; Orderic Vitalis described the ruthlessness with which, for fifteen years, he dominated the Welsh of that area. In Domesday Book,

Robert was recorded as paying the king £40 for north Wales; that can only mean the kingdom of Gwynedd. He even revived ancient claims of the principality to hold Arwystli. However limited his tenure, his career marked a sad period in the history of the northern kingdom. His death had something of the qualities of an epic. Gruffydd ap Cynan, the dispossessed prince of Gwynedd, landed with three ships on a predatory raid; his men captured prisoners and stock and herded them down to the coast. Robert was roused from sleep, ordered the alarm, and with one attendant scrambled down to the beach where he was overwhelmed and killed. He had been knighted by Edward the Confessor, and when he died he must have been well over fifty. Orderic could claim that neither Snowdon's high mountain nor Conwy's rapid river could hold him in check. Robert's career brings out very clearly a major feature of the Norman invaders: they were not primarily interested in the value of their conquests. Their material gains might seem slight and could be precarious, but for many of them it was the combination of battle, action and possessions which made life worth while.

The border earldoms share common features. They were established by the Norman king primarily for the defence of the frontier; there were opportunities for expansion into Welsh territory; in the early phases of that expansion, the initiative lay with the local magnate, not with the king. It is worth asking why the pattern and extent of expansion differed along the frontier, and what checks were imposed upon the three earls. Much depended upon the political conditions in Wales. Since 1063, Gruffydd ap Llywelyn's half-brothers had kept north Wales stable, Bleddyn in Gwynedd and Rhiwallon in Powys. They were able to exploit the weakness of the Normans in England by supporting revolts led by Eadric the Wild and Earl Edwin of Mercia. In Wales, Bleddyn took advantage of the weakness of Deheubarth: with Rhiwallon he won a significant victory at Mechain in 1070. There, Rhiwallon was killed, and Bleddyn succeeded him as ruler of Powys; there, too, an immediate threat to Bleddyn's authority was removed with the death of the two sons of Gruffydd ap Llywelyn, one in the battle, and the other soon afterwards. In 1073, Bleddyn had a dangerous and costly encounter with Norman forces commanded by Robert of Rhuddlan, where he might easily have been taken prisoner. His end came, however, not fighting the Normans, but at the hands of Rhys ab Owain of Deheubarth, and Gwynedd was then claimed by Bleddyn's cousin, Trahaearn ap Caradog. He was something of an outsider whose family ruled Arwystli, and he could not count on the loyalty of the leading men of Gwynedd. His claims were challenged by a representative of the old ruling house returning from a long exile, Gruffydd ap Cynan, who had to establish himself as a credible contender for the principality. Already, the Normans in Chester and north-east Wales could sense political weaknesses in Gwynedd and Powys; for them, conditions favoured an aggressive policy. In the south, Rhys ab Owain had only a tenuous hold on his kingdom, for he was challenged by one rival from south-east Wales, Caradog ap Gruffydd, and another from the north, Trahaearn ap Caradog. In 1078 Trahaearn overwhelmed Rhys, but he showed no sign of taking over his kingdom. His victory cleared the way for another member of the southern dynasty, Rhys ap Tewdwr, to claim Deheubarth. This complex pattern of rivalries was clarified at the battle of Mynydd Carn in 1081. There, two leading figures were killed, Trahaearn and Caradog ap Gruffydd, whose deaths left Gruffydd ap Cynan and Rhys ap Tewdwr as the leaders of Gwynedd and Deheubarth. A third casualty at Mynydd Carn was Meilyr ap Rhiwallon of Powys: although he was himself a minor figure, his death led to the undisputed succession of Bleddyn's sons in Powys and, through Maredudd ap Bleddyn, his heirs continued to rule that principality until the end of the thirteenth century.

In the north, Gruffydd ap Cynan rapidly fell victim to Norman treachery. He was taken prisoner by Earl Hugh of Chester, with the connivance of the earl of Shrewsbury, and for many years his career was in total eclipse. When he escaped from captivity and returned to Gwynedd he began a new phase of a long and remarkable reign. These were the conditions in which Earl Hugh and Robert of Rhuddlan could sweep through north Wales and which made possible Robert's tenure of Gwynedd in 1086. In south Wales, Rhys ap Tewdwr fared better. He was never free from challenge, and he suffered a number of reverses, but he maintained his hold on Deheubarth. In 1081, William the Conqueror journeyed through south Wales as far as St David's. It was a show of force, presented perhaps euphemistically as a pilgrimage to the saint's shrine, and it achieved two things. It signalled the establishment of friendly relations between the two rulers which gave Rhys security in Wales and the Conqueror peace and security along the southern stretch of the frontier. That accord held firm until William's death, and it is a major factor in the lull which marked Norman activities in south-east Wales. It also signalled the Conqueror's interest in territory beyond the frontiers of the kingdom which he claimed by inheritance. There is no surviving edict or statement of policy, but by the 1080s William had assumed something of the role of overlord which his Anglo-Saxon predecessors had long exercised in Wales. In 1086, Rhys ap Tewdwr owed the king £40 as a render for his kingdom; so, too, did Robert of Rhuddlan for north Wales: the inference is clear – William had a direct interest in Wales and he did not see his magnates as free agents beyond the boundaries of his kingdom.

By the late 1080s, any check on the activities of border magnates and any immunity which Rhys might enjoy were wearing thin. William Rufus was ready to sanction and encourage new advances into Wales and to give the opportunity for profitable ventures to new men from his own entourage. Bernard of Neufmarché was active in Brycheiniog, and perhaps Robert fitz Hamo was already moving towards, if not in, Morgannwg. Bernard's family had served the duke of Normandy with distinction, but his father was disgraced and dispossessed and Bernard had to make good his loss by service with William Rufus. At some date after the Domesday survey he acquired estates in Herefordshire and he married the heiress of Osbern son of Richard. By 1088 he was established at Glasbury, and over the next five years he and his men were probing the defences of Brycheiniog. Rhys ap Tewdwr of Deheubarth was called in to defend the kingdom against their attacks and in 1093 he and 'the Normans who were living in Brycheiniog' met near the point where the Honddu falls into the Usk. There he was killed, and with his death the way was cleared for conquest and settlement in Brycheiniog and, as contemporary writers acknowledged, in other parts of south Wales. Bernard established his castle at Aberhonddu which the Normans named Brecon: there he founded a priory church and a small borough. The invaders gave it protection by building a series of mottes as an outer line of defence, and Bernard's knights, endowed with lands in the river valleys, established their own castles. Bronllys and Hay guarded the approach from Herefordshire; Tretower and Crickhowell controlled the route which would lead to Abergavenny and Gwent; Aberyscir and Trecastell were the defences on the western side of Brecon towards Cantref Bychan. The mountainous country which formed the Great Forest of Brecknock was slowly provided with a series of small castles and hunting lodges. North of Brecon, towards the inhospitable uplands of the Epynt, the displaced Welsh dynasty established a base; the remains of two earthwork castles, one a ringwork and the other a motte, mark the defences of their principal residence. The stages by which this lordship was taken, settled and controlled can be seen in broad outline. At the beginning of the twelfth century, Bernard of Neufmarché used very general terms to describe it; he spoke of his castle on the Honddu and of the lands, churches and tithes which he and his men had given Battle abbey in Wales. In 1121, when Bernard's daughter was given in marriage to Miles of Gloucester, Henry I confirmed to them Bernard's possessions, describing the lordship of Brecknock in some detail: in particular, he laid out the western extent of the lordship 'to the boundaries of the land of Richard fitz Pons at Cantref Bychan'. By that year Brycheiniog had become a well-defined lordship, still, of necessity, dominated by castles, with the rich lands of the river valleys firmly in Norman hands. The Great Forest was exploited during the twelfth century and the building of small castles continued throughout that period and well into the thirteenth century. To the north, the Normans seem to have had only nominal control. It is clear that the invaders imposed their own patterns on the lordship. The ancient centres of power had been Talgarth and perhaps Trecastell, in Llywel, but Bernard chose a new site for his principal castle at Brecon, and he and the barons of his honour built up a new network of nodal points to provide for the defence of the lordship.

South of Brycheiniog, the kingdom of Morgannwg was under attack during the last years of the eleventh century; there, Robert fitz Hamo, a member of a distinguished Norman family led the attack. His grandfather had died in Duke William's service in 1047 and his father was serving in the Conqueror's administration as early as 1069 and continued in office as sheriff of Kent throughout William II's reign. Robert represented the third generation of this curial family, and in the crisis of rebellion against William Rufus in 1088 he had stayed firm in his loyalty. The king needed men he could trust at court and in different regions of the kingdom; he needed their active support and he could also use them to constrain or exclude more dangerous rivals. The Conqueror's queen had been given the rich estates of a Gloucestershire thegn, Beorhtric son of Aelfgar, and this inheritance William Rufus gave to Robert fitz Hamo. That removed a powerful temptation from the king's younger brother, Henry, who wanted these estates, and who might have proved a dangerous vassal. William II selected a number of men to hold lands in Wales and it is highly likely that Robert fitz Hamo undertook his attack on Morgannwg at the king's instigation. In personal terms there is no obvious reason why Robert should have become interested in conquests in Wales, but his direct concern with Bristol and its trade across the Bristol Channel is the most probable link. Robert set up his castle at Cardiff, and secured a limited range of territory stretching westwards to Coity (the Welsh spelling, Coety, is now in regular use) and southwards along the coast. The river Ogmore marked the limits of his advance; his gifts to religious houses lay to the east of that line, and the castles of Ogmore, Newcastle (Bridgend) and Coity have the appearance of a frontier defence. Morgannwg became the lordship of Glamorgan, but the work of subduing and settling the lordship was long-drawn-out. Expansion westwards was the work of Robert's son-in-law and successor, Robert, earl of Gloucester, who died in 1147, while the work of consolidating and fortifying the northern areas of the lordship was still being continued in the thirteenth century. Morlais castle was a valuable addition to the northern defences on the border of Brecknock, and Caerphilly, built by Earl Gilbert the Red, was established to ensure defence. He began to build the castle in 1268; after a major reverse, it had to be redesigned and rebuilt in the 1270s, and work was still in progress at the turn of the century. Along the coast and in the vale of Glamorgan, Norman knights and their tenants were established; for example, the family of Robert le Sor settled at Peterston, the Humfravilles at Penmark, the Turbervilles at Coity and the family of de Londres at Ogmore.

The upland territories of Morgannwg remained in Welsh hands, and the survival of Welsh power is a major theme in the history of the lordship. In the earliest phase of Norman infiltration in south-east Wales two Welsh dynasties were directly involved. One was the line of Rhydderch ab Iestyn, whose son, Gruffydd ap Rhydderch, and grandson, Caradog ap Gruffydd, controlled Gwynllŵg and Morgannwg. Their involvement in the larger sphere of Welsh politics has already been examined. Caradog's position was compromised by the attacks and settlements of William fitz Osbern and his successors, but Caradog's heirs regained possession of Caerleon and had a recognised and honoured place in Gwent. In 1081, a second dynasty was established when Iestyn ap Gwrgant took advantage of the death of Caradog ap Gruffydd at Mynydd Carn to seize power in Morgannwg. From that point different dynasties claimed power in Gwynllŵg and Morgannwg. But both areas formed part of Robert fitz Hamo's lordship, and he and his successors were frequently involved with both dynasties. In the middle decades of the twelfth century the lords of Glamorgan were attended by Morgan ab Owain ap Caradog (of the Gwynllŵg family), and attesting charters he still used the style, Morgan the king.

In terms of tenure the important family was that of Iestyn ap

Gwrgant which controlled all the upland territory from the river
Taff to the hill country above Neath and what is now Port Talbot. In
the second quarter of the twelfth century Caradog ab Iestyn was lord
of Neath and Afan with a stronghold and borough on the coast at
Aberafan. His brother, Rhys, held the territory of Ruthin (not now
easily identifiable as a territorial unit), with his main residence at
Llanilid, lying between Coity and Llantrisant. Ruthin did not survive for long in Welsh hands: at some point in the twelfth century it
was taken over by Norman settlers, apparently led by one of the St
Quintin family, and it was later associated with lands held by
Richard Siward of Llanblethian and Talyfan. The estates of Caradog

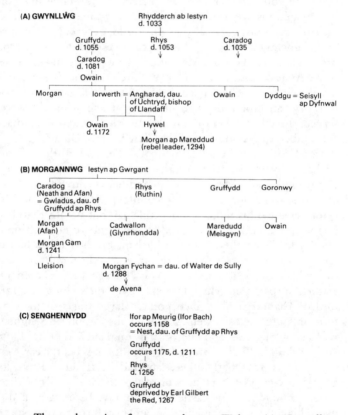

Figure 2 Three dynasties from south-east Wales: (a) Gwynllŵg,
(b) Morgannwg, (c) Senghennydd
Note: not all the lesser members of these families are shown.

ab Iestyn remained in the hands of his heirs until the thirteenth century, one line retaining Afan, another Glynrhondda, and a third Meisgyn. On the eastern boundary of Glamorgan lay Senghennydd, an upland territory which marched with the hill country of Brecknock. Here the third Welsh dynasty was established. Its origins are obscure, but in 1158 its leading figure was Ifor ap Meurig, nicknamed Ifor Bach, 'the small'. He demonstrated his power in two ways. In 1158 he clashed with the forces of his Welsh neighbour, Morgan ab Owain of Gwynllŵg and killed him, and in the same year he mounted a daring raid on Cardiff castle and carried off William, earl of Gloucester, his wife and child. These may be isolated episodes but they reinforce the fact that Senghennydd was both independent and dangerous. Ifor's power was personal but there is one hint that he was anxious to ensure that it should be maintained after his death. He left three sons, but only one, Gruffydd, occurs as a man of power in Senghennydd; he and his successors held the lordship. His brothers, Cadwallon and Maredudd, were both found in the service of the Angevin kings late in Henry II's reign and in the reign of John. They seem to have been excluded from the succession in their Welsh territory, and the unity and integrity of Senghennydd were preserved. In the thirteenth century Welsh and Norman magnates succumbed to the pressure of the Clare lords of Glamorgan. In 1247 the earl took over Llanblethian, Talyfan and Ruthin, depriving Richard Siward of these estates, while the Welsh dynasty lost Glynrhondda and Meisgyn. Afan and Senghennydd, now isolated outposts, were more exposed to comital pressure. In Afan, Morgan Gam defended his judicial independence, but before 1250 his son, Lleision, had been forced to cede these rights of jurisdiction to his overlord. His brother, Morgan Fychan, married a daughter of the Anglo-Norman baron, Walter de Sully, and the family began to use the style *de Avena*; despite their Welsh lineage, they merged into the anglicised society in which they had lived for so long. By 1289 the lord of Glamorgan had incorporated large tracts of their upland territory into his own demesne. The absorption of Senghennydd was a slow business, and Henry III in England and Prince Llywelyn ap Gruffydd in Wales disputed the legality of what the earl was trying to do. In 1267 Earl Gilbert captured Gruffydd ap Rhys, lord of Senghennydd, and kept him prisoner. In Gruffydd's territory he began to build his new castle at Caerphilly. By 1272 he had established his control of Senghennydd, and he refused to allow his tenure to be shaken. It was the end of a long process. Whatever the first two generations of settlers in Glamorgan may have claimed, Welsh dynasties and Welsh tenure remained a major part of the structure of the lordship until the last quarter of the thirteenth century.

It is possible to concentrate on these eastern lordships principally because the sources relating to their early development are comparatively plentiful. Domesday Book provides revealing glimpses of what was happening on the frontier in the Conqueror's reign; for later phases of settlement the cartularies of Brecon priory and Llanthony abbey, the *Book of Llandaff* and the resources of Margam and Neath, as well as of St Peter's, Gloucester, and Tewkesbury abbey, all provide valuable material. The slow expansion of Norman settlement and of the lord's influence in Glamorgan is well documented, and the whole story presents an important case history. If nothing else, it should serve as a warning against easy assumptions about the history of lordships for which the evidence is very limited.

In the far west, early probes by Roger of Montgomery's men were followed in 1093 by a sustained attack, and Roger's son, Arnulf, was established at Pembroke. For a Welsh annalist this sweep into west Wales was an immediate consequence of the death of Rhys ap Tewdwr. It overshadowed another Norman incursion centred on the castle built at Rhyd y Gors, near Carmarthen, by William fitz Baldwin. As with Norman advances in north Wales, the campaigns in west Wales and their achievements were spectacular but fragile. Lines of communication were stretched far beyond any practical limit, and military resources available in Shrewsbury (or, further north, in Chester) were less than adequate. Resolute local leadership might expose and exploit that basic flaw. There is every indication that the ruthlessness and brutality of the Normans could goad the Welsh into violent reaction, however strong the odds might be against success. Between 1094 and 1098 the reaction occurred, and the weaknesses of the Norman invaders were exposed. Sir John Lloyd saw this as a 'national' movement which began in Gwynedd, was consolidated in west Wales and spread eventually to Brecknock, Gwynllŵg and Gwent. It might be dangerous to underrate the spread of information and the direct response which that could invoke, but that will scarcely transform the reactions of the 1090s into a 'Welsh' resistance. Events in north Wales suggest a strong element of opportunism. Robert of Rhuddlan was killed in 1093 in the first direct encounter which Gruffydd ap Cynan, newly escaped from captivity, had had with the Normans. Cadwgan ap Bleddyn, of Powys, saw the chance to cut the earl of Chester's extended lines of communication. The earl himself took over Robert of Rhuddlan's role, but there was a distinct loss of momentum. In west Wales the leaders of the attack on Arnulf's strongholds were minor figures, while Rhyd y Gors was abandoned after the death of its founder. The leaders of resistance in Gwynllŵg are never identified. In Brecknock, Gruffydd ab Idnerth and his brother, Ifor, inflicted a substantial defeat on the Normans at Aber Llech, but it was noted as significant that the castles of the lordship did not fall, and on that slender basis recovery could rest. Two royal expeditions in 1095 and 1097 signalled the king's interest in Wales but achieved very little. By the end of the century, the Normans in north Wales had retreated to the line of the Conwy; in west Wales, Pembroke was still in their hands; Glamorgan, Gwynllŵg and Brecknock had been held despite the scale of the threat.

The reign of Henry I (1100–35) was a period of harsh but effective government in England. The new king strengthened the administration and exploited the financial resources of the kingdom systematically. He relied heavily on a group of magnates and administrators of unswerving loyalty and did not hesitate to limit, and where necessary break, powerful families which threatened the security of the kingdom. When he won Normandy from his brother, Duke Robert, in 1106, he introduced the same hard efficiency into the duchy. It is no surprise that he showed a sustained interest in Wales where his dealings bore the same stamp of vigour and ruthlessness. He intervened in the affairs of Anglo-Norman dynasties on the border and in Wales itself: he bargained, and at times intrigued, with Welsh princes; he commissioned new men to take part in the subjugation of south Wales; and he was directly responsible for settlement in depth, notably by Flemish immigrants in the west.

The changing fortunes of great magnates ushered in major changes. Roger of Montgomery died in 1094, to be succeeded in Normandy by his eldest son, Robert of Bellême, and in England by his second son, Hugh, whose tenure of the earldom of Shrewsbury was brief. Joining Hugh, earl of Chester, in an invasion of Anglesey he was killed in the summer of 1098 by a Scandinavian force which mounted an unexpected raid on the island. Robert of Bellême claimed his inheritance, combining his family's Norman and English possessions. His loyalties lay with Duke Robert of Normandy, and on the accession of Henry I he joined a rebellion against him. In due course, in 1102, he was deprived of his earldom and his English estates and forced to retire to Normandy, and with him, his brother, Arnulf of Pembroke, suffered disgrace and forfeiture. At the same time, the role of the earl of Chester was much diminished. Earl Hugh died in 1101, leaving a boy of seven as his heir, and the young Earl Richard remained in wardship until 1114.

These events altered the balance of power on the frontier: royal officials were active in the earldom of Shrewsbury, and no independent initiative could be expected from Chester. In Wales, the overthrow of Arnulf of Pembroke had far-reaching consequences. No single magnate was allowed to succeed him: instead, Pembroke was gradually organised as if it were an English shire. Those who had held land and authority under Arnulf emerged with a greater independence. Gerald of Windsor, his steward, was the most prominent: as constable of Pembroke castle he controlled the strongest castle in the west, and he and his family were firmly established at Carew. He was a key figure in Anglo-Norman society, and his marriage with Nest, daughter of Rhys ap Tewdwr of Deheubarth, involved him in a violent feud with the ruling house of Powys. A pattern of smaller lordships emerged; Cemais, for example, was in Norman hands by 1115, and about the same time Manorbier was held by Odo de Barry. The migration of that settler family from the lordship of Glamorgan to Pembroke still requires explanation. It has to be seen in a wider context of French immigration, not only from other parts of Wales but also from across the Bristol Channel. The fitz Baldwins, from Devon, and tenants associated with their Devonshire honour of Okehampton, de Brian, Punchardon and Moreville, held lands in Dyfed or influenced the formation of place-names in west Wales. The fitz Martins and their tenants had their origins and lands in Somerset. As with the magnates of the eastern frontier zone, one of the most intriguing, and at times intractable, problems is to determine where they found and recruited the knightly tenants who served with them in Wales. Henry I's introduction of Flemish settlers in west Wales belongs in this setting, if only because their leaders became men of note in the area. The king negotiated the migration of Flemish settlers in the two *cantrefi* of Rhos and Daugleddau; his agents worked with prominent leaders who could control a sizeable body of workers, and in at least one instance their negotiations were carried through in Flanders. Wizo, who called himself 'the prince', made a grant to Worcester cathedral priory, on his first journey from Flanders to Wales. It was the grant of the church which he proposed to build on his new land once he arrived there. His gift suggests the mechanics of his business deal, and reflects the substantial advantages he expected to gain in Wales. He established his castle at Wiston, and he was plainly a man of standing. He was not alone: a contemporary from Flanders, Letard called himself 'Litelking' and gave his name to Letterston, while another, Tancard, became castellan of Haverfordwest. William of Brabant, whose name betrays his origins, was called *primas*; he was killed by Owain ap Cadwgan in 1110. Flemish settlers were not confined to Dyfed; they were to be found in Kidwelly (the anglicised form of the Welsh Cydweli) and in Ceredigion, where the name Castell Fflemish identifies an area of Flemish settlement.

The lordships of Glamorgan and Pembroke were separated by territory which became an intricate network of Norman lordships and Welsh enclaves. The Welsh areas of Ystrad Tywi, Kidwelly and Gower were handed over in 1102 to one of the lesser figures involved in the struggle for power, Hywel ap Goronwy, who was put to death in 1106, and within a few years Norman lords were firmly established in most of this territory. Richard fitz Pons was given Cantref Bychan, the eastern part of Ystrad Tywi, and Henry de Beaumont, earl of Warwick, began the process of building up the lordship of Gower. Henry I gave Kidwelly to his leading administrator, Roger le Poer, bishop of Salisbury, and the assumption must be that Roger used lesser men to secure this area for him. Before the end of Henry's reign, the lordship of Kidwelly had passed to Maurice de Londres who, like Odo de Barry, moved west from his base in the lordship of Glamorgan; what induced him to add this new lordship to his possessions can only be a matter of conjecture. Throughout its history, the Norman hold on Kidwelly was precarious; they appear to have had little success in establishing a network of defences for the lordship and their principal castle was frequently under attack and repeatedly taken by the Welsh. The neighbouring area of Carnwyllion was never strongly fortified, and left Kidwelly exposed, while Welsh forces could move easily from Cantref Mawr and take advantage of the hill country which extended to within only a few miles of Kidwelly castle.

There remained the eastern section of Dyfed, outside the range of Arnulf of Pembroke's territory, where William fitz Baldwin, sheriff of Devon, held the castle of Rhyd y Gors before his death in 1096. His brother, Richard, re-established the castle in 1105; it is usually assumed that he was asserting a family claim, but he may have been acting as a royal agent. Within a few years, by 1109, the area was certainly in the king's hands and under the control of one of his most experienced administrators, Walter of Gloucester. The defence of this territory now depended upon the castle built on a bluff above the river at Carmarthen. That was to remain a royal castle and the centre of royal influence in south Wales.

The circumstances which made these advances politic are to be found in the violent history of the leading Welsh dynasts, at that time the princes of Powys, and of the lesser families of mid- and south Wales. The death of Hugh, earl of Shrewsbury, and the appearance of Robert of Bellême as his successor were critical events. The new earl and his neighbour, Earl Hugh of Chester, drew back from renewed warfare in Wales, and that gave the opportunity for two Welsh princes to reassert their claims. Gruffydd ap Cynan was able to continue building up his power in Gwynedd, and Cadwgan ap Bleddyn was re-established in Powys, where he depended upon Earl Robert as lord and patron, a position which may have meant more to Robert than to Cadwgan. Robert set up a strong alliance with Cadwgan and his brothers, Iorwerth and Maredudd, and he made good use of their combined strength in his confrontation with Henry I. The king was determined to break this Welsh connection and Iorwerth was detached from the alliance with extravagant promises. He was to have Powys and Ceredigion, with Arnulf of Pembroke's lands, and with a compact block of territory in south Wales, Ystrad Tywi, Gower and Kidwelly. Once the threat of Robert of Bellême had been removed, Henry I defaulted. Powys was confirmed to Iorwerth, and Cadwgan was established in Ceredigion; in their heartland the family was secure, but the southern territories were never handed over. A Norman, Saer, was given Pembroke, and Hywel ap Goronwy (from Meirionydd) was given Ystrad Tywi, Gower and Kidwelly. It was cynical and unprincipled, but it gave Henry I the immediate security he needed, and after a brief interval Norman lords were endowed with these lands. When Iorwerth tried to claim his rewards he was imprisoned, and from 1103 until 1110 he remained in the king's custody. With him out of the way, his brother Cadwgan was established in Powys and Ceredigion, but his position was always inherently weak. Henry I held two of his brothers, each of whom could be released as a rival claimant, as Iorwerth was eventually released in 1110. Meanwhile, Cadwgan had to deal with his son, Owain, who was a courageous fighter but completely devoid of political skill, and perhaps even of political ambition; he also had to deal with two nephews, Madog and Ithel, who were undoubtedly ambitious for themselves and who could be used as puppets by Henry I. In 1109 Owain carried off Nest, the wife of Gerald of Windsor. It is said that 'when Cadwgan heard that story, he was grieved and was frightened for two reasons: because of the violation of the lady, and because of fear of king Henry on account of the injury to his officer'. His fears were well founded, for he was made to pay a heavy price for his son's offence. The king sent Madog and Ithel to ravage his territories and made them rulers of Powys. Their inadequacy led Henry's officers to restore Cadwgan in Ceredigion, and eventually to send Iorwerth as ruler of Powys. Owain continued his maverick career until, in 1116 he was trapped and killed by Norman troops who eventually expunged the wrong he had done to Gerald of Windsor. Many of the other leading characters in these events died by violence: Iorwerth and Cadwgan were murdered by Welsh enemies; Madog was captured and blinded by his kinsmen. This intermixture of family rivalries, the struggle for power between Welsh claimants, and the often unscrupulous political manoeuvrings of the king and his administrators, produced a sordid and unedifying sequence of events which sapped the political strength of the princes of Powys. When, at a later stage, other dynasties found new strength and rebuilt their political fortunes, the ruling house of Powys remained a comparatively weak and ineffectual force.

In terms of the Norman settlements in Wales, the major consequence of the conflict between Henry I and the rulers of Powys was the introduction to west Wales of one family, the Clares, which was to play a major role in the history of the southern marchlands. The *Brut y Tywysogyon*, a thirteenth-century compilation based on earlier annals, reports the advent of this dynasty with interesting overtones. Gilbert fitz Richard was already lord of Clare and Tonbridge; he and his family had grown rich in England. As the *Brut* has it, Gilbert had frequently asked the king for land in Wales. That, in itself, is a rare insight into the motives of the Normans who settled in Welsh territory: the sense that here were rich pickings, even for the most powerful of Norman families, is not often expressed so openly. Exasperated with Cadwgan and his kin, Henry determined that one part of their territory should be made safe in the hands of an immigrant lord. In a famous phrase, which all those who have written about this period have cited, Henry said to Gilbert, 'Now I will give you the land of Cadwgan ap Bleddyn. Go and take possession of it.' It is reminiscent of the terms on which so many Normans received their estates in England: given the name of their Anglo-Saxon *antecessor*, they had to go and find out for themselves what land they had acquired and where it lay. Gilbert was given an area, traversed by Normans working from Shrewsbury, with one major castle at Cardigan already in use, but with the hinterland little explored, and he took up the challenge with great vigour. He secured Cardigan and established himself at Aberystwyth (with his stronghold not on the site of the later Edwardian castle but on high ground overlooking the lower reaches of the river Ystwyth). He commissioned a number of castles, some of which bore, or came to bear, Welsh names, while others were identified by the name of their French castellans. Walter's castle, held by Walter le Bec, Razo's castle, held by Razo the steward, Stephen's castle, whose castellan has long been forgotten though his name survives in Llanbedr Pont Steffan (Lampeter), and Humphrey's castle, later rebuilt and renamed Castell Hywel: all these were identified in the *Brut*. Another castle, built around the same time but soon destroyed, was identified as Richard's castle, and the stronghold at Blaenporth was known as Ralph's castle. Each castle stood in a separate commote; of the ten commotes in Ceredigion, only one, Creuddyn, did not have a major Norman stronghold at this time, and even that area could be kept under surveillance from Aberystwyth. This is not a pattern produced by accident; Gilbert fitz Richard planned his enterprise. He imported English and Flemish settlers to colonise his new territory, and it looks very much as if his military dispositions, as well as his economic arrangements, were carefully thought out.

The Clares had wide interests, and Wales did not command a full share of their attention. Gilbert's eldest son, Richard, is said to have been more concerned with his Welsh lands than with his English possessions, but he lacked the elementary caution necessary in frontier territory and was ambushed and killed as he travelled through Abergavenny and Brecknock on his way to Ceredigion. His sons showed very different interests. The elder, Gilbert, was made earl of Hertford in 1138 and seems to have been chiefly concerned with his English estates. The younger son, Roger, who succeeded him as earl in 1152, had time for campaigning in Wales, and he either built or reconditioned a number of castles at strategic points, at Ystrad Meurig, Castell Hywel, Aberdyfi (Aberdovey), Dineirth and Llanrhystud. This marked a vigorous campaign in 1158, but already the political conditions in west Wales were changing; Rhys ap Gruffydd was establishing himself as the dominant prince in west Wales, and by 1165 he had overrun Ceredigion and Roger de Clare had withdrawn from his Welsh lordship. He lived until 1173 and was succeeded by his son, Richard, who held the earldom of Hertford until 1217. Unexpectedly, a dynastic marriage brought this branch of the family back to Wales. Richard married Amicia, second daughter of William, earl of Gloucester, one of three co-heiresses who inherited Earl William's estates when he died in 1183. In the end, she outlived her sisters, and in 1217, only a few weeks before he died, her husband secured her inheritance, and his successors became lords of Glamorgan and Gwynllŵg.

The junior branch of the Clare family had also built up considerable power in Wales before the male line died out in 1185. Gilbert fitz Gilbert was the younger son of that Gilbert who was given Ceredigion in 1110. When he was a young man, he had little in the way of lands and wealth himself, though close relatives were powerful men. In particular, an uncle, Walter, held the eastern lordships of Strigoil, Caerleon and Usk, and when he died without direct heirs in 1138 these were given to Gilbert who also received the lordship of Pembroke from King Stephen. When Stephen made him an earl, he took the formal title of Pembroke, though he often used Strigoil as a popular style. Gilbert fitz Gilbert was a younger son who was fortunate to acquire a large landed holding in his own right, and he passed on to his heirs, Richard Strongbow and his son Gilbert, a rich inheritance. That Gilbert was still under age when he died in 1185, and he was never formally invested with the earldom; when he died his estates passed to an heiress, Isabel, whose husband, William Marshal, eventually acquired both the lands and the earldom of Pembroke.

The Clares, like many other families, owed their fortune to royal patronage and to changing political patterns outside Wales. Robert fitz Hamo, of Glamorgan, rendered one last service to Henry I, joining him in his invasion of Normandy in 1106. At Tinchebrai Robert received serious head wounds from which he never recovered. When he died, leaving a daughter as his heiress, the king took his lands into his own custody, enjoying their revenues for perhaps as long as fifteen years. Then Henry determined to keep this rich inheritance in his family circle and gave the woman in marriage to his bastard son, Robert, whose new estates extended over many shires with a heavy concentration in Gloucestershire and Glamorgan. The whole transaction was a matter of family advantage, with Henry disposing of a major English fief, but it affected the Norman settlement in south Wales, and it linked the lordship of Glamorgan with a central figure in English politics. The earldom of Gloucester, with the lordship of Glamorgan, rarely lost that central position, but remained closely associated with the crown and its interests in the reigns of John, Henry III and Edward I, and that connection continued well into the fourteenth century.

At a less exalted level of the king's court, another family acquired interests in Wales. Walter of Gloucester, hereditary sheriff of

Gloucestershire, like his Norman predecessors, had served the crown well, and he reaped a succession of comparatively minor rewards in lands and offices. He had played his part in the Norman expansion into south Wales, with responsibilities at Carmarthen. His family was enriched in 1121 when Henry I gave the heiress of Bernard of Neufmarché to Walter's son, Miles of Gloucester, with all her father's possessions. That included the lordship of Brecknock. The king also gave another useful administrator, Brian fitz Count, the lordship of Abergavenny which he held for some twenty years and then, in 1141–2, transferred to Miles. By that arrangement Miles consolidated a substantial block of territory: an English honour with its *caput* at Caldicot, in Gwent, and some of its richest manors in Gloucestershire, and the lordships of Brecknock and Abergavenny. The marriage of his son, Roger of Gloucester, to a daughter and co-heiress of Payn fitz John (yet another of Henry's administrators) added new land to the family's holding notably in Herefordshire. Miles was made earl of Hereford in 1141 and he and his family controlled a compact area lying north of the territories dominated by the earl of Gloucester. In terms of land and military power, the two men were a formidable combination, and they shared an unshakeable loyalty to Henry I. The augmentation of their estates and standing overshadowed less spectacular advances made by men whose names would recur in the story of Wales and the frontier: the Braose family settled in Builth and the Mortimers, firmly established in Herefordshire with the *caput* of their honour at Wigmore, moved steadily into Maelienydd (part of the later county of Radnorshire), and began in a very modest way their progress to the position of influence and power which they enjoyed in the thirteenth and fourteenth centuries. Further north, more new men were introduced along the frontier; they seem to be men associated with Henry before his accession when he held lands in western Normandy in the Cotentin; Alan fitz Flaad was settled at Oswestry and the name Lestrange first appears at Knockin.

It may seem odd that a king who exercised so much influence in the country should have mounted only one full-scale expedition into Wales. In 1114 he set in motion three separate armies intended to overawe the ageing prince of Gwynedd. Potentially it was a dangerous moment, but Gruffydd ap Cynan saw no advantage in open hostilities and made peace with the king. It was an unnecessary campaign but it was also a tacit recognition that Henry had achieved his ends by other means. A second punitive expedition was mounted

against Powys in 1121. It was intended to strengthen the defences of
Cheshire, and, although it 'approached the bounds of Powys', it did
not develop into a major invasion of Welsh territory. Direct intervention was not needed chiefly because, for some fifteen years,
Henry was able to rely upon Richard de Belmeis, bishop of London,
who served as sheriff and justiciar in Shropshire, and who manipulated the Welsh princes unmercifully for the king's advantage. Other
royal officers held much of south Wales in check. All this contributed
to make Henry I a dangerous enemy for Welsh aspirations. The
influence of the English king has never been underestimated, but in
recent years it is the feature which has been most firmly emphasised
in the story of Anglo-Norman advances into Wales. For Rees
Davies, Henry I 'towers in the history of the subjugation of Wales
and of the making of the Welsh March as no other monarch before
the reign of Edward I'.

The princes of Powys were not the only Welsh rulers to be
demoralised by him. In south Wales the claims of Rhys ap Tewdwr
were maintained in feeble fashion by his son, Gruffydd. He was
brought up in exile in Ireland and he returned to Wales in 1113. From
then until 1135 he was content with a quiet existence in remote but
safe territory around Caeo, between Lampeter and Llandovery. He
made a late attempt to claim greater power after Henry I's death in
1135, but he himself died two years later before he had done anything
of note. In north Wales the key figure was Gruffydd ap Cynan,
whose activities were significant for half a century. His early
attempts to return to Gwynedd – for he, too, spent his formative
years in Ireland – met with disastrous failure, and from 1081 until the
early 1090s he was a prisoner of the earl of Chester. When he escaped
he had to spend some years establishing his authority. Henry's
expedition of 1114 is one of the strongest indications of the position
which he had achieved. So, too, is the fact that later in the twelfth
century a *Life* of Gruffydd ap Cynan was written: in that sense he is
unique among medieval Welsh princes. Gruffydd outlived Henry I
and continued to rule Gwynedd until his death in 1137. By that time
he was blind and senile. He was fortunate in his sons with whom, in
his prime, he extended his power beyond the mountain stronghold
of Gwynedd into Meirionydd in the west and Rhos, Rhufoniog and
Dyffryn Clwyd in the east. Before the end of his long life, these sons
had become restless and anxious to be active in their own interest,
and Gruffydd was accused of failing to control them. One,
Cadwallon, died in 1132, and Owain Gwynedd was able to succeed
their father in 1137 without immediate challenge from a younger

brother, Cadwaladr. There was no long period of recovery and reconstruction before the new prince could rule effectively, and Owain embarked upon one of the most constructive reigns the northern kingdom had experienced.

3

THE MARCHER LORDSHIPS

———— • ————

Between 1100 and 1135 Norman expansion in Wales reached its peak, and it would be easy to present this period as one of steady Norman advances and of uncertainty and decline for the Welsh princely dynasties. But that would obscure two major elements in the story. The first is that conquests in Wales were achieved slowly and were confined to a limited area. The Norman onslaught on England under William the Conqueror was swift and devastating in its results and it affected the whole kingdom. The English aristocracy had no time to learn the tactical lessons of the Norman invasions, and they could not match the advantage which the conquerors drew from their use of castles and mounted knights. In Wales, by contrast, there was no wholesale conquest; only parts of the country were overrun. The Welsh had ample time to learn the tactical lessons on which survival might depend. They never matched the skills and advantages of the Norman cavalry, but in a country which favoured guerilla warfare and the use of lightly armed, mobile foot-soldiers, that was not a matter of critical significance. Welsh leaders did learn the advantages of fortifications, and from the earliest decades of the twelfth century they began, tentatively but effectively, to use defensive earthworks and, more slowly, to repair and use Norman castles once they had been taken. The second major element is that the Normans were never able to pour men and money into Wales on a scale which would guarantee secure tenure of their conquests. Gerald of Wales, writing much later, pointed the weakness precisely, foreshadowing in his analysis the methods and the scale of operations which Edward I would one day use against the Welsh. Without that intensity of attack Norman gains and Welsh losses were far from permanent. Welsh survival in some strength in Glamorgan, Brecknock, Builth and Kidwelly, to use only four examples, is one manifestation of that fact. Welsh resilience and the re-establishment of Welsh princely power in Ceredigion, and in disputed territories between the Conwy and the Dee, demonstrate the same factor in sharper terms.

More intangible is the influence of reputation. Gruffydd ap Cynan achieved much by patient and steady progress rather than by heroic measures and major advances, but he was a man of wide influence. His reputation is greater than the record of his reign might justify. Even in his decline, his heirs found restraint irksome but they had to wait for him to die before they were free to follow their own policies. His son, Owain Gwynedd, could be seen as a man of power to be treated with respect by his English and Welsh opponents alike, and that mark of quality and achievement was equally clear in the princes of Gwynedd in the thirteenth century. In England and Normandy, Henry I was a man to be feared, even at the end of a long reign. The moment he was removed from the scene there was, in Wales as in England, a release of tension and a realignment of power and influence. The same strength attached to Henry II and Edward I, and by contrast Stephen, John and Henry III lacked stature and might be disregarded with greater impunity. In each case they were more capable than their reputation would suggest. Had Henry III been taken more seriously, the prince of Wales might not have underestimated the threat posed by Edward I: there was a closer similarity between father and son than many of their contemporaries realised.

The death of Henry I in 1135 was the signal for more vigorous and more hostile policies by the Welsh, though firm action by Stephen and the marcher lords held the promise of successful defence. An attack on the settlers in Gower early in 1136, the ambush and death of Richard fitz Gilbert at Crickhowell later in the year, and the death of Payn fitz John in a skirmish in 1137 were set-backs. Much more serious for the Normans was the renewed activity of Gruffydd ap Cynan's sons in Gwynedd. They threatened Ceredigion, capturing a number of castles, and drawing Gruffydd ap Rhys of south Wales into alliance against the Clares. From the lordship of Pembroke a Norman force marched against them but at Crug Mawr, some 2 miles from Cardigan, they were overwhelmed. They lost control of Ceredigion: only the castle at Cardigan survived as a refuge. At this stage Stephen showed some of the drive which had brought him to the English throne; he sent Miles of Gloucester to rescue the survivors and that difficult operation was carried through success-fully. But to move from rescue to an effective defence, much less to the offensive action which was needed, was beyond the king and his resources. Ceredigion had been won back by the Welsh, and their control was firmly established. The territory held by the Cliffords in Cantref Bychan was reclaimed and Llandovery ceased to be a Norman bastion. Carmarthen was captured.

These were not merely short-term gains. In England, Stephen lost the support of Robert, earl of Gloucester, in 1138, and a year later Matilda, daughter of Henry I and wife of Count Geoffrey of Anjou, made her bid for power, landing in England to claim her father's kingdom. The administrative cadre which had served Henry I with loyalty rallied to her; especially important was the support of Miles of Gloucester. Magnates offended or disappointed by Stephen trans-ferred their allegiance to her or began to play the political game for their own best interests. Civil war divided the kingdom for some eight years, and jealousies and rivalries survived long after hostilities had died away. For Wales, it was particularly important that Ranulf, earl of Chester, became deeply involved in English politics as he sought to extract the greatest advantage for his family from the civil war. For those who had settled in the marches these developments meant continual weakness: for the Welsh, they meant greater oppor-tunity to extend their powers and to reclaim lost lands. In the south, the combined territories of Earl Robert and Miles of Gloucester formed Matilda's main power base; their resources in money and manpower were directed primarily to further her cause. Stephen was deprived of the traditional centres from which campaigning in Wales could be mounted, Bristol, Gloucester and Hereford. The nearest city which was within his sphere of influence was Worcester. In the north, the earl of Chester was diverted from the problems of the frontier which were left for his agents to resolve, and Stephen could not intervene since Chester was no longer in loyal hands. From Powys, Madog ap Maredudd moved into border lordships; his advance was marked by the capture of Oswestry. From Gwynedd, Owain Gwynedd could move into the disputed _cantrefi_ between the Conwy and the Dee: the fall of Mold castle indicated the range and scale of his successes. This lack of unity was not exclusively an English problem for, at the time of their greatest opportunity, Welsh leaders were divided. Owain Gwynedd was involved in con-flict with his brother Cadwaladr on one flank, and with Madog ap Maredudd of Powys on the other. That, and the absence of any obvious successor in south Wales when Gruffydd ap Rhys died in 1137, robbed the Welsh recovery of some impetus. Even so, the combination of renewed drive among the Welsh princes and political weakness in England made for extensive Welsh gains and for the loss of castles and land by the Norman settlers. The attendant toll of captives carried off by the victors added to the sense of triumph in the Welsh principalities and to the sense of disaster in the marcher lordships most closely affected.

Not for the first time, the permanence of these gains rested upon events in England. Henry II succeeded Stephen in December 1154, determined to restore royal authority in the kingdom and to repair the damage caused by civil strife and by the lack of a strong central administration. At the same time he was directly concerned with his lordships in France where he could rarely resist the temptation to extend his power in border territories and in areas where his predecessors had claimed rights as overlords. By 1157 he was ready to turn his attention to Wales and the marches. Two princes carried Wales through these difficult years, Owain Gwynedd in the north and Rhys ap Gruffydd in south Wales. Both were aware of the complex problems to be faced: to deal with rival Welsh dynasties, to deal with the marcher lords, and to live in the shadow of a rich and powerful neighbour. Both resolved this problem to their own advantage by accepting the formal obligations of English overlordship and, when necessity demanded, by accepting the limitations implicit in the status of a client-king. Owain gauged the political realities of the day quickly and, however often he had to yield, he did not lose the initiative. Rhys, coming to power as a young man during these critical years, learned the lessons more slowly but applied them with maximum effect in his maturity.

In 1157 Henry planned an attack on Gwynedd, isolating Owain by forming an alliance with influential men in north Wales – Cadwaladr (Owain's brother), Madog ap Maredudd of Powys and his brother Iorwerth Goch (the Red), and a lesser figure, Hywel ab Ieuaf of Arwystli. A fleet was sent north to operate with the king's army. The campaign was remarkable for a near disaster which brought Henry II close to death. While his main army was secure on the coastal route to Basingwerk, Henry cut across the heavily wooded hill country south of Hawarden where he was ambushed by Owain's sons. There, at Coleshill, his companions were thoroughly demoralised, and the king was lucky to escape. He met with a second reverse when the men on his ships attempted an unsuccessful raid on

Moelfre, in Anglesey. His main force remained formidable, and Owain had to fall back on Gwynedd and to accept unfavourable terms. He was required to do homage to Henry and to cede the commote of Tegeingl, which bordered directly on the lands of the earldom of Chester, and he had to receive back into Wales his brother, Cadwaladr. It was not long before Owain was acting with complete independence. When Madog ap Maredudd died in 1160, he attacked Powys and Arwystli to extend his influence to the east. He took full advantage of a vacancy in the diocese of Bangor to defy Henry II and Archbishop Becket, and to seek the support of the papacy for his own candidate. In 1165 Henry set out on a second major campaign clearly intended to bring Owain into submission, but it proved to be a barren failure. All the leading Welsh princes with their forces gathered in Edeirnion, but English and Welsh forces never met in battle. The weather conditions in which the English army had to travel across mountain routes were so atrocious that a prompt and ignominious withdrawal was unavoidable. The retreat was as decisive as any battle might have been, and the king never again attempted a major attack on Gwynedd. The sequel demonstrated the worst side of Henry's nature. He had a number of well-born Welsh hostages and they were blinded; they included two sons of Owain Gwynedd – their ultimate fate is not known – and two sons of Rhys ap Gruffydd, Cynwrig who died in 1237, and Maredudd Ddall (the Blind) who died in 1239. The Welsh would have lost many more casualties in battle, but that would have caused much less resentment. So much did Owain feel released from Henry's overlordship that in 1168 he set on foot negotiations with Louis VII of France to build an alliance between Gwynedd and France against their common enemy. All told, it was a course which required great finesse and firm judgement. In one direction it pointed to a policy which would be used to good effect by later rulers of Gwynedd, the search for recognition and alliance in Europe. The tragedy, recurrent in Welsh history, was that Owain was not followed immediately by a strong ruler who could build on his achievements. On his death in 1170 open warfare broke out between his sons: Dafydd and Rhodri killed their elder half-brother, Hywel, and in the next twenty years Gwynedd was divided between them and their kinsmen. Dafydd was sufficiently influential to secure a half-sister of Henry II as his wife, but at home he could be forced out of the old territory of Gwynedd into lands between the Conwy and the Dee centred on Rhuddlan. Gwynedd had to wait for the

emergence of Llywelyn ab Iorwerth in the last years of the century
before unity and strength could be restored.

In south Wales the major event was the establishment of Rhys ap
Gruffydd as the ruler of a reinvigorated kingdom of Deheubarth.
After Gruffydd's death in 1137 his four young sons worked closely
together to defend and consolidate their territory. Each son,
Anarawd, Cadell, Maredudd and Rhys took the lead in succession,
and there seems to have been no discord between them. Their raids
extended from west Wales to the lordship of Glamorgan. Anarawd
was assassinated by men from north Wales in 1143; Cadell and his
younger brothers achieved the reconquest of Ceredigion, making it
once more part of Deheubarth, before Cadell was wounded so
severely by Normans from Tenby that he was effectively removed
from the political scene. Maredudd died in 1155, leaving Rhys as
ruler of the southern kingdom. It was a remarkably peaceful and
bloodless succession. Between 1158 and 1165 Rhys was under heavy
pressure from Henry II. He was persuaded to submit, despite the loss
of territory involved when Ceredigion and Cantref Bychan were
restored to their Norman lords. Immediate retaliation by Rhys and
his kinsmen, an attempt to take Carmarthen in 1159, and a successful
attack on Llandovery in 1162 pointed for Henry II a recurrent
danger: the Welsh prince would not accept an enhanced Anglo-
Norman presence in west Wales. For Rhys, submission and defiance
were part of the dynamic of border conflict. For Henry, in west
Wales as in the north, the first objective was to suppress a trouble-
some prince. So long as that phase lasted the king's natural affinity
was with the lords of the southern march. In the late 1160s the political climate in south Wales changed and Henry had to reassess the
place of the Welsh prince and the marcher lords in his polity.

The change sprang from Richard Strongbow's interest in Ireland.
Dermot MacMurrough's control of the kingdom of Leinster
depended upon his alliance with Murchetach MacLochlain, king of
Munster, and when that alliance failed he had to find allies elsewhere.
He gained the sympathy of Henry II and began to recruit support in
south Wales. While a number of lesser magnates were attracted, his
chief prize was the earl of Pembroke, Richard fitz Gilbert (Richard
Strongbow). With the grudging (and ambiguous) approval of the
king, Richard came to terms with Dermot and set off for Leinster.
From 1167 onwards, Ireland was a magnet for men from west Wales,
and in particular for the sons and grandsons of Nest, daughter of
Rhys ap Tewdwr. To check their independence in Ireland, Henry

embarked on his own expedition in 1171; he and his successors
retained a close interest in Irish lands conquered by Anglo-Norman
settlers, and royal officials played an important part in their affairs.
In Wales, it was a valuable expedient for the king and the prince of
Deheubarth to make common cause; how soon this was mooted is
hard to say, but by the autumn of 1171 the terms of their rapproche-
ment had been agreed. For Rhys, the first and most important result
was the confirmation of his tenure of the lands he had conquered,
Ceredigion, Cantref Bychan, Emlyn, and two commotes near
Carmarthen. The final confirmation of his standing came with the
style justiciar for south Wales; an English title which carried the clear
delegation of royal authority was used to cover jurisdiction over
Welsh leaders and communities which looked to Rhys from the lordships of Gwynllŵg, Usk, Caerleon, Glamorgan, Elfael and
Maelienydd. Long ago Stubbs wrote that Henry II preferred a willing ally to an unwilling vassal, and it is a good description of the
change which was brought about by the formalities of 1171–2. While
Henry lived, Rhys was a trusted agent and ally – never more so than
in the years of crisis for Henry, 1173–4, when he faced rebellion
throughout his territories. For his part, Rhys was content to make
full use of his relationship with the king, but he continued to think
and act as an independent Welsh prince. He rebuilt Cardigan castle
for his own use, and he used marriage alliances to consolidate his
position. One daughter married William fitz Martin of Cemais,
while his eldest son, Gruffydd, married Matilda de Braose from the
Norman lordship of Brecknock. Rhys made his large family a source
of strength by creating marriage links with the leading Welsh
families of south and mid-Wales. In 1175 he was at Gloucester, acting as the king's intermediary and presenting a large cross-section of
his own clientele to Henry, and most of them were linked to him by
blood or by marriage. As the twelfth century drew to a close, Rhys
was once again engaged in campaigning against the crown and the
greater lords of the southern march, and at the same time he was
deeply implicated in internal feuds among his kindred. These
struggles presaged the decline of his dynasty and the eclipse of his
kingdom. By the time of his death in 1197 he had been an active
participant in war and politics for sixty years, and he had been the
dominant ruling prince in Wales for more than forty years.

   The second half of the twelfth century saw the emergence of a new
phenomenon in the marches: at different times, one family emerged
to a position of dominance in south Wales and, often, to a position of

great power in the English kingdom. The succession is clear: Braose, Clare, de Burgh, Bohun, Mortimer and Despenser. It might be matched by a shorter list of magnates emerging to prominence in the north. At times, the dominant role might fall to one of the royal kindred, to John, and pre-eminently to the Lord Edward. The rise in family fortunes was often the result of luck and opportunism rather than of deliberate planning. The expansion of Braose interests in Wales is a case in point. A marriage with Bertha, daughter of Miles of Gloucester, which did not appear to offer great landed wealth, brought Brecknock and Abergavenny to William de Braose. Miles died, still in his prime, at the end of 1143. His eldest son, Roger, was deprived of the earldom of Hereford for treason in 1155 and died within a few months. He had three brothers; one, Henry of Hereford, was certainly married, and the male line looked secure, but they all died without children. Walter of Hereford died in the Holy Land (or on the journey home); Henry was killed by Seisyll ap Dyfnwal, the leading figure in Gwent Uwchcoed, and Mahel was killed in 1165 by falling masonry from the burning castle of Bronllys. Three sisters shared Mahel's inheritance, and Bertha and William de Braose took the lordships of Brecknock and Abergavenny. He was already lord of Builth and Radnor and his combined holding made a strong power bloc in the middle reaches of the march. The sons of Miles had concentrated on their Welsh lordships and William continued in the same tradition. He marked his succession by avenging the death of Henry of Hereford, luring Seisyll and other local Welsh leaders to Abergavenny and murdering them there. He further outraged local opinion by pursuing Seisyll's wife and killing her infant son as she was protecting him in her arms.

William made Brecknock the centre of his marcher interests. His son, another William, rose to power in the last years of Henry II's reign and served Richard I. He was at Chalus when the king was fatally wounded in 1199. In the early years of John's reign he became one of the king's intimate circle and by his services he gained Gower, Kington and the lordship of the three castles – Whitecastle, Grosmont and Skenfrith – which created a formidable and compact block of lands in the southern march; he was also given custody of Glamorgan, Monmouth, Gwynllŵg and some Lacy lands. 'Given' is an ambiguous term to use; he bargained and promised very large payments for the custodies from which he hoped to draw large profits. With the Irish lordship of Limerick and his ancestral lands in Normandy and England, these acquisitions made him one of the richest and most influential men at the king's court. In 1207 he fell

foul of the king who stripped him of his custodies and forced him to
seek refuge, with his family, in Ireland. In 1210 he fled to France,
where he died in the following year. His wife and son were handed
over to the king who had them starved to death, perhaps at Windsor
or at Corfe castle; his grand-children, the younger William's sons,
were kept in prison until 1218. There followed an intriguing battle of
wills. John was anxious to reconcile Giles de Braose, bishop of
Hereford, and promised him restitution for his family, but he was
not willing to carry out his promise. Llywelyn ab Iorwerth, prince of
Gwynedd, was anxious to reap the best advantage for himself and his
allies in Deheubarth; on the one hand, the eclipse of the house of
Braose gave him added strength in Wales, while on the other hand
the family's ambitions might be used to attack King John. Reginald
de Braose, brother of John's victim, was the obvious man to take a
lead in regaining the family's lands, but he saw an opportunity to
gain land for himself at the expense of his imprisoned nephew, the
true heir to the Braose inheritance. In 1213, with the support of the
Welsh prince, Bishop Giles and Reginald de Braose moved to open
war against the king and regained all the lordships in which the
family had enjoyed long tenure. In recognition of their dependence,
Reginald married a daughter of Llywelyn ab Iorwerth who made
sure that Gower was also restored to him. When, in 1217, Reginald
decided in favour of coming to terms with Henry III, he angered his
father-in-law, and found his Welsh lordships under attack. In 1218
John de Braose and his brothers were released; their father's

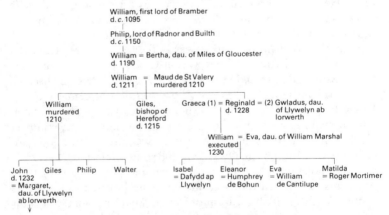

Figure 3   The family of de Braose
Note: not all the lesser members of the family are shown.

lordships of Bramber and Barnstaple passed to John without difficulty, but when he challenged his uncle and tried to regain his Welsh
territories by legal action, he failed. Only one lordship was restored
to him in the march: in 1219, Llywelyn arranged a marriage between
his daughter, Margaret, and John de Braose, and handed over to him
the lordship of Gower. The restoration of the family's fortunes was
short-lived. In 1230, when William, son of Reginald de Braose, was
hanged by Prince Llywelyn, he left four daughters who shared his
inheritance. Isabel was married to Llywelyn's son, Dafydd, and she
was given Builth on the occasion of her marriage; Eleanor and her
husband, Humphrey de Bohun, secured Brecknock; Eva married
William de Cantilupe and took Abergavenny to a new dynasty;
Matilda married Roger Mortimer who added Radnor to his lordships. The Braose family's domination had been created and broken
in one generation, and in the next their name disappeared from all
their Welsh lordships except Gower.

King John's grasp of Welsh affairs sprang from his tenure of the
honour of Gloucester and the lordships of Gwynllŵg and
Glamorgan. They had long been used as a valuable endowment of
Henry I's son, Earl Robert (*c.* 1122–47), and grandson, Earl William
(1147–83). When William died he left three daughters, and in 1189
his earldom and estates passed with his youngest daughter, Isabel, to
John. These rich lands were not easily to be prised from the royal
hands. For eleven years before his accession, John had control of
Gwynllŵg and Glamorgan and could claim first-hand, if fitful,
experience as a marcher lord. In 1199 he divorced his wife but he
retained the greater part of her estates for another sixteen years,
allowing the title of earl of Gloucester to pass to a succession of
claimants. As king, and especially after 1204, he was frequently in
the English border shires, while in Wales he secured Cardigan castle
from Maelgwn ap Rhys in the west, and he took control of the
Braose lordships in the south-east. His expedition to Ireland in 1210
embarked from, and returned to, west Wales, and increased his
direct awareness of the southern marches. His illegitimate daughter,
Joan, was married to Llywelyn ab Iorwerth of Gwynedd. When,
twice in 1211 and again in 1212, he planned major campaigns against
Gwynedd, they were based upon a formidable body of experience
and personal knowledge. His second venture, in the summer of
1211, penetrated deep into Gwynedd and reduced Llywelyn ab
Iorwerth to his lowest ebb. The full measure of the king's control in
south Wales is to be found in his use of three of his ablest and most
ruthless mercenary captains in his marcher lands, Fawkes de

Breauté, Engelard de Cigogni and Gerard d'Athée. From their harsh rule, English shires and Welsh lordships alike found relief through the grant, and ultimate implementation, of Magna Carta.

The residuary legatee of their work was another able servant of the Angevin kings, Hubert de Burgh. His short career in the march was ominous, for he was a man of the court, well placed to acquire grants of land and the custody of minors and estates, and he chose deliberately to garner in Wales. If evidence were needed that marcher lordships were valuable property, de Burgh's activities provide it. In 1201 he was granted the three castles of Whitecastle, Skenfrith and Grosmont, only to see them transferred to the king's confederate, William de Braose, in 1205. He had to wait for Braose to fall before he could reassert his own claims. Then, during the early years of Henry III's reign, he began a systematic process of extending his influence: Montgomery, in 1223, where he built the splendid cliff-top castle which still dominates the town; Archenfield in 1227; and Carmarthen and Cardigan, with their lordships, in 1229. The limits of Carmarthen were extended eastwards by making Gower part of that lordship as a subordinate tenure. Two accidents of succession completed his tally: in 1230 the earldom of Gloucester with its Welsh lordships passed to an eight-year-old boy, and Hubert was given custody of him and his lands; and in the following year the custody of the Braose lands in Wales was transferred to him. In some eight years, Hubert had transformed a small tenure on the march into a major collection of lordships. In the short run, he used his power as a check on the ambitions of Llywelyn ab Iorwerth of Gwynedd in central and south Wales. But in a long career, de Burgh had made many enemies, and in 1232, in the first major constitutional crisis of Henry III's reign, he was overthrown.

In the late thirteenth century, the Bohuns emerged as a powerful influence. They did not attempt to accumulate lordships, and their lack of strength in Wales was all too apparent, but they brought with them great wealth and they had the benefit of their political influence in English affairs. For that reason, the conflict between Clare and Bohun which reached crisis point in the late 1280s had far-reaching consequences in south Wales and made possible direct intervention in the marches by Edward I. The Bohuns were no strangers in Brecknock. By marriage with Margaret, daughter of Miles of Gloucester, the Bohuns acquired the family's English lands, the honour of Caldicot. In 1230, another marriage alliance brought them into Miles' old lordship of Brecknock, but their power there was weak. The lordship was under the strong influence of the princes of

Gwynedd, and for a number of years after 1262 was held firmly by Llywelyn ap Gruffydd. Their changing fortunes in the barons' wars in England added to the Bohuns' weakness in the march. The death from wounds of Humphrey de Bohun, earl of Hereford, in 1265 while he was the king's prisoner, left another Humphrey, a son of seventeen, to succeed him, and the wardship of the youth was given to the earl of Gloucester. When he reached his majority in 1270, Humphrey bought the right of making his own marriage for £1,000, but twenty years later this transaction was still a matter of sharp conflict, and not much more than a quarter of the money had been paid. There were other causes of dispute, notably whether the new Clare castle at Morlais had been built within the limits of Glamorgan, or beyond those limits in the upland territory of Brecknock. Their quarrel reached flash point, with the earl of Gloucester prepared to follow the custom of the march and resort to open war to settle their dispute. But Bohun was not strong enough in the march to risk that possibility; instead, he preferred to play to his strength in England, and to appeal to the king for judgement. Edward was by no means unwilling to intervene, especially because the earl of Gloucester had tried to assert his right, as lord of Glamorgan, to determine the succession to the diocese of Llandaff. He met with a check in that long process in 1290, and Edward was anxious to press the rights of the crown within the marches. Gloucester consistently refused to appear in the courts, and both earls resorted to local violence in south Wales. They were brought to trial at Abergavenny in 1291 and sentenced to imprisonment; there were urgent consultations with Edward's trusted administrator, Otto de Grandson; and in January, 1292, both earls submitted themselves to the king's will in parliament. Their sentences were, on the surface, harsh; both were imprisoned, the earl of Gloucester was fined 10,000 marks (£6,666 13s. 4d.) and Glamorgan was declared forfeit for his lifetime, while the earl of Hereford was fined 1,000 marks (£666 13s. 4d.) and Brecknock was taken from him for his lifetime. But the king had, as it seems, overreached himself, and quietly these penalties were dropped. The earls were quickly released, their marcher lordships were soon restored to them, and the fines were never paid. What could not be undone was the direct intervention by Edward I in marcher affairs and the deliberate overriding of marcher custom. The Bohuns suffered a temporary eclipse after the death of the reigning earl of Hereford at Boroughbridge in 1322, but they recovered and survived as lords of the march until the extinction of the male line in 1373. One feature of their tenure of the lordship of Brecknock which deserves particular notice is the accord which they established with the leading Welsh dynasty of their lordship. Over a number of generations community of interest and loyalty marked their relationship and gave the lordship an element of stability which served it well in times of strife and upheaval.

The men of power in Edward I's reign may have found him a difficult and dangerous adversary. In war, whether in Gascony or England, in Wales or Scotland, he was a hard fighter who enjoyed the taste of success. At home, he spared no one, however close to the royal cir e, if he considered that rights and privileges were being exercised without adequate warrant. Things were very different in the reign of his son, Edward II, when the king's homosexual predilections impinged directly on politics, and the king's favourites could win for themselves great power and wealth. The first of Edward's special friends, Piers Gaveston, acquired honours and lands in England but, despite his marriage to Margaret de Clare, he was not directly interested in Wales and the march. That changed after he was executed, in June 1312, and Edward fell under the influence of the Despensers, father and son. The older Despenser was not himself unduly greedy for land, though he gained the rich lordship of Denbigh, but his son was a man of very different calibre. By marriage with Eleanor de Clare, he shared in the division of the Clare inheritance in 1317, with Glamorgan as his immediate share of their Welsh lands. He was soon to be identified as the most covetous magnate on the marches. In thoroughly unscrupulous fashion, he secured Gwynllŵg from Hugh Audley in 1317–18, and at a later stage, Usk from the third Clare heiress, Lady Elizabeth de Burgh. By the end of 1317 he had obtained a life grant of Dryslwyn and Cantref Mawr; two years later he controlled the old lordship of Emlyn (now more regularly known as Newcastle Emlyn) through a compliant nominee, and he had made his first attempt to secure Gower. When Edward II defeated his enemies among the magnates at Boroughbridge in 1322, the younger Despenser was on hand to claim Brecknock, Hay and Huntington (from the earl of Hereford's estates), Blaenllyfni (from Mortimer of Chirk) and Iscennen, in Cantref Bychan (from the Giffards). Chepstow and Goodrich were added to his list of possessions, and then he secured from the king the profitable custodies of the earldom of Pembroke and of the Hastings lordships, including Abergavenny and Cilgerran. His greed was a by-word: by his opportunism and unscrupulousness he held lordships from west Wales to the Wye which rendered about £4,000, with perhaps another £1,000 from the lands he held in custody.

The Despensers' most implacable enemy was Edward II's queen, Isabella of France, and on her determination to escape from her humiliating position in England and its consequence, there is little need to dwell. Her value as a negotiator between the two countries gave her the means of travelling safely to France, where she made common cause with the exiled Roger Mortimer. To complete the formalities of making peace, Edward II or his heir was to do homage to Charles IV for Aquitaine; and the Despensers, failing to see the full implications of their decision, sent the young Prince Edward. The queen and prince became the centre of a growing party of men disenchanted with the Despensers and their administration. In September 1326 Isabella and Mortimer landed in Suffolk. Edward found himself abandoned by many of his leading administrators, and he and the Despensers were isolated and exposed. They made for Wales and for the apparent strength of the younger Hugh's lordships, but that proved a vain hope. The older Hugh surrendered at Bristol and, after a travesty of a judicial hearing, was executed. Edward and the younger Hugh made a bid to escape from Chepstow by sea, but they were only able to reach Glamorgan, and at Neath abbey they were taken into custody. Despenser was sent to Hereford for trial and executed with crude brutality. With whatever justification, dislike of and disgust at sexual aberration in the king's immediate circle sharpened the vengeance which the Despensers' political opponents sought on purely political grounds.

The alarming power bloc built up by the Despensers collapsed, and their enemies were able to profit from the disaster. Even so, by a mixture of tenacity and resilience, Despenser remained a name of significance on the march. The younger Hugh's original stake in the march, his wife's lordship of Glamorgan, remained with Eleanor and her second husband, William Mortimer de la Zouche, until their deaths in 1337, and continued to be held by her Despenser successors until 1413. In the 1370s, the Despensers drew about one third of their total income from their Welsh lordship alone. It deserved their close attention, and it was symbolic that, in 1375, Edward Despenser should have died in the lordship while he was visiting his Welsh estates. That they were so restricted in south Wales owes much to the tenacity of the Clare family: Hugh Despenser's plans to wrest Gwynllŵg from Hugh Audley and his wife were frustrated, and that lordship continued in the possession of their line until 1347; and the third co-heiress, Elizabeth de Burgh, regained Usk and enjoyed her possession of that lordship until a great age before she passed it on to her successors.

The Mortimers had long been established on the frontier, with their honour based on their Herefordshire castle at Wigmore where they had been established from the first half of the reign of William the Conqueror. They made modest advances into Maelienydd and then into the neighbouring district of Gwrtheyrnion but their gains were less spectacular than those of their neighbours. A fortunate marriage with one of the co-heiresses of William de Braose brought new lordships under their control after his death in 1230: from her father's lands she acquired Radnor, and from the Marshal inheritance of her mother she gained Narberth and part of St Clears. If marriage brought new estates, so, too, did service under the crown; the rise in Mortimer fortunes in the second half of the thirteenth century is part of the story of Edward I's conflict with Prince Llywelyn ap Gruffydd: Ceri and Cydewain and Llywelyn's castle and lands of Dolforwyn consolidated the family's hold in mid-Wales, while the grant of Chirk to a younger son was a major enhancement of their power. When Roger Mortimer died in 1282, he left his son, Edmund, with a much-enriched inheritance, though not with the ambition to play a large role in English politics. A generation later, the family had to survive the problems of Edward II's reign. Edmund's son, Roger, and the representative of the Chirk line were both among the king's enemies in 1322 and suffered heavy losses after Boroughbridge. Roger Mortimer of Wigmore, awaiting execution, escaped from the Tower of London and made his way to France, and with Queen Isabella, was responsible for the defeat and murder of Edward II. Then, from 1327 to 1330, with the young Edward III as a puppet-king, Mortimer controlled the English kingdom: he assumed an unparalleled display of dignity and status, overshadowing the young king. For his family, the permanent acquisition in these years of power was the earldom bestowed on him in 1328. He chose the style, earl of March, a marcher dignity for which there were precedents in central France, but which was a new departure in England. His liaison with the queen and the political danger he presented to the young king combined to mark him down for destruction, and he fell and was executed in 1330. Almost a generation passed before the family was properly reinstated. In 1354, Edward III removed the judgement passed against Earl Roger in 1330, at the same time as he suspended the judgement passed against Edmund fitz Alan, earl of Arundel, in 1326. From that point on the earls of March resumed their place as leading figures on the march and in the king's court. Roger, the second earl, lived to enjoy his restoration for six years. His son, Edmund, held the earldom from

1360 to 1381, and married a grand-daughter of Edward III, Philippa, daughter of Lionel, duke of Clarence, and heiress of Elizabeth de Burgh. As with the Clares and the Bohuns, the Mortimers were locked into the pattern of politics of the English kingdom and the royal dynasty.

It is easy to make the assumption that new lands in Wales brought wealth to the Anglo-Norman, and later English, lords, but it is far from easy to make the case in any detail. They had to exploit all the resources of their lordships, whether they were used by immigrants and settlers or by a native Welsh population. Conquest and settlement determined the main lines of division between these racial groups, with the territorial distinction between Englishry and Welshry. The Englishry was that low-lying area in which the invaders settled and established a manorial form of organisation. The land was easily farmed, and could be defended adequately, and here the settlers engaged in arable farming, and made good use of meadowland and river pastures for feeding their stock. The lord's lands were farmed by a dependent, servile population, often made up of English peasants, and from these estates he derived the profits associated with demesne farming, or with the rents and payments made by those who farmed his land. The lord would also enjoy the normal profits from the courts in which he claimed jurisdiction, whether honorial or manorial.

The Welsh were relegated to the less profitable lands in the upland areas of the lordship. They were no strangers to these areas, which they had learned to exploit as pastoral farmers. Much of their time was traditionally taken up with substantial herds of cattle, and they were accustomed to the system of transhumance by which they moved from their winter quarters (the *hendre*) to the summer quarters on the upland pastures (the *hafod*). The place-names themselves indicate how fundamental the practice was. One early and clear indication of the importance of their herds is to be found in the use of one word – *da* – for 'cattle' and also for 'wealth' or 'goods'. When they were forced out of the lowland areas, the Welsh moved into those upland areas which they knew so well. They adjusted in their use of land to continue producing cereal crops from hill farms; the process can be seen clearly in the lordship of Brecknock. Their wealth remained largely in cattle. Their new Norman lords could exact from them traditional payments in kind. *Cymorth* was originally an ancient render of cattle, a means by which the Welsh lord (and later his Norman supplanter) might tax the herds which made up so much of the wealth of his people. The payment of a death duty, *ebediw*, was the equivalent of the English *heriot*. For a military leader or a freeman it would be his horse and arms; for a lesser figure, his best beast, or his second best beast, according to custom. The women folk of the community were the occasion of another payment, *amobr*, basically a payment protecting virginity, which seems to have had something of the quality of English payments for permission to marry.

For the twelfth and thirteenth centuries, the evidence bearing on these issues is very limited. It is hard to assess the numbers of Welshmen living within any lordship, or the wealth which they could build up. It is equally difficult to assess how profitable was the change from an economy subject to frequent raids and incursions, with plunder as an appreciable element in terms of gains or losses, to a more settled and productive economy. In 1965, Professor M. Altschul estimated that the Clare honour of Gloucester may have produced a revenue as high as £600 in the latter part of the twelfth century and that the lordship of Glamorgan was producing about £225 a year. He thought that the revenue from these two honours might represent about half of the total income of the Clare earls of Gloucester and Hertford in the early thirteenth century. In that case, Glamorgan may have provided something like 15 per cent of their revenues. The indications are that, as the thirteenth century advanced, that proportion increased to 23 per cent in 1266 and 40 per cent in 1317. More recently, in 1978, Professor Rees Davies produced an intensive study of the marcher lordships in the later middle ages and for the fourteenth century he could cite a large body of material, all of which tended to the view that the value of the greater Welsh lordships was increasing steadily throughout the century. Two types of revenue, in particular, were being collected and exploited by the marcher lords. One was a body of gifts, grants and subsidies which were being exacted at such regular terms that they constituted a form of casual income. The other was the profits of judicial lordship, the income derived from the lord's jurisdiction over his Welsh tenantry. Here again, the scale is notable; those who held large lordships in England and in Wales were drawing much more from their jurisdiction in Wales than they could draw from their English lands, sometimes by as much as 70 per cent or 80 per cent of the revenues produced through their courts. One illustration may point to the scale of these financial advantages. Over some twenty-one years, from 1337 to 1358, the lord of Brecknock was obtaining about £4,000 by way of casual income from his Welsh tenantry. At the same time, he was mulcting the same community on what appears to be a massive scale in his courts. In 1352, for one offence alone, for assarting lands in the Forests of Brecknock without permission, he exacted a fine of £400. But that was only one payment for one offence; during the five years, 1352–7, he fined his Welshmen 100 marks (£66 13s. 4d.) for wrongful judgements, £500 for evading tolls, and £750 for attacking the men of Builth: a total of £1,717 in fines over five years. Were they excessive, or could they be absorbed easily by the community? There are three indications which may help establish an answer to that question. In 1375, when the Welsh of Brecknock were given the chance to provide a suitable gift, rather than face the rigours of major activities in the lord's courts, they paid £1,800 for that purpose. The gross income of the lordship in the fourteenth century was of the order of £1,400 (£1,405 in 1398). If the fines of 1352–7 are averaged out, they would amount to some £343 in each year; and against the scale of the figures which can be cited, that is a small sum. What would be of crucial importance would be to know the number of Welshmen who might have to contribute towards these exactions. In 1302, at a mass ceremony, 2,000 Welshmen from Brecknock gave their allegiance to the king. If that figure is a reliable pointer to the size of the Welsh population in Brecknock during the century, the burden on any individual would have been comparatively small. The general conclusion seems to be that in uplands Brecknock there was a flourishing and profitable husbandry. Estimates from the fifteenth and sixteenth centuries point to a large-scale animal farming, with large herds of cattle and sheep. The lords of Brecknock were drawing a large profit from all this, but the critical question is whether the Welsh tenantry retained a reasonable share of the profits after their lord had exacted his dues. In Wales, as in England, the material which would allow such a comparison is sadly deficient. It may be helpful to gauge the tone of legislation or the scale and frequency of fines and exactions, but the pressures which bore upon the peasantry cannot be measured in precise terms. The Welsh community of Brecknock leased the Great Forest and its pastures from their lord, and presumably they were able to make considerably more than the basic demand; the additional payments which their lord could exact suggest that their initial profits may have been quite high, but it is still impossible to say how much or how little advantage they could claim when the final accounts were cast.

A large proportion of their herds of cattle was destined for English estates of marcher lords, and for feeding their large households in

England. The Beauchamps used their lordship of Barnard Castle, in County Durham, as a large cattle ranch from which their drovers took regular herds as far south as Warwickshire, Worcestershire and Berkshire. There can be little doubt that Welsh estates provided the same facilities for the Clares, the Bohuns and the fitz Alans and their neighbours on the march. There was also a profitable trade in stock cattle for English markets. Herds numbering several hundreds could be nurtured and fed in upland pastures.

Sheep, too, provided great wealth. In the twelfth century the pioneers were the Flemish settlers in west Wales, and above all the Cistercians of south and mid-Wales. The monks pastured large flocks on upland ranges in the summer months, but they geared their acquisition and use of land to ensure adequate lowland pasturage for their flocks in the winter season. Other houses followed their example: Talley abbey had ample upland grazing, and good sheltered land around Llandeilo for winter use. Houses like Margam and Strata Florida grew rich on large flocks. Secular magnates were not slow to follow their example, nor, in fact, to take over on lease some of their upland territories. Elizabeth de Burgh had 7,862 sheep on her pasture lands in 1340, while the fitz Alans were credited with 15,000. At Clun, 26 per cent of their income was drawn from their flocks. The number of fulling mills in use in the marches points to the scale of cloth production: over 200 can be identified in use from the thirteenth to the sixteenth centuries. Trade statistics are not easy to establish, but the scale of trade in wool with Shrewsbury, or of wool, cloth and hides with Bristol, cannot be doubted. Nor can the significance of the concentration of cloth production at Ruthin or of leather work at Brecon and Swansea.

There remains one further export to England, that of manpower. From early on, Norman magnates took with them contingents of Welsh soldiers, and the kings of England began to make use of Welsh mercenaries. From the twelfth century to the fifteenth this flow of fighting men grew steadily. The value of the Welsh as mobile, lightly armed troops, and especially as bowmen, was widely recognised, and their courage in fighting without the slightest of protection earned admiration. Until the late thirteenth century, lack of discipline in battle was a criticism voiced by contemporaries. Welsh fighters played a part in the civil strife in England during the reign of Stephen; they formed part of the professional mercenary armies of the Angevin kings. The pipe rolls of the reigns of Henry II, Richard I and John contain many entries relating to the recruitment and equipping of Welsh troops. Edward I and his captains, many of them drawn from the marches, employed Welsh fighters in the campaigns against Gwynedd in 1276, when Edward I had some 9,000 Welshmen from the marches serving in his armies. They were prominent again in 1282–3. It was a matter of adjustment to recruit and deploy them for the campaign in Flanders, when more than 5,000 Welshmen saw service, and for Edward's campaigns in Scotland. The royal castle at Builth was ideally placed to serve as a collecting depot and staging post for troops destined for Scotland. In 1319, the king's justiciar in south Wales, Rhys ap Gruffydd, mustered 1,200 men from south Wales there for service in Scotland, and a second contingent was assembled there in 1321 under Gruffydd ap Llywelyn. Smaller contingents were raised for the more routine operations of a later period; 450 men left for Roxburgh in 1334, and at the end of the century, in 1385, 215 Welshmen were mustered at Builth to serve in Scotland. In two respects, this affected Wales directly. It ensured that there was not a large cadre of disaffected men after the defeat of Welsh ambitions in 1282–3. It also produced profitable employment for many men from the marches whose economic prospects might otherwise have been very poor. In that respect, what was happening in Wales ran parallel to what was happening in other areas where a surplus of men and a lack of opportunity for them at home made mercenary service seem an attractive alternative. Perhaps the nearest parallel is with Brabant and the Low Countries. What happened in the thirteenth century could be matched by what happened in the fifteenth century; after the collapse of the Glyn Dŵr revolt, many Welshmen found a welcome outlet through Henry V's campaigns, or served under Bedford. Many of them returned from France to England to take part in the fighting which marked the conflict between Lancaster and York.

Trade, defence and race are inextricably bound up in the history of the marcher boroughs. The problems of the history of Welsh boroughs are more clearly discernible in terms of the great Edwardian plantation towns, for which there is a substantial body of evidence. For the twelfth and thirteenth centuries there is a sad lack of evidence relating to the boroughs in the marcher lordships, but as material becomes richer in the later middle ages and in the sixteenth century, the scale of operations and the profits to be drawn from boroughs stand out more clearly. In Glamorgan, the lord and his knightly tenants encouraged the development of a number of boroughs, with Cardiff pre-eminent among them. In Brecknock, by contrast, the burgesses of Brecon were given such firm privileges

that no other market developed within the lordship. These settlements were primarily garrison towns, planted in an age of conquest,
and it is almost impossible to assess how far Welsh people were
allowed, or encouraged, to settle in them. Burgesses shared with
garrisons the responsibility for defence. At Swansea, in recognition
of that fact, the burgesses were allowed to pasture their horses with
those of the soldiers in the castle. Charters addressed to the lord's
faithful men, French, English, Flemish and Welsh, point in general
terms to a Welsh element in borough society, but only in the later
middle ages does documentary evidence throw some light upon
them. At best, a small minority of Welshmen appear among the
burgesses. In 1411, six out of eighty-six burgesses named in Brecon
were unmistakably Welsh (with perhaps a hidden element in the
number of men using trades names in place of surnames), and by
1442 about 25 per cent of another list of burgesses were Welsh.
Morgan ap Dafydd Fychan was deprived of the three burgages he
held in Brecon when he went over to Owain Glyn Dŵr's party. At
Cardiff, a number of burgesses were drawn from neighbouring vills
and took their names from their home villages, Llandaff, Barry,
Penarth and Llancarfan. By the mid-sixteenth century, perhaps as
many as 35 per cent of those holding property were of Welsh stock,
but how long that proportion may have held cannot be determined.
At Tenby, too, it was not until the late fifteenth century that Welsh
names appeared in any number. This racial imbalance may owe
much to the lack of documentation, but it was encouraged at times
of crisis by legislation insisting that no Welshman hold property in
the boroughs, and that local defence should be seen to be secure in
English hands. How effective such panic legislation was, or even
how permanent it was intended to be, varied sharply even over a
limited time-span.

   The boroughs raise in sharp terms the major problems of finding
language to describe the exploitation of Welsh lands and Welsh
people, first by Anglo-Norman conquerors and then by English
lords. French, English and Welsh magnates would all have agreed
that the wealth and power of the great depended upon the exploitation of those who worked the land. The language in which that
might best be expressed is the language of lordship. What could the
lord exact from his tenants, or from the servile and semi-servile
population on his estates, or from his burgesses? What obligations,
if any, did he owe in return? It is difficult, in those terms, to draw a
sharp distinction between the way in which the abbots of Cirencester
exploited their borough of Cirencester, or the lords of Glamorgan

exploited their borough of Cardiff. Equally, it is difficult to draw a sharp distinction between the way in which profits were drawn from a great manor like Tidenham on the English side of the frontier, or a manor like Ogmore or Meisgyn on the Welsh side. Lordship and exploitation were the common language of much of European society. Robert de Bellême, drawing resources from Normandy, from his English estates, or from the lands of conquest in Wales, was not using a markedly different approach in each area.

In Wales, conquest introduced a note of racial hatred which has marked historical writing on both sides of the border. It can be seen most clearly in the twelfth century in terms of those men, like Gerald of Wales, who belonged to both races but at different times felt rejected by both races. But this seems to have been, and to have remained, an emotional overtone; it does not appear to have added any extra weight of burdens for a conquered Welsh population. In the search for analogies which may help to clarify these issues, there has been a tendency in recent decades to use the language of colonialism in order to explain the Welsh experience. Some aspects of colonial practice may be illuminating: the deliberate settlement of a working population of Flemings or English; the introduction of laws and customs alien to the local population; the use of military force to bolster a regime. Other aspects are not so relevant to the Welsh experience: excessive mulcting of a subject population; limitations on the prospects of education and, to a lesser extent, of career; and racial apartheid. Intermarriage was taken for granted and honourable status was recognised and acknowledged. Fear produced defensive legislation for the protection of borough and castle, but neither fear nor its product were permanent features of the Welsh scene. Like all analogues, this colonial analogy may be pushed too far and it must be used with great sensitivity. Conditions in medieval Wales should be interpreted in terms of the standards and conventions of that age. They must be understood in terms of lordship, a concept which has its own overtones and subtleties.

A similar sensitivity is needed when questions of right and power are raised. The marches produced their own custom. When the Great Charter was drawn up in 1215, it was accepted that disputes over disseisin or the loss of liberties should be settled 'for tenements in England according to the law of England, for tenements in Wales according to the law of Wales, for tenements in the march according to the law of the march'. That enshrined custom of long standing; it echoes the innate conservatism of an aristocratic society. It cannot be doubted that, from an early stage in the Norman incursions into

Wales, the new lords assumed for themselves rights and privileges in their lordships. There was a time when historians concentrated heavily on the constitutional implications of this assumption, and sought to define, often in overprecise terms, what the custom of the march might be. In the thirteenth century, at times of crisis, the custom is brought into sharper focus: in the Charter, or in Edward I's intrusions into the lordship of Glamorgan and the conflict between Bohun and Clare. In recent studies the emphasis has shifted and the tendency is to seek the customs of the march through the detailed exercise of the rights of lordship as they can be seen in the fourteenth century. The advantage of such an approach is the greater precision which is made possible by the rich documentation of the period. The disadvantage is that it implies that later developments are all-important and it discounts the nature and the significance of marcher custom and marcher independence in the eleventh and twelfth centuries.

4

THE CHURCH IN WALES

·

When the Normans began to settle in Wales they found a church which they could not easily understand and which was virtually without defence against their depredations. The *clas* church struck no chord of experience or memory. It was not obviously related to the church with which they were familiar. It did not match the monastic foundations which they took for granted. Though it had something in common with the minster churches of England, there was not time enough to take such comparisons into account. Norman invaders claimed many estates to which the church could make a claim. From the 1060s right through to the 1150s and 1160s, the diocese of St David's was being robbed of lands by Norman settler stock. For the southern dioceses of Llandaff and St David's, their depredations were part of a massive and long-drawn-out process of despoliation. The stages by which historians can trace the gradual build-up of a viable church structure in Wales extend over a long period of time, and they represent a large measure of repair and restoration.

In the earliest phases of conquest, the Normans used their successes to provide new endowments for monasteries which had attracted their patronage in France. William fitz Osbern gave churches and lands from his English and Welsh conquests to the two monasteries which he had founded in Normandy at Lire and Cormeilles. It is one of the indications that he was associated with lands in conquered territories that churches, lands and tithes were later to be found in the possession of these two abbeys. Those who followed him had different loyalties. So, the fact that the church (and priory) of Monmouth should have been given by Wihenoc de Ballon, lord of Monmouth, to St Florent of Saumur is a clear indication of a change of lordship and of interest. Bernard of Neufmarché is an interesting personality: he seems not to have had a direct interest in the church at Neufmarché, with its eleventh-century chancel. His patronage was attracted to Battle abbey, in Sussex. There, William the Conqueror wanted to establish a monastery which should be a memorial to his great victory of 1066. His son, William Rufus, with an unexpected display of filial devotion, made sure that Battle was brought to completion and dedicated. Bernard was one of Rufus' new men, and might have been expected to support his lord. The parallel of the Conqueror's success at Battle and Bernard's success in his Welsh territory must not be ignored. It was said that Bernard had in his entourage monks of Battle. Whether by design or by the accident of their influence, the church of his new lordship was deliberately associated with Battle abbey, and throughout the middle ages, the priory of Brecon was directly subject to the abbot of Battle. Priors of Brecon were appointed and removed at his will, and the fortunes of the priory were closely linked with those of the parent house. That pattern was followed in many instances in Wales. The earliest lords of Gower were closely associated with Evreux, and the church at Llangennith, with other ecclesiastical benefits, were given to the abbey of St Taurin at Evreux. The remains of the romanesque church at St Taurin are a direct reminder of that link.

In terms of diocesan structure there can be little doubt that the Welsh church appeared to be backward and archaic. By chance, the first opportunity to appoint a French bishop occurred in north Wales. In 1092 the Normans appointed as bishop in Bangor, Hervé, a Breton, but his tenure of the see was very brief. When the Normans were driven back towards the Clwyd, Hervé took refuge in England where he eventually found a new sphere of activity at the abbey of Ely, and when Henry I founded the new diocese of Ely in 1109, Hervé became its first bishop. His experiences in Wales occasioned much shrill criticism of those who had rejected him. There was a long vacancy before a new bishop was consecrated for Bangor in 1120, David 'the Scot', who was certainly a Celt, and probably a Welshman. In the south-east and in the west, dioceses were ruled by bishops long past their best, and until the beginning of the twelfth century there was little opportunity for change. Then, in 1107, a vacancy in south-east Wales was filled as part of a general move towards greater efficiency in the English church. Bishop Herewald died in 1104, and his eventual successor was Urban who, as archdeacon in the diocese, had shared in the general improvement under Herewald and in the decline of Herewald's last years. How Urban gained royal support is a question which cannot be answered, but it may have been important that, when a new bishop was to be appointed, a local candidate was available and was regarded as acceptable by the crown and the archbishop of Canterbury. Urban was one of five bishops to be consecrated by Anselm after the settlement of his quarrel with the king. Since 1070, following a practice which can be discerned earlier, English bishops had made a promise of obedience to the archbishop of Canterbury and had left a written statement of their promise in the cathedral archive. In 1107, the bishops consecrated for English sees made their profession of obedience to Anselm; so, also, did Urban. His example was followed by all bishops appointed to Welsh sees in the future and in that sense it marked the formal submission of the Welsh bishops to Canterbury and the incorporation of the Welsh dioceses into the province of Canterbury.

Urban styled himself bishop of Glamorgan, but he was concerned to establish the boundaries of a diocese which was larger than that title would imply. He claimed churches in the east, in Archenfield, which had been under Bishop Herewald's jurisdiction but which had since then been incorporated into the diocese of Hereford. He claimed churches to the west associated with the cult of St Teilo which had been absorbed into the diocese of St David's. Urban was indefatigable in building up and presenting his case. He travelled to Rome three times to seek favourable judgements from the papal curia, and it is not clear whether he died at Rome or on his return journey after his third visit. In the end, he did not win for the diocese the expanded boundaries for which he fought, but his search for a firm title and the vigour with which he presented his case left their mark on the history and the records of his diocese. Much of the evidence is to be found in the *Book of Llandaff*, part cartulary, part a collection of saints' lives, which reached its final recension in the 1120s. From the early twelfth century, the centre of the diocese was the cathedral church at Llandaff. When Urban became bishop, there was a small church at Llandaff, 'twenty-eight feet in length, fifteen wide and twenty high, with two aisles on either side of but a small height, and with a porch twelve feet long'. It was a small church, perhaps more like an oratory than a major church, and Urban set out to rebuild it on a larger scale. He was responsible for rededicating the

church to St Peter and St Euddogwy, and he added the name of St
Dyfrig, plainly in the hope of establishing his claims to jurisdiction
over the ancient area of Dyfrig churches. The cathedral was also
dedicated to St Teilo, and until comparatively recently the case could
be argued quite strongly that Urban added that dedication to his
cathedral church as a means of strengthening his claims to the area
and churches covered by the cult of St Teilo. The key to his policy
remains the extent to which the material in the *Book of Llandaff* was
re-edited by his clerks in the interest of his case. The last and most
radical recension of the material belongs to the 1120s and to his
attempts to establish his diocese. The most important change in
recent years in the treatment of these questions has been the vindication of earlier recensions of the *Book of Llandaff*. Wendy Davies has
argued persuasively that the church at Llandaff was associated with
St Teilo by the end of Bishop Joseph's episcopate in 1045. She has
identified a group of charters which link Joseph with the area of
Llandaff itself. The evidence is very slight, with perhaps four grants
near Llandaff, and half a dozen in more distant places like Whit-
church, Splott and St Bride's super Ely. There is nothing to suggest
that Bishop Herewald maintained this interest in the eastern fringe of
Morgannwg, and continuous development of Llandaff as an episcopal centre could not be established. But it would be hard to ignore
these indications and to deny to Urban and his clerks a sense of
historical development. The factor which made Llandaff a valuable
centre for the diocese in the twelfth century was the establishment of
the castle and borough at Cardiff. The agents of Urban's policy were
the clerks of Llancarfan, not of Llandaff. The palimpsest of the *Book
of Llandaff* remains difficult to read and to interpret, but the lines
along which the discussion is proceeding have changed perceptibly
over some fifteen years of study and analysis.

Bishop Urban faced the major problem of despoliation within his
diocese. A succession of Norman magnates had taken advantage of
Bishop Herewald's age and weakness to acquire lands and churches
held by the bishop or to hand them over to monastic foundations of
their own choosing. Against men like William fitz Baderon of
Monmouth or Payn fitz John and Brian fitz Count in Gwent, and a
dangerous neighbour, Bernard of Neufmarché in Brecknock, Urban
invoked the authority of the pope to condemn their greed. His most
difficult task was to reach accord with Robert, earl of Gloucester and
lord of Glamorgan. In 1126, in a careful salvage exercise, he secured
an agreement defining his rights and privileges; for that, he and the

earl called on the full authority of Henry I, and their settlement was witnessed by many of the leading barons of the kingdom.

Bishop Urban's successors at Llandaff were essentially local men. Uchtryd (1140–?8) and Nicholas ap Gwrgant (1148–83) were Welshmen. Henry of Abergavenny (1193–1218) had been prior of Abergavenny before his appointment. His successor, William (1219–29), was prior of Goldcliff. Later in the thirteenth century, Elias and William of Radnor and John of Monmouth were drawn from the marches. One of the sources of strength for the diocese was that there were no long vacancies. The see was filled with commendable speed, and was not subjected to the periodic diversion of its income to the royal treasury. The use of archdeacons can be traced from the eleventh century; the formal establishment of a cathedral chapter was completed by Bishop Henry of Abergavenny before his death in 1218. The transformation from an inchoate and partly organised bishopric to a diocese with formally recognised boundaries, rights and privileges was achieved in one generation; the emergence of a full diocesan structure required a much longer period of development and definition.

In the eastern areas of the bishopric of St David's, Norman infiltration and despoliation could be identified from the late 1080s, and further west the process continued well into the twelfth century. The first Norman nominee in this diocese was Bernard, the queen's chancellor, appointed in 1115. He brought to his diocese two elements which featured in the work of any royal administrator, the experience of getting business done efficiently and a capacity to weigh up alternative policies. He was responsible for the organisation of the diocese into archdeaconries and deaneries, and he displayed great sensitivity in his arrangements, using the ancient kingdoms of Dyfed, Brycheiniog and Ceredigion to form the archdeaconries of St David's, Brecon and Cardigan, and using the familiar commotes to form the basic rural deaneries. (The archdeaconry of Carmarthen was a more complex structure.) To have adopted this scheme implies that Bernard was ready to listen to local advisers. He could do little about the widespread alienation of church property, but he was careful to ensure that local religious houses which had received endowments from Norman settler families should have the full protection of his authority. St Dogmael's, Brecon priory and Carmarthen priory all benefited from his protection and good will. At St Dogmael's, he presided over a major occasion when, in 1121,

Fulchard, the first abbot was installed. All the grants which had been made to his house were recorded in one document, and the bishop confirmed them to the monks. It might be interpreted critically, as Gerald of Wales chose to interpret it, as a prodigal alienation of the rights and lands of the see with very little to show for it, but it had the advantage of establishing a clear title for the lands claimed by the monastic community.

At the cathedral church Bishop Bernard drew together the Welsh *claswyr*, who included two of the sons of Bishop Sulien, and those Anglo-Norman clergy who formed his own immediate circle to make a recognised chapter of canons. He clearly listened to those who might claim to be the custodians of memory and custom, and he allowed their reading of the past to direct his own policy for the future. They preserved and passed on traditions that St David's had been a metropolitan church, and that the bishop had performed some of the functions of a metropolitan as recently as the eleventh century. They also preserved vague and conflicting memories that St David had himself been an archbishop. In 1119 Bernard secured from the papacy the formal canonisation of St David: if that is too strong a claim for the very slight evidence to bear, at least his cult was given formal recognition. During the 1120s he was canvassing the view that St David's should be the seat of an archbishop and the centre of an independent province. At the end of his life, in 1148, Bernard was ready to bring this case to a papal council at Reims for adjudication, but he died before the council met, and his case fell by default. There were other bishops in England and Europe for whom the problem of status was critical. In the English church there was the long-standing quarrel between Canterbury and York to settle whether York should be subordinate to Canterbury. At the same time, Henry of Blois, the ambitious and embittered bishop of Winchester, was actively pursuing the attempt to have his cathedral made the centre of a separate archbishopric in southern England. In France, the Breton church was made subordinate to the archbishop of Tours in 1144, and at Lyons, Bourges and Vienne ambitious prelates were seeking to enhance their authority. A little later, in 1152, the Irish church was released from the oversight of Canterbury. While the prospects of success were not very great, Bernard was arguing a fashionable cause.

After his death, St David's was drawn in two contrasting directions. Should it become a local bishopric, linked closely with the ruling house of Deheubarth? Or should it be a Norman bishopric linked closely with the English crown and the Anglo-Norman lords of the march? From 1148 to 1176 the bishop was David fitz Gerald, son of a Norman father and a Welsh mother, the grandson and nephew of Welsh princes. The recurrent talk that his nephew, Gerald of Wales, might be appointed to the see pointed to the continuation of that local, family tradition. Henry II and his sons maintained a persistent determination that St David's should not be regarded as a bishopric subject to princely patronage. Men with strong local interests might be appointed, but their appointment was to remain firmly under the influence of the Angevin kings. Gerald of Wales had the misfortune to represent the two concepts least likely to find support from the Angevin dynasty. He represented the local family, and he represented in the most belligerent form the local pressure for the creation of a Welsh archbishopric centred on St David's.

No other bishop of St David's in the twelfth century, and few in the thirteenth, matched Bernard for his statesmanship and ability. A majority of his successors were men with local connections, either in Wales or the march: David fitz Gerald (1148–76), Geoffrey of Henlaw (1203–14), Iorwerth (1215–29), Anselm le Gras (1231–47), Thomas the Welshman (1248–55) and Richard of Carew (1256–80). The two exceptional figures who could be distinguished as curial bishops were Peter de Leia (1176–98) and Thomas Bek (1280–93). It is no surprise that the bishopric was recognised as a marcher lordship, and its fortunes were associated particularly with the crown and the marcher baronage. The organisation of the chapter at St David's was basically the work of Bishop Bernard, though the emergence of formal offices was a slow process. The senior office in the chapter, that of the precentor, was created in 1224; the treasurer can be traced from the 1250s, and the chancellor first appeared in 1287. The office of dean was a nineteenth-century addition to the historic chapter.

After the abortive attempt to appoint a French bishop at Bangor in 1092 there was a long hiatus until 1120, when David the Scot was elected. Under Gruffydd ap Cynan and Owain Gwynedd, Welsh control over Bangor was effectively established. David held the see probably until 1139, and his successor, Meurig, consecrated early in 1140, died in 1161. There followed a long vacancy as Owain Gwynedd fought to secure his own right to nominate to the see and to avoid the imposition of a candidate chosen by Henry II. With the aid of Dafydd, the resourceful archdeacon of Bangor, Owain held the king and the archbishop of Canterbury at bay, threatening at times to ignore Canterbury's claims and to have a bishop of his own choosing consecrated in Ireland. That remained a threat, and Owain and his immediate successors were never able to establish an independent position. The succession, when it continued, was largely, though not entirely, Welsh: Gwion (1177–90), Alan (1195–6) and Robert of Shrewsbury (1197–1213). From 1215 until his resignation twenty years later, the bishop was Cadwgan, a Cistercian monk and writer of some note.

At St Asaph, the weakness of the bishop and the diocese could not be disguised. No bishop was appointed until 1143, when Bishop Richard was consecrated. The diocese could scarcely claim to have achieved stability before the end of the century. Politically there were two problems: the first was that the prince of Powys was a thoroughly ineffective patron, and the second was that St Asaph lay in the disputed territory of the Perfeddwlad, a no man's land in the twelfth century. The only protection the bishop could find was that which the prince of Gwynedd could offer him; the more distant patronage of the English crown was almost without value. The early bishops had short episcopates. Geoffrey of Monmouth, for example, author and romancer, held the see for some two years. Another Geoffrey was bishop from 1160 until 1175, but he was scarcely able to maintain a foothold in north Wales. He spent many years living at Abingdon, carrying out episcopal functions in England in defiance of Archbishop Thomas Becket. In 1186 the bishopric passed to Bishop Renier, who gave the diocese some stability until his death in 1224. Of the six bishops who held the see in the thirteenth century, one survived for one year, two others each held the see for five years, and Bishop Abraham (1225–33) had eight years in office. Only Anian I (1249–66), with seventeen years, and Anian II (1268–93), with twenty-five years, had any length of time to impress their personality and policy on the bishopric.

Against this background of a weak episcopal succession and lack of any sense of unity, the attempt of Bishop Bernard of St David's, and after him of Gerald of Wales, to create a province in Wales can be seen at their full value. Gerald first came to prominence as an enthusiastic young reformer in St David's. Family influence secured for him the archdeaconry of Brecon in about 1174. From then on he was near the centre of ecclesiastical politics in Wales. Twice he was a potential candidate for the diocese of St David's; for a few years at the end of the century he was acknowledged as bishop-elect of the diocese, though he was never to be consecrated. On three occasions, as he reports, there were offers of other bishoprics, one in Ireland, and the other two in Wales, at Bangor and Llandaff.

Gerald was a man with a deep affection for west Wales and for his boyhood home at Manorbier. In his maturity he was devoted to the cathedral of St David's, and to the interests of the diocese. He could withdraw from practical affairs to the seclusion of the study, for he was by training and inclination a scholar with a passion for writing. Educated at St Peter's abbey, Gloucester, and later in the schools at Paris, he was at home in the world of scholarship. In a long career, he could move to the forefront of controversy, and withdraw with apparent indifference to write his scholarly books. He was a compulsive writer, capable of vitriolic attacks on his enemies, and of passages of bombast and self-adulation which irritated many of his contemporaries and have continued to irritate his readers ever since. A touch of humour or of self-deprecation could have worked wonders for him: as it was, people often laughed at him, rarely with him. He was a man of the marches and of mixed blood. Through his grandmother, Nest, he was descended from the princes of Deheubarth, and he was very proud of the connection. His father, William de Barry, was a minor figure in the Anglo-Norman aristocracy of the marches. Gerald was proud of both sides of his inheritance. Critics note that he is not always consistent, and that he can speak with approval of his Welsh connections or with dismissive contempt of 'the Welsh'. He was proud of the achievements of the fitz Geralds, whether in Wales or in Ireland. At his best, his writings betray a sense of curiosity which no other scholar applied to the study of the Welsh, or of the Irish. He was a sharp observer of the church: in his dislike of the monastic orders, and especially of the Cistercians, he allowed prejudice to cloud his judgement, but in his vignettes of Welsh ecclesiastical life in his *Gemma Ecclesiastica*, he was capable of warm and perceptive observation of the simple virtues of local clerical life. He documented the struggle for St David's at great length, and without his works historians would know surprisingly little of that conflict. With so large an output, he dominates the story of the church in Wales in the second half of the twelfth century and the first two decades of the thirteenth. What the modern historian may see must be seen very largely through Gerald's eyes and with his insights.

The struggle for St David's was a secondary theme in the early years of Gerald's career, and it became the major theme of his life in 1198. He believed that David fitz Gerald in 1148 and Peter de Leia in 1176 had each been required to give, in addition to their promise of obedience to Canterbury, an undertaking that they would not raise the question of the independent status of St David's. He also believed and reported that in 1176 Henry II vetoed his own nomination for the diocese and held it as 'neither necessary nor expedient for king or archbishop that a man of such honesty or strength should be bishop of St David's, lest the crown of England or the cathedral of Canterbury should suffer loss'. The king's choice of a safe man was distinguished, Peter de Leia, prior of Much Wenlock, who was responsible for rebuilding the cathedral church. Gerald was happy to serve him for a few years as commissary. He was also happy to accompany Archbishop Baldwin on his journey around Wales in 1188; with his connections, Gerald could smooth the way for the archbishop and his entourage as they passed through the territory of different Welsh princes. The ambition for independence was voiced on rare occasions, at a synod in London in 1175 and at the third Lateran Council in 1179, though on neither occasion did it form part of the formal business to be discussed. At that stage, Gerald seems not to have been directly concerned with the issue. His interest was mobilised when his name was put forward for the vacant bishopric in 1198. The chapter of St David's was anxious to have Gerald as their bishop but there were a number of other candidates. Two archdeacons and two canons were summoned to meet Hubert Walter, archbishop of Canterbury, to discuss the appointment and they put forward four names: Gerald, whom they particularly wished to see elected, Walter, abbot of St Dogmael's, Peter, abbot of Whitland, and Reginald Foliot, a canon of St David's and the representative of a well-known English family. Gerald himself could not be present, but he wrote to the archbishop to say that he would ratify the choice of any suitable person accepted by his colleagues. He defined a 'suitable person' as one who would acknowledge the customs of both peoples, Normans and Welsh, and who would devote himself as bishop to his pastoral office. Hubert Walter showed his hand: he had already picked the men he was prepared to see at St David's, Alexander, abbot of Ford, and the candidate whom he preferred, Geoffrey of Henlaw, prior of Llanthony. He rejected Gerald as an unsuitable candidate, since he was a Welshman connected with Welsh princes, and he also rejected the two Welsh abbots.

Technically, this was a preliminary foray with Hubert, the king's leading adviser. The chapter still had to send a formal delegation to the king to appoint the new bishop. Late in 1198 the chapter was instructed to send a delegation to Richard I, then in his Norman stronghold at Château Gaillard. Four canons were to be sent, with instructions to elect Gerald, though they were aware that they might have to wait for, and follow, the king's directive. Then it was agreed

that two canons should seek out Richard and ask for the election to
be made at Westminster. By the time they reached the court
Richard was dead, and they travelled back to Chinon, in Anjou, to
find his brother, John, now king of England. John was well disposed
towards Gerald and he tacitly accepted his nomination, but when
Hubert Walter gained the king's ear the chance of a peaceful election
began to recede. There was delay, and in June 1199 a full chapter at
St David's reaffirmed their intention and unanimously elected
Gerald as their bishop. In view of Hubert Walter's hostility, the
canons sent Gerald, with a few companions, to Rome to seek
consecration from Innocent III. They informed the pope that Hubert
Walter and the king's officers 'by violent intrusion against their election and privileges, wished to set over them a stranger, wholly
ignorant of their language and the customs of their country'. So they
were sending the question of election to the papal curia. They also
feared that 'an unlawful oath might be extorted from their elect, in
prejudice of the rights of their church, as had often been done from
their prelates', and that meant that they were remitting to Rome the
question of the status of St David's. Gerald, as bishop-elect, was
committed to pursue both causes in the curia.

There ensued four years of sharp and increasingly bitter conflict.
Gerald made three journeys to Rome, and attended a series of judicial
hearings in England. He found that he could make considerable head-
way, and occasionally gain a great advantage, at Rome, but his chief
opponent, Archbishop Walter, was wily and experienced, and was
not easily outflanked. Gerald started with the support of the full
chapter, but to maintain the loyalty and commitment of all the
canons over a long period of time was no easy matter, for Hubert
Walter was very successful at dividing them and frightening some of
them into silence. By the final stages of the long process, Gerald had
no support from the chapter and he stood alone as the defender of his
own claims as bishop-elect and of the ancient rights of his church.

On his first visit to Rome he found that Innocent III was prepared
to appoint a commission to inquire into the disputed election to St
David's, but he could see no grounds for initiating an inquiry into the
status of the see. To sanction that he would require evidence that the
bishopric had once claimed metropolitical status. Gerald was
allowed to consult the registers of Eugenius III, under close and careful supervision, and there he discovered a copy of a letter which
Eugenius had sent to Theobald, archbishop of Canterbury, when
Bishop Bernard had been campaigning for the restoration of the
independence of St David's. At Rome, Gerald found slight further

evidence which gave some support to his claims. In a list of bishoprics arranged under metropolitans, Canterbury was named with its
suffragan sees in England. The Welsh bishoprics followed immediately, but they were not included in exactly the same form; they
appeared under a separate rubric: 'In Wales there are four dioceses:
the churches of St David's, Llandaff, Bangor and St Asaph.' For the
present this was enough to persuade Innocent to grant a commission
to hear the question of status. These matters would be heard in
England before judges-delegate. After some altercation, Innocent III
appointed Gerald as administrator of the see during the vacancy, so
that when he returned to Wales he would control the bishopric
effectively for the time being.

When he was once again at St David's, Gerald began to explore the
cathedral archives and there he found the original of the letter of Pope
Eugenius which he had discovered at Rome, together with a number
of other documents bearing on the earlier phase of the struggle.
Before the papal commissioners in England, and later in Rome, he
secured judgement against Hubert Walter for failing to appear in this
cause, and the archbishop was required to pay half of Gerald's
expenses. Outwardly defeated, Hubert Walter turned the reverse to
his advantage. The pope issued instructions for a new commission to
meet to deal with the cause of status, but Hubert Walter was able to
influence the drafting of the terms for this new commission. Gerald
was to be heard in this cause only if all, or a majority, of his fellow-
canons should stand with him. When he returned to England, Gerald
discovered how far his support had already been eroded. When he
asked the canons formally if they would stand with him at a session
of the papal commission to be held at Worcester on 26 January 1202,
they refused. Throughout that year Gerald maintained the struggle,
but there was a series of attempts at compromise. Most important
was the suggestion that St David's should be an archbishopric but the
archbishop should be subordinate to Canterbury, while Gerald's
own position was weakened when he suggested that he would withdraw as bishop-elect of the see. The final judgement came in April,
1203, when Innocent III ruled on the question of Gerald's election
which, together with the election of the abbot of St Dogmael's, was
set aside. Gerald was allowed to pursue the cause of the status of the
bishopric, but he knew that his effectiveness as an advocate had been
fatally weakened, and before long he had capitulated. He accepted as
bishop Hubert Walter's nominee, Geoffrey of Henlaw, prior of
Llanthony. It was agreed that the question of status should not be
raised again during the lifetime of Hubert Walter, and within a year

Gerald had promised the monks of Canterbury that he would never again raise this vexed question. At the end of a long and exhilarating struggle, Gerald had to accept total defeat. The fact that there was another vacancy at St David's in 1215 seems not to have stirred him, and his name was not considered on that occasion. It remained for him to write up the story of his epic struggle, and it is largely from his own work that the story can be reconstructed in such detail. Gerald was fighting a partisan cause, and he could not be expected to concede a major point of principle to his opponents. That the king and the archbishop of Canterbury were fighting for the unity of a province which, as they defined it, had political as well as ecclesiastical significance did not come into his view of events. Nor did he gauge with any accuracy the value of Hubert Walter as a royal adviser; that the king should allow the archbishop to be defeated on such a major issue is almost inconceivable, and in the same way, that Innocent III should disregard Hubert's work as papal legate, or alienate the English crown at that stage, could scarcely be considered practical politics. It would mean reading into the first years of the century the bitterness engendered by the dispute between John and Innocent III over the appointment of Langton to Canterbury. With almost touching naïvety, Gerald seems to have believed that if he won the argument in hearings, whether in Rome or in England, he might win the case. No doubt, the excess of loyalty which he felt for the diocese, and the zeal with which he pursued his cause, coloured that judgement. The ambition which Bishop Bernard, and after him Gerald, had hoped to achieve remained as a temptation on two later occasions. Thomas Bek, at odds with his archbishop, John Pecham, tried briefly to promote the independence of St David's, but he was very quickly brought back into line. With a deeper understanding of the whole problem, but with a less secure political judgement, Gruffydd Young, Owain Glyn Dŵr's bishop of Bangor, proposed sweeping reforms which would have created a new province for Wales and much of western England.

For Gerald, there was a price to pay for defeat. He retired to Lincoln, ageing fast, and finding solace in study. He called to Lincoln his nephew, another Gerald, expecting that he could mould the boy to be a companion for his old age. The two never found accord, and it is plain that the scheme did not work. By an arrangement, reprehensible even by the standards of his own day, Gerald ensured that his archdeaconry and the rich prebend of Mathry should remain in the family; he transferred them to his young nephew, perhaps expecting that he might himself control them until the young man was old enough to take over. The boy had a tutor, who acquired the living of Llanhamlach, and who encouraged the lad in habits of independence. They wasted the assets of the manor of Llanddew, one of Gerald's favourite possessions, and there was little he could do about it. They boasted that they would keep the old man out of Wales, and to his great regret, the bishop joined with them in making good their boast. It was an unhappy end for his life. The querulousness and bitterness which he had so often displayed in his prime remained the key notes of his old age. It may be thought that one who had served Wales and the church so well deserved better, but it is entirely in keeping that a man of his character should end his life, as he had so often used it, in controversy.

The Welsh church was much handicapped by poverty. The bishoprics were notoriously poor. Even the richest of them, St David's, with its possessions deliberately increased by Edward I, was worth appreciably less than Chichester and Carlisle, and no English see had an income as inadequate as those of St Asaph, Llandaff and Bangor. There was a particularly heavy increase in papal taxation levied in the second half of the thirteenth century when Bangor's assessment was increased by 438 per cent and St Asaph's by 414 per cent, and this clearly affected the profitability of the northern dioceses. The range of income of the Welsh bishops may be assessed when firm figures become available in the early sixteenth century: St David's was then rated at £457 a year, St Asaph at £187, Llandaff at £144 and Bangor at £131. Other indices point in the same direction. The churches granted to religious houses left Llandaff and St David's impoverished. When figures become available in 1291 a clear measure of the problem is possible. Tewkesbury abbey was given churches which then had a value of £108 13s. 4d., all of them in the diocese of Llandaff. Gloucester abbey had rich possessions, with Llancarfan in Llandaff and Llanbadarn Fawr in St David's, but the richest gains were incorporated in the possessions of daughter houses; churches held by Goldcliff were valued at £53 6s. 8d., and those belonging to Ewenny were valued at £42. Benedictine houses founded in Wales gained in the same way by the grant of parish churches, and, again, diocesan resources were heavily depleted. Brecon, with Hay, Llanigon, Talgarth, Llangors and Brecon itself, held churches valued at £70; Abergavenny had six churches valued at £38. The valuation placed on religious houses in 1291 provides another index: among the Benedictines, Goldcliff was at the head of the list (£171 14s. 1d.), followed by Brecon (£122 10s.)

and Monmouth (£85 18s. 8d.). Estimates of landed possessions place Goldcliff high on the list (1,346 acres), with Monmouth and Llangua well endowed, each having 480 acres. One house of Augustinian canons was pre-eminent, Llanthony, valued at £233 7s., and credited with estates of 1,094 acres. These were all foundations linked closely with Anglo-Norman settlers, and they drew their monks from settler stock. The monastic churches were normally close to the principal castle of the local magnate. Ewenny may, at first sight appear to be an exception, for it lay about a mile from the de Londres castle at Ogmore, but the two sites were not intended to be separate *foci* for interest or settlement.

The new orders of Cîteaux, Savigny and Tiron were also established in the marches, and were largely intended for settler stock rather than for Welsh monks. A Savigniac house was founded at Neath by Richard de Granville in 1130, and the Cistercian monastery at L'Aumone sent a colony to Tintern in 1131. The Tironians settled at Llandudoch, which became the abbey of St Dogmael's. From Clairvaux, one of the four elder daughters of Cîteaux, colonies were sent to Treffgarne in 1140 and to Margam in 1147. In each case, the new house received large grants of upland territory, and in due course built up its wealth from cattle and sheep farming. Margam was estimated to have 6,937 acres, Neath, 5,208. There was some friction between the two abbeys. In 1147 the Savigniac houses were absorbed into the order of Cîteaux and one consequence was that Margam and Neath were in close rivalry for land grants to extend their Welsh possessions. The monks of Neath were seriously concerned to migrate to north Somerset, though such radical plans were never put into operation.

The colony at Treffgarne was refounded in 1151 and became the monastery of Whitland, a house which was to play a major role in the history of monasticism in mid-Wales and the north, for a family of daughter houses was set up (see figure 4): in 1143 Cwmhir was founded (and re-established in 1176), and in due course the monks of Cwmhir sent out a colony to Cymer. From Strata Florida (founded in 1164) another colony was sent to Aberconwy in 1186 (resited in 1190), and the abbots of that house were to be closely linked with the princes of Gwynedd, serving them as advisers and emissaries. Llywelyn ab Iorwerth was buried there. In Powys, Strata Marcella (Ystrad Marchell) was founded under the patronage of the ruling dynasty in 1170 and sent out a colony to Valle Crucis in 1201. The princes of Powys used both monasteries for royal and family burials. Strata Florida was never as wealthy as Tintern or Margam, but has strong claims to be regarded as the most influential of the Welsh Cistercian houses. In 1291 it was valued at £98 6s. 9d., and credited with 6,260 acres of land, and in terms of sheep flocks and wool production it was remarkably successful. The principal feature of houses established from Whitland is that they were founded under Welsh patronage and recruited from Welsh stock. They were strongly Welsh in their loyalties, and they contributed substantially to the Welsh tradition of historical writing associated with the *Brut y Tywysogyon*. One curious foundation was the single house of Premonstratensian canons established in Wales. Their monastery, Talley abbey, was founded at Talyllychau in Cantref Mawr by the Lord Rhys. The canons shared much of the outlook and practice of the Cistercians, but they were a singularly isolated community.

The military orders acquired a number of estates in Wales. The most important house of the Templars on the marches was at Garway, in Herefordshire. Those lands which the Hospitallers held in north Wales were associated with their Shropshire house at Halston. In south Wales they had a commandery at Slebech. The Augustinian canons were firmly established in Wales. The Lacy family foundation at Llanthony was by far the wealthiest of their Welsh priories, and from the beginning the remoteness and beauty of the site occasioned comment. In 1136 Miles of Gloucester set up a second Llanthony beyond the fortifications of the royal castle at Gloucester, but the Welsh house, Llanthony Prima as it came to be known, continued to flourish. At Bardsey, an Augustinian community maintained the traditions of the Celtic church and ensured the continuity of the *clas* church on the island of the saints. They ensured the same element of continuity at Penmon, in Anglesey. There, close to the Welsh borough of Llanfaes and to the Edwardian borough at Beaumaris, the canons fulfilled their traditional role as

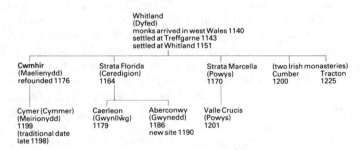

Figure 4   Cistercian monasteries: the family of Whitland

secular priests with responsibilities within the community. Their houses at Carmarthen and Haverfordwest were ideally placed for them to serve within the communities of those boroughs. Like the Cistercians, the Augustinians recruited from the local Welsh population for their northern houses. Despite the small scale of the Welsh towns the orders of friars were slowly established in Wales. The Dominicans had settled in Cardiff by 1242, and were found in Haverfordwest before 1246. They had been established in Bangor and Rhuddlan by the 1250s, and their friary beyond the walls of Brecon was in use by 1269. The Franciscans did not set up many friaries in Wales. In 1237 Llywelyn ab Iorwerth buried his wife, Joan, at Llanfaes, and during the next few years he established the Franciscans there. Some forty years later they had acquired houses at Cardiff and Carmarthen.

One legacy of the religious orders in Wales was a series of large churches, some of which have survived as parish churches, while others are now splendid ruins. The Benedictine priories and cells, sited in towns (some of which already had a parochial function). tended to be converted to parish use. Some, like Kidwelly, have been so altered by the change of use, rebuilding and restoration that it is difficult to identify any trace of their monastic function. The graceful church at Monmouth with its ancillary buildings retains some hint of its former use. Ewenny priory, with its fine romanesque work, and Brecon priory (now a cathedral church) retain much of the character of a monastic church. Each has an impressive and well-preserved enceinte, but modern adaptation of the site for secular buildings and the disappearance of conventual buildings have, in each case, obscured the pattern of the priory. At Brecon, a tithe barn and a fragmentary wing, much altered in the 1920s, which was probably used to house pilgrims in the later middle ages, still survive, and the building line of the cloister and the conventual buildings has been retained. At Penmon, an ancient well, the medieval church and the continued use of part of the buildings as a residence make it possible to reconstruct in general terms the use and evolution of the site. Chepstow, with its early romanesque west front and nave, and Abergavenny and Carmarthen, from later centuries, are now substantial parish churches. The scale of the Dominican friary at Brecon may still be gauged from the remains of the friary church incorporated into the chapel of the school founded on the site in Henry VIII's reign by Bishop Barlow. At Margam, part of the church survives in use, and there are fragmentary remains of the chapter house. The ruins of Tintern have a noble beauty, and, like those of Llanthony, they owe much to the dramatic qualities of their position. At Valle Crucis, a surprisingly large area of conventual buildings, adapted for secular use, survives; if the first impression of the site is that of the beauty of the ruined church, the second impression is that of a small but well-designed and well-built Cistercian house. Neath abbey, overshadowed by industrial development, still shows in its ruined state the quality of the facing stone and the pattern of different surfaces which once made the abbey church an austere but beautiful building in its marshland setting. The abbot's house, extended and adapted in the sixteenth century, is one of the notable features of this complex of buildings. Talley abbey is a valuable reminder that the founder's intentions could not always be carried out. The church was planned on a large scale, and the east end and transepts were built without difficulty, but the nave was never completed. After three bays had been built, and the foundations for the remainder of the pillars had been laid, a temporary west end wall was necessary, and the money was never found to complete the nave on the scale of the original plan. On rare occasions materials from monastic buildings have been transferred elsewhere and preserved in a new setting. The thirteenth-century arcade in the parish church at Llanidloes was transferred from the abbey of Cwmhir. In the south nave of Cilcain church there is a fifteenth-century roof in which arch-braced trusses alternate with hammer-beam trusses, and it has all the appearance of a roof brought from another site and adapted to fit this building. One possibility that has been canvassed is that it was once the roof of the refectory at Basingwerk abbey.

Small medieval churches have suffered much from neglect and from late and overzealous restoration. While some remote churches, like Cwmyoy and Patricio, have been maintained and restored with great delicacy, many have been made over with little care for their earlier style. Sometimes, minimal development and repair in Tudor times and timely restoration in the seventeenth century have given way to a long period of neglect in the eighteenth century. At St Mary's, Swansea, the nave was so severely damaged by storms and gales that it was cheaper to demolish the medieval nave and replace it with a barn-like structure, singularly ugly, and quite unworthy of the town. In the 1890s a zealous vicar demolished this eighteenth-century nave, together with the Norman tower and chancel, and in its place Arthur Blomfield built a grand church in his best Early English style. Destroyed by fire in 1941, the church has now been rebuilt on Blomfield's foundations.

The cathedral churches of Wales, larger, more expensive and more regularly used than many parish churches, owe much to nineteenth-century restorers. St David's had been built in contemporary style by Bishop Bernard (1115–48), but when Peter de Leia became bishop in 1176 there was urgent need to rebuild, and he began the church of which the nave still survives. Work continued throughout the middle ages. The tower fell in 1220, and Bishop Iorwerth gained some reputation for his building work (1215–29). Bishop Henry of Gower (1328–47) is better known for his building work at the bishop's palace at St David's, at Lamphey and at Swansea than he is in the cathedral, where he seems to have followed a single scheme of improvement, and his work on the aisles and chapels went well beyond embellishment. Right at the end of the fifteenth century the fine wooden ceiling of the nave was built, and early in the sixteenth century Bishop Vaughan was building his own memorial chapel. The medieval church must now be seen through the work of George Gilbert Scott, who regarded the restoration of St David's as the most dangerous commission he had undertaken. The main arcading and the aisle walls were dangerously out of true, the tower was expected to fall almost at any moment, and major structural work was necessary to remove these threats. The eighteenth-century west front had to be replaced, and the south transept had effectively to be rebuilt. St Asaph, the smallest cathedral church in England and Wales, owed much to two medieval builders. Between 1310 and 1320 the nave and transepts were rebuilt, and from comparison with work which was being done at Caernarfon, it appears to have been done by Master Henry of Ellerton. The tower was added by Robert Fagan, a mason from Chester, in 1391–2. The cathedral was badly damaged during the Glyn Dŵr revolt and repair was a slow business. The roof was rebuilt by Bishop Robert of Lancaster (1411–33) and completed by Bishop Richard Redman (1471–95). Substantial changes were made in restorations carried through in 1780 and 1822, but reading the medieval sequence was made even more difficult by Scott's restoration of the 1860s. Bangor suffered frequent damage, not only during the turbulent years of the thirteenth century, but during the Glyn Dŵr revolt. Repair was slowly achieved as the fifteenth century drew to a close. Bishop Henry Dean (1496–1500) was responsible for repairs to the transepts and chancel, though the basic fabric of the church of the late twelfth and thirteenth centuries is clear to see behind his work. The tower was not completed until the time of Bishop Thomas Skeffington (1509–33). The building sequence at Llandaff could be traced from the romanesque church built by Bishop Urban and dedicated in 1120 to the tower of the west front

which took its name from Jasper Tudor at the end of the fifteenth
century. The first major tragedy which affected this medieval church
was the neglect and destruction of the nave in the eighteenth century
and its replacement by a classical temple. When that was remedied by
the restorers of the nineteenth century, the cathedral met with
disaster in the Second World War, and once again long and careful
reconstruction was necessary. The romanesque church of St Woolos
at Newport, which was made the cathedral for the new diocese of
Monmouth in 1921, was a dependency of St Peter's abbey,
Gloucester. There was a long dispute to decide whether it was a
priory or a chantry foundation, and the church was never
refashioned on a large scale during the middle ages.

A pressing requirement of the Welsh church was for books, and
especially works of practical guidance for parish priests and popular
works of devotion. Gerald of Wales' *Gemma Ecclesiastica* was a collection of sound instructions for clerics working in country communities, and it might be matched by similar work produced by the
Cistercian, Cadwgan, bishop of Bangor (1215–35), whose homilies
included simple instructions on how to deal with confession. To
provide basic texts in Welsh was a substantial achievement. Trans-
lations of parts of the Bible were in circulation, together with popular but apocryphal writings, the *Efengyl Nicodemus* (the *Gospel of
Nicodemus*) and the *Breuddwyd Pawl* (*The Dream of Paul*). The *Oculus
Sacerdotis*, attributed to William de Pagula, offered extensive
guidance on the practical problems of confession and preaching, and
an exposition of the seven sacraments. Other works which owed
much to the writings of the Spanish Dominican, Raymond of
Peñaforte came into circulation, the *Regimen Animarum* and the
Penityas, while a book called *Y Gysegrlan Fuchedd* (*The Consecrated
Life*) was widely used. The most ambitious collection of medieval
writings in Wales was *Llyfr yr Ancr* (*The Book of the Anchorite*),
compiled by an anchorite at Llanddewibrefi for a lay patron. Sparse
though the evidence is, the Welsh gentry could build up their own
collections of books. One of the items of his personal belongings
which the Glamorgan Welshman, Llywelyn Bren, placed in safe-
keeping before he embarked on his rebellion in 1316 was a small
collection of seven books. The only volume named was a secular
work, the *Roman de la Rose*; three others were identified as Welsh.
Thirty years later, about 1350, the manuscript now known as the
White Book of Rhydderch was produced for Rhydderch ab Ieuan
Llwyd who lived near Llangeitho, in Ceredigion. It was probably

written at Strata Florida, and it included secular and religious texts, one of which was a Welsh version of the story of the crucifixion from St Matthew's gospel. To search for religious works in use in Wales solely from the surviving manuscripts of religious foundations would be unwise.

Nowhere is the state of the Welsh church more clearly laid out than in the extensive, if critical, analysis drawn up by Archbishop Pecham (1279–92). In his first eight years as metropolitan he carried through a visitation of every diocese in his province and by 1286 he was looking forward to undertaking the whole formidable process for a second time. He certainly carried out a second visitation of Canterbury and London and perhaps of Exeter and Worcester. He could, as a result, claim a quite exceptional knowledge of his province. Much of what he saw, he did not like. There were too many non-resident clerics, too many livings held in plurality, too many signs of neglect. The laity he regarded as 'a stiff-necked people, kicking against the pricks and determined to resist all exhortations to obey the word of God'. He gave clear instructions to enable priests to improve their ministry, and where they could not make progress, especially in the matters of preaching and confessions, they were to call in the friars. His criticisms of the Welsh dioceses must be set against this background. The clergy he found ostentatious and loose-living, with concubinage and drunkenness as common causes of offence. Many of them were grossly ignorant, and he declared that he could never remember having seen such illiterate priests and clerics as he had found in Wales. At the same time he was aware of the problems created by the use of the Welsh language. When he visited the western part of the diocese of Coventry and Lichfield – that part which extended to the borderland between Powys and Chester – he recognised the need for ministrations in Welsh and ordered that a Welsh-speaking suffragan should be appointed to deal with the problems of that area. In Wales itself he discerned and valued a greater measure of freedom from the control of a secular ruler than was possible in England, but despite this he was himself to be responsible for a considerable tightening up of secular control in the newly conquered territories of north Wales. He was essentially a just man with a sharp eye, and his comments about the Welsh dioceses deserve serious attention. Though he was aware of the problem of two cultures and two languages, it would be expecting more than his age could produce to look for solutions at his hands. Yet, in a curious way, he deserves, in Gerald of Wales' terms, to be seen as a sympathetic observer, and as a metropolitan who was not insensitive to Welsh aspirations. One practical step was of particular value. Pecham laid down that in St Asaph his injunctions should be read each year as a reminder of what needed to be done, and in the northern dioceses some improvements were made in Pecham's last years. The insoluble problem was one of education. While promising men might be sent to border monasteries, as Gerald of Wales had earlier been sent to St Peter's, Gloucester, and a few would make their way to the universities, the opportunities for training Welsh-speaking clerics for service in Welsh parishes were very limited. John of Monmouth, bishop of Llandaff from 1297 to 1323, had been chancellor of Oxford before his consecration. He attracted scholars to his cathedral chapter and tried to make the cathedral a centre for scholarship and a place where clerics might be trained. But, at best, that was a temporary expedient which left the basic problem largely unsolved.

These problems were exacerbated by changes which occurred in the nature of the Welsh episcopate in the later middle ages. Edward I was fortunate that two bishops held the northern sees for long periods at the end of the thirteenth century, Anian of Bangor from 1268 to 1305/6 and Anian II of St Asaph from 1268 to 1293. They had already come to terms with him and with the English regime in north Wales, but their long experience and strong Welsh loyalties made for a slow transition to English rule. Both Edward I and Edward II and their advisers continued to appoint the same type of bishops in north Wales, and did not seek a sudden break in the succession. No doubt they chose safe men, but at St Asaph two Welshmen carried the succession, Llywelyn of Bromfield (1293–1314) and Dafydd ap Bleddyn (1315–45), and at Bangor Gruffydd ab Iorwerth (1307–9) and Anian Sais (1309–28) continued the tradition. Anian's nickname indicates English leanings, if not English loyalties, and perhaps his appointment should be regarded as ambiguous. However, critical changes came, not through the workings of an 'English' policy, but through changes in papal practice. In the fourteenth century, papal provision became the normal method of making episcopal appointments. The changes can be seen in Wales from the 1320s to the 1350s. In 1323 there was a vacancy at Llandaff and the pope translated John of Eaglescliffe from the Irish see of Connor. The change can be observed at St David's from the 1340s and at St Asaph and Bangor from the late 1350s. The appointment of Welshmen to Welsh sees became more exceptional and, in the fifteenth century, rare. At Llandaff, men with local associations continued to be chosen. The appointment of a new bishop turned on negotiation between king and pope, and the weight of evidence is that the English kings of the fifteenth century were more willing to support men from the marches than men from north Wales.

One diocese derived great benefit from the changes of the later middle ages, the diocese of St David's. There, a succession of prominent royal officials held the see between 1280 and 1414. Edward I made the see more attractive by adding to its resources, but he and his successors used it to good advantage to support a succession of curial bishops. Thomas Bek, appointed by Edward I in 1290, had been keeper of the wardrobe; John Thoresby (1347–9) was keeper of the privy seal and later chancellor; Adam Houghton (1362–89) was chancellor, and his successor, John Gilbert, in addition to being a royal confessor, served as treasurer. Guy Mone (1397–1407) was a very experienced royal servant as keeper of the privy seal and later treasurer, while Reginald Brian (1350–2) had been a royal clerk and Thomas Fastolf (1352–61) had served as an ambassador. When Henry Chichele became bishop in 1408 he took his place in a line of distinguished bishops. His task was to bring order back to a troubled area and to reconcile schismatics who had looked to the papacy at Avignon for support. In 1414 he was translated to Canterbury and to a wider sphere of responsibility. Before his departure, there was an ominous note: Chichele could not maintain himself on the income of the bishopric of St David's alone. Like his predecessors, he relied on other appointments to supplement the meagre resources of his diocese and it has been noted that he did not limit himself to important and lucrative benefices but was happy to hold a prebend in his own college at Abergwili, small though the income was. Like many pluralists of his day, he was too experienced to despise the small but useful sinecure. After his time the diocese ceased to attract leading administrators and was given to lesser figures. There was also a marked tendency to translate bishops from Welsh sees to richer dioceses in England. The routine work was being done, ordinations carried out and vacancies filled, but there was little sign of vitality: the note is muted, and the history of the Welsh church in the later middle ages must be written in a minor key.

5

CRISIS OF IDENTITY:
TOWARDS A PRINCIPALITY OF WALES

The close of the twelfth century marked a turning point in the history of Wales. Princely authority was gravely weakened in south Wales, and much attenuated in Powys. In the southern kingdom, the Lord Rhys had held in check the forces which might lead to disintegration, but his death in 1197 brought to an end the great days of his dynasty. Inspired by pleasure rather than politics, he had produced eight legitimate sons and seven bastards, and conflict over lands and power was the dominant theme of the story of Deheubarth in the early decades of the thirteenth century. The full effects of family rivalry were delayed for a few brief years. Gruffydd, eldest son of the Lord Rhys, succeeded his father and retained Dinefwr and the principal estates of the dynasty in Ystrad Tywi, and despite harassment by his rivals, he held his own until his death in 1201. From that point on, disputes produced a bewildering and constantly changing pattern of land tenure and power. Deheubarth, no longer a centre of effective power, became a kingdom of many memories. In Powys, the shift in power was more subtle. The death of Madog ap Maredudd in 1160 was followed by the division of his lands. His sons shared the land which formed northern Powys and which was later to be known as Powys Fadog: Gruffydd Maelor retained that part of Powys as a principality, and his brothers, Owain Fychan and Owain Brogyntyn, held the lesser territories of Mechain, Penllyn and Edeirion. Northern Powys remained in the hands of a single ruler until 1236, when division between heirs broke up the unity of this principality. But in 1160 it had been necessary to do justice to

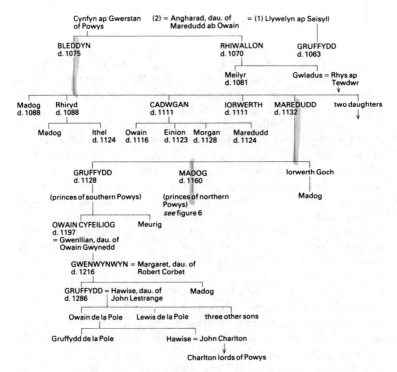

Figure 5   The princes of Powys from 1039 to 1160, and of southern Powys to 1286

Note: princes of Powys are indicated in capitals.

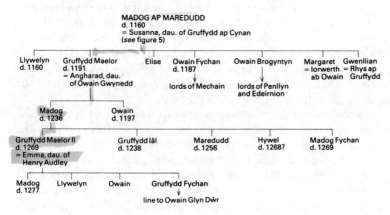

Figure 6   The princes of northern Powys, 1160–1277

Owain Cyfeiliog, the son and successor of Madog's brother. His share of the family inheritance formed the principality of southern Powys (later to be called Powys Wenwynwyn) which he held until his death in 1197, and which was to remain as a weak but undivided unit until 1286. The rulers of each part of Powys were significant political figures, but they were no longer the equals of the princes of Gwynedd in terms of resources and influence.

Increasingly it is difficult to find apt descriptions of territories and the men who held them. 'Principality' becomes steadily less appropriate as the landed possessions of individual leaders grow smaller. Although 'prince' is useful as a generic term and retains value for a small number of men, it becomes much more of a courtesy description than a real title. 'Men of gentle birth', or 'of the lineage of princes' has more meaning. The *Brut y Tywysogyon* shows a tendency to limit the title of prince to a small number of leaders, six in 1211, ten or eleven in 1215. In 1211 they are Gwenwynwyn of Powys, Hywel ap Gruffydd ap Cynan (Llywelyn's distant cousin), Madog ap Gruffydd Maelor, Maredudd ap Rhobert of Cydewain and two sons of the Lord Rhys, Maelgwn and Rhys Gryg. In 1215, they and others from their dynasties are linked with specific territories: from Gwynedd, Hywel ap Gruffydd ap Cynan and Llywelyn ap Maredudd; from Powys, Gwenwynwyn, Maredudd ap Rhobert and perhaps Madog ap Gruffydd Maelor whose war-band was part of Llywelyn's forces; from Deheubarth, the two sons of the Lord Rhys, Maelgwn and Rhys Gryg, were joined by their nephews Rhys Ieuanc and Owain ap Gruffydd, and there were two representatives of the local dynasty which ruled in Maelienydd, the sons of Maelgwn ap Cadwallon. Their names were not recorded, but they were clearly 'of the lineage of princes'. Modern writers find it easier to avoid concepts of rank and to speak of chiefs and chieftains, and sometimes of princelings. The English administration found it profitable to use feudal language and to think in terms of lordships and barons, but it would be anachronistic and unhelpful to use such language until the closing decades of the thirteenth century.

In this setting the princes of Gwynedd were able to maintain and build upon the pre-eminence achieved in the twelfth century. The foundation for this new development was laid by Llywelyn ab Iorwerth who, like many outstanding Welsh rulers, had to make his way against powerful odds. He came of distinguished stock: his father was Iorwerth, son of Owain Gwynedd, and his mother was Margaret, daughter of Madog ap Maredudd of Powys. Iorwerth died soon after the birth of his son, and power was seized by his brothers, Dafydd and Rhodri. Llywelyn probably grew up in Powys, and he emerged in the 1190s as a threat to the security of his uncles and their possessions. In 1194 he joined in a family coalition and attacked Dafydd, then well established as ruler of Gwynedd, and forced him to cede land and responsibilities in Perfeddwlad and to make substantial concessions to the cousins who were Llywelyn's allies in this episode. It might have been merely another upheaval in family alignments, but it was transformed into a permanent political settlement. Rhodri died in 1195. Two years later, with Dafydd as his prisoner, Llywelyn had taken over completely in Perfeddwlad and was beginning to rule Gwynedd. Dafydd spent the last six years of his life as an exile living on the English manors of Ellesmere and Hale which Henry II had given him. One of Llywelyn's cousins, Gruffydd ap Cynan, died in 1200 and Llywelyn took possession of his land; the other, Maredudd, was deprived of his lands in Llŷn for treachery in 1201, and at that point Llywelyn was established firmly as prince of Gwynedd. The attitude of the English administration had still to be determined, but in 1205 Llywelyn married Joan, the illegitimate daughter of King John, and this alliance was to have great importance for himself and for his family. In Joan he found an able and intelligent partner, who could exert a strong influence at her father's court. In due course, their son, Dafydd, could write to Henry III as 'prince of north Wales and his faithful man and devoted nephew'. Marriage was the culmination of a process of expediency; Llywelyn made no problems of his dependency on the English crown, swearing fealty to King John in 1201, and performing homage three years later. That, too, was to be part of the framework within which his ambitions might be achieved.

Neither homage nor marriage could prevent conflict between Llywelyn and John, for with both Gwenwynwyn of Powys and Llywelyn himself ambitious for power, the English king could play one off against the other. From 1207 Llywelyn was in the ascendant, invading southern Powys, and taking control of Ceredigion; but in 1211 John switched his support to Gwenwynwyn, who was re-established in Powys, and the prince of Gwynedd was hard put to survive. Already, the earl of Chester had overrun Perfeddwlad and later John advanced deep into Gwynedd 'planning to dispossess Llywelyn and to destroy him utterly'. Checked at Degannwy on his first attempt, he resumed the attack late in the summer, taking Bangor and forcing Llywelyn into submission. Despite his volatile nature, it was always dangerous to underestimate John's capacity for planning and carrying out an effective campaign. The king intended to follow up these successes in 1212, and as a preliminary move he installed two of Llywelyn's nephews, Owain ap Dafydd and Gruffydd ap Rhodri, each a potential claimant for Gwynedd, in Perfeddwlad; but as John's problems elsewhere escalated the campaign was never set in motion. The balance of power swayed violently during these years. In the first years of the thirteenth century Llywelyn could style himself prince of north Wales, and he appeared as a dominant figure in Welsh politics; in 1211–12 he was lucky to survive. That was, however, John's last hope of success, for as his domestic and international problems increased, Llywelyn's fortunes grew steadily. He regained the lands he had lost in 1210 and 1211, and in the next few years he carried the war southwards, taking Shrewsbury in 1215, while his confederates in south Wales reduced Anglo-Norman power in Dyfed, taking Narberth, and in Gower, capturing Swansea and five local castles. When Llywelyn joined them, they took Carmarthen, Llanstephan, St Clears, Laugharne, Trefdraeth (in Cemais), Newcastle Emlyn, Cardigan and Cilgerran. Conflict between King John and his barons, culminating in civil war, did much to create the opportunity which Llywelyn could exploit, but these military successes demonstrate the authority which he was able to impose in mid-Wales and the south. Three separate incidents illustrate the full extent of that authority. In 1216 he punished Gwenwynwyn of Powys for defecting to King John by assuming control of southern Powys, and in the same year he settled the terms on which the territories of the old kingdom of Deheubarth should be distributed between rival claimants. A year later, in a combination of family and national politics, he mounted a show of force in the south. His son-in-law and ally, Reginald de Braose, abandoned him and made peace with the magnates acting for the infant Henry III; in retaliation, Llywelyn attacked Brecknock, pursued Reginald to Swansea, and there accepted his submission. Swansea he handed to Rhys Gryg, and he continued to control the disposal of the castle there. Five years later, when John de Braose rebuilt Swansea castle, he did so with Llywelyn's permission and approval.

The death of King John and the accession of Henry III made the re-establishment of peace between the king and the rebel barons in England an urgent necessity. The confirmation of Magna Carta as an immediate declaration of intent in November 1216, and a major victory over the insurgents at Lincoln in May 1217, led to a formal peace settlement in the treaty of Kingston in November and the reissue of the Charter with significant emendations. The Welsh princes gained from the relaxation of John's stern discipline and the release of hostages, but they felt that at Kingston they 'had been scorned and ignored in that peace', and they held back. They made their own peace in the treaty of Worcester in March 1218. For practical purposes Llywelyn's power was tacitly accepted. The royal administrators sought his good offices to bring the princes of Wales to do homage to Henry III, and the *Brut y Tywysogyon* recorded that when Rhys Gryg went to the king's court and did homage he did so by Llywelyn's counsel and advice. Llywelyn's power in Gwynedd and his tenure of Perfeddwlad were taken for granted. In fact, the earl of Chester had acknowledged that Llywelyn should retain Mold, with its important castle, just south of the frontier of Tegeingl. No attempt was made to define the position in the sensitive area of mid-Wales where Llywelyn's ambitions clashed with the interests of a number of marcher dynasties. The minority government in England had accepted the important principle that royal lands and castles should not be alienated in perpetuity during the king's minority, and this reluctance to make permanent grants was reflected in the treaty of Worcester. Llywelyn was to retain the two major castles of Cardigan and Carmarthen and to hold them in custody until Henry III came of age. He was also left with the principality of southern Powys and the border territory of Montgomery to hold in custody until Gwenwynwyn's heir came of age. In theory, Llywelyn stood in the same position as Henry III's English magnates, but there was a distinct difference between the actual powers which he exercised in Wales and the more limited power defined in the treaty, to say nothing of the areas in which the treaty made no provision. Worcester restored peace and amity, but it did not provide any formal or constitutional recognition of Llywelyn's authority beyond the limits of Gwynedd. The prince made no problems about renewing his homage to Henry III.

This settlement established the pattern for the next twenty-two years. There was some whittling away of Llywelyn's gains but no major change in his basic position. He and the powerful English administrators who were responsible for the young king's policy – and, as he grew older, Henry III himself – were always ready to exploit a chance opportunity. Llywelyn wanted political stability, but not necessarily peace. The king, the Marshal earls of Pembroke and Hubert de Burgh were anxious to extend their influence in the marches; their ambitions, mutually exclusive as they were, created serious clashes at the royal court and in Wales. In 1223 the southern marches were disturbed by the determined attempt of William Marshal to recover his father's position in west Wales. He captured the castles of Cardigan and Carmarthen, which passed out of Llywelyn's control; so also did Cilgerran. All this represented a marked limitation on Llywelyn's influence in south and west Wales. What had started as a baronial campaign was reinforced by royal forces, and in this conflict Llywelyn also lost Montgomery to the crown.

Further royal campaigns followed in 1228 and 1231. On the first occasion Henry III was said to be 'planning to subdue the Lord Llywelyn and all the Welsh', but the royalist forces achieved little success. Henry drew diplomatic advantage from the encounter by receiving the homage of prominent Welsh leaders. For Llywelyn the campaign produced a bitter harvest. William de Braose, the lord of Brecknock, was taken prisoner, and as part of the price of his release he was obliged to hand over the castle and lordship of Builth. While he was in custody, William was involved in a liaison with Llywelyn's wife, Joan. He returned to Llywelyn's court in 1230 to continue the negotiations for his ransom, and while he was there Llywelyn discovered what was happening. The punishment prescribed in Welsh law for his offence was death, and by the judgement of the magnates of Llywelyn's court, William de Braose was hanged. Joan had been Llywelyn's wife for twenty-three years; he regarded her as a close companion and confidante, and he was deeply injured by her infidelity. William's death was part justice, part personal vengeance, and it might have cost the Welsh prince dearly in terms of his power in mid-Wales. He was negotiating a marriage between his son, Dafydd, and Isabel, daughter of William de Braose, and despite the execution, he was anxious that the marriage arrangements should be completed. The whole episode is a fascinating amalgam of personal feeling and policy, and Llywelyn managed to satisfy both. His attachment to Joan survived the crisis, and she continued to be a trusted adviser. When she died in 1237, he founded a community of Franciscan friars at Llanfaes, where she was buried.

For Henry III, the one major advantage of his next Welsh campaign in 1231 was the rebuilding of Painscastle as a key stronghold for the defence of mid-Wales. For the rest, the year was dominated by one of Llywelyn's sweeping attacks through south Wales. He destroyed castles at Montgomery, Brecon, Hay and Radnor, then turned to the east and burned Caerleon; on the same campaign he took Neath and Kidwelly. Two years later he was again disturbing the peace of the southern marches, but this time his activities were linked with political upheavals in England. Hubert de Burgh, already powerful at the king's court, had built up a formidable collection of castles and lordships in south Wales but in the summer of 1231 he was overthrown, and a struggle for power broke out. At the centre of it was the new earl marshal, Richard, who had succeeded his brother in April. He had opted to have the French lands belonging to his father, believing that this must exclude him from holding the family's English possessions. When he assumed the earldom and his estates in England, Ireland and Wales, Henry III and his leading advisers viewed him with hostility. Conflict broke out when royal troops invested his castle at Usk, and he joined forces with Llywelyn, wreaking havoc in south-east Wales, destroying a number of castles, including Monmouth, Abergavenny and Blaenllyfni. Cardiff was taken, but spared, while in the west Carmarthen fell to their combined forces. Richard died by treachery in Ireland, and peace was restored between Henry III and Llywelyn at the treaty of Middle in 1234. Throughout these years, it is clear that both the Welsh prince and Henry III were watching the military situation closely, and were able to intervene promptly to their own advantage.

The same is true in terms of politics, but here Llywelyn was at a disadvantage, and as the 1230s drew to a close his princely authority was adversely affected. It would be simplistic to suppose that a Welsh prince could bind others to himself by only one means. Like other rulers, he could make use of various bonds and exploit different motives. In the crudest terms, military conquest or punitive raids could bring a neighbouring prince into submission. Llywelyn ab Iorwerth used such tactics firmly against Gwenwynwyn of Powys. Here, military and political domination were essential since the rulers of southern Powys had the potential to speak for Welsh aspirations and to make their principality a bulwark of defence for Wales and, perhaps, the focus of Welsh loyalty. When Gwenwynwyn succeeded Owain Cyfeiliog in 1197 he was a man of high ambition, but his first attempt to challenge English power on the marches met with defeat at Painscastle in the following year. He was to find that, instead of a successful policy of aggression and growth, he would be forced to reign under the shadow of his powerful neighbours. As early as 1202, Llywelyn ab Iorwerth signalled his intention to harass Powys, but for a while King John found it expedient to encourage Gwenwynwyn as a makeweight against Gwynedd. By 1208 the prince of Powys had come into open conflict with John for which he paid dearly. Summoned to the king's court in 1209, he was forcibly detained and his lands were declared forfeit, and in the aftermath southern Powys was invaded by Llywelyn. Although Gwen-

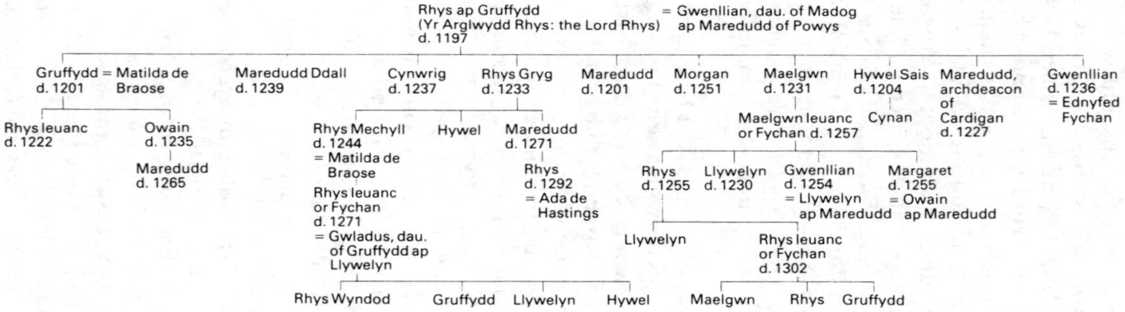

Rhys ap Gruffydd
(Yr Arglwydd Rhys: the Lord Rhys) = Gwenllian, dau. of Madog
d. 1197   ap Maredudd of Powys

Gruffydd = Matilda de Braose, d. 1201 | Maredudd Ddall d. 1239 | Cynwrig d. 1237 | Rhys Gryg d. 1233 | Maredudd d. 1201 | Morgan d. 1251 | Maelgwn d. 1231 | Hywel Sais d. 1204 | Maredudd, archdeacon of Cardigan d. 1227 | Gwenllian d. 1236 = Ednyfed Fychan

Gruffydd = Matilda de Braose, d. 1201
— Rhys Ieuanc d. 1222
— Owain d. 1235
  — Maredudd d. 1265

Rhys Gryg d. 1233
— Rhys Mechyll d. 1244 = Matilda de Braose
  — Rhys Ieuanc or Fychan d. 1271
    — Rhys Wyndod | Gruffydd | Llywelyn | Hywel
— Hywel
— Maredudd d. 1271
  — Rhys d. 1292 = Ada de Hastings
    — Gwladus, dau. of Gruffydd ap Llywelyn

Maelgwn d. 1231
— Maelgwn Ieuanc or Fychan d. 1257
  — Rhys d. 1255 | Llywelyn d. 1230 | Gwenllian d. 1254 = Llywelyn ap Maredudd | Margaret d. 1255 = Owain ap Maredudd
    — Llywelyn
    — Rhys Ieuanc or Fychan d. 1302
      — Maelgwn | Rhys | Gruffydd
— Cynan

Figure 7 Rhys ap Gruffydd of Deheubarth and his descendants in the thirteenth century
Note: it is assumed that Gwenllian was the mother of all the children of Rhys in this genealogy, but clear evidence exists only for Gruffydd, Rhys Gryg and Maredudd (d. 1201). The use of a limited range of personal names and of the descriptive name, Ieuanc, Fychan (Junior, Young or Little) makes identification very difficult.

wynwyn was restored in 1211, royal officers remained active in Powys, with Robert de Vieuxpont, the king's lieutenant, retaining an uneasy hold on the old centre of power at Mathrafal. As John's fortunes declined, Llywelyn increased his influence in Powys, securing Gwenwynwyn's homage and, when the prince sought to escape from this unwelcome tutelage, invading Powys and driving Gwenwynwyn into exile in England. There, in 1216, he died. Within the year, his lands were entrusted to Llywelyn to hold until the infant Gruffydd ap Gwenwynwyn came of age. For the child, the future was bleak: he had to wait for twenty-five years before he was allowed to claim his inheritance in Wales. He lived to be at least seventy, but in that long life he was to spend some thirty-four years in exile. Llywelyn was able to keep southern Powys under subjection until his death in 1240; he relied heavily on his sons, Dafydd and Gruffydd, who acted as his agents and held territories in Powys. The nature of their tenure and authority is not easily defined, but two analogies may provide some insight. It could be compared with English domination of Gascony, and in that case the analogy would be with a colonial administration, or, alternatively, it could be compared with French control of the northern lordships of the old duchy of Aquitaine, in which case the analogy would be with the creation of an *apanage* as a means of extending royal power into a disputed area.

Llywelyn ab Iorwerth won over other leading Welshmen by fear or favour. Fear of the king's anger and appreciation of the benefits which came from the king's friendship were fundamental to the exercise of Angevin kingship, and they were recurrent elements in Welsh politics. With the numerous claimants to the inheritance of the prince of Deheubarth, the favours which could accrue from Llywelyn's benevolent patronage outweighed the advantages of internecine warfare. This can be seen especially in the changing fortunes of two young brothers in south and west Wales, Rhys Ieuanc and Owain, the sons of Gruffydd ap Rhys. Unusually for the family of the Lord Rhys, they were the children of an Anglo-Norman mother, Matilda de Braose, and perhaps that accounts for the close and unbroken association between them. Their father died in 1201, when they were both very young and very inexperienced, and they had to survive, to learn political wisdom and to retain some portion of their patrimony. With wily and aggressive uncles anxious to seize their lands, it was no easy inheritance. In their early years, they may have deserved J. E. Lloyd's critical comment that they 'had the misfortune always to espouse the losing cause'. They depended upon a strong patron, and family quarrels meant that for brief periods they could count on one of their uncles, Rhys Gryg and Maelgwn ap Rhys. Then, for a longer and happier period, they enjoyed the patronage of Llywelyn ab Iorwerth of Gwynedd. For a decade they contested, with violent changes of fortune, the tenure of lands and castles in Cantref Mawr and Cantref Bychan, and slowly they learned how to deal with their uncles on more advantageous terms. In 1211 they suffered as Llywelyn's allies, their lands were taken from them, and they were forced to make peace with King John, but as John's troubles increased they found greater security. Rhys appears at times as the leading partner. He was credited with taking Llandovery castle in 1202, and he complained in 1213 that he alone had no portion of his family's lands, though it is clear that he was speaking for his brother as well as for himself. He played a leading role in the Welsh attacks of 1215 which saw the fall of Kidwelly, Carmarthen, Gower (with its castles of Loughor, Talybont and Oystermouth) and finally the castle and town of Swansea. He seems to have spent part of his time in the lordship of his mother's family, Brecknock; in 1216 he was a useful intermediary between Llywelyn ab Iorwerth and the burgesses of Brecon. It is not surprising that, when he died in 1222, the *Brut y Tywysogyon* recorded a long and graceful eulogy for 'a young man eminent for his praise and his eloquence and his sense and his prudence and his wisdom'. After a painful illness he died at Strata Florida where he had taken the Cistercian habit. If Rhys is picked out for particular notice, it remains clear that the brothers shared a common inheritance. In 1216 Llywelyn ab Iorwerth arranged a formal distribution of the family's lands which left the two brothers with possessions concentrated largely in Ceredigion. When Rhys died, Owain was not strong enough to take over these lands *en bloc*, and Llywelyn obliged him to share the inheritance with Maelgwn ap Rhys. Even then, his problems were not over, for William Marshal ravaged the family's lands in 1223, and two successive attempts at arbitration were necessary before Owain recovered what was due to him. In 1235 he too died at Strata Florida where he was buried beside his brother. Over a period of twenty-one troubled years, Rhys Ieuanc cannot have been able to spend more than five or six years in full enjoyment of his lands; Owain, surviving for a further thirteen years, had at least another decade of reasonably settled conditions in which to husband his resources and to make some use of them.

In one instance, patronage and alliance sufficed to maintain peace between Llywelyn and a powerful neighbour, Madog ap Gruffydd

Maelor of northern Powys, until his death in 1236. He was one of a number of princes who entered into a formal agreement with Llywelyn in 1212, but for the most part their successful partnership was informal and personal. He could attest charters of the prince of Gwynedd, and give open acknowledgement of Llywelyn's status in Powys in his own charters; a dispute about land in Llangollen was to be settled at a time appointed by his lord, the prince, and the prince's seneschal. There was a price to pay for the mutual advantage to be derived from their relationship, and, with no sense of subservience, Madog was ready to pay that price.

In his dealings with other princes, Llywelyn knew the value of formal links. In 1212 he 'made a solemn pact with the princes of Wales', Gwenwynwyn, Maelgwn ap Rhys, Madog ap Gruffydd Maelor and Maredudd ap Rhobert, and together they went to war against King John. In the same year, when he was negotiating a treaty of alliance with Philip Augustus of France, he sealed his undertaking 'in the presence and with the advice of his great men (*procerum*) and with the common assent of all the princes of Wales'. Both seem to have been *ad hoc* arrangements, but in each case he was the leading figure, speaking for as well as acting with the other princes. Increasingly, he came to value the formal links of a feudal society. When, in 1208, Innocent III placed John's lands under interdict and released his subjects from their obligations of fealty and homage, his directive had strong political overtones for Wales. Llywelyn made use of these same obligations when he secured Gwenwynwyn's submission by taking his fealty and homage. Like King John, he went further and demanded a charter recording Gwenwynwyn's loyalty, and he wanted hostages as a guarantee of compliance. The accession of Henry III reinforced the importance of these ties. In 1218 Llywelyn gave his homage to the new king, but in the treaty of Worcester a number of his closest associates had to promise to withdraw their homage from Llywelyn if the prince broke the terms of the treaty. Again, in 1228, Henry III used the opportunity to take renewed homage from a number of Welsh leaders; it was said that they rendered homage 'without kingly honour', but a gloss on that obscure phrase suggested that the king was not strong enough to impose terms and had to be content with reconciliation through this formal procedure.

Llywelyn was content to work within this intricate pattern of loyalties and allegiances, partly because his approach to politics was essentially practical, and partly because he had plans which could only be achieved with English co-operation and he had to tread

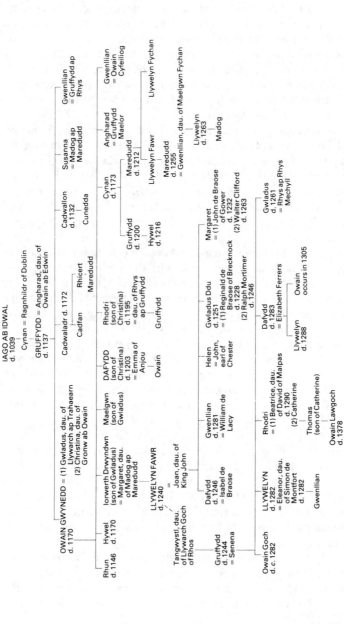

Figure 8   The princes of Gwynedd and their descendants, 1039–1378

Note: ruling princes are indicated in capitals. Hywel and Rhodri, sons of Owain Gwynedd shared authority with their brother, Dafydd.

warily. His concern was with the future. How could he ensure that the structure of power which he had built up would continue? That question could be simplified: who would succeed him? He had two sons, Gruffydd, born out of wedlock, whose illegitimacy was a cause of offence to the pope and to Henry III, and Dafydd, son of Llywelyn and his wife Joan. If tradition were followed, both would count as heirs and share the inheritance, and Gwynedd would suffer as Deheubarth and Powys had suffered. Llywelyn determined that Dafydd should be his sole heir, and over a period of eighteen years he negotiated for the recognition of Dafydd as his successor. In 1220, the leading figures of Henry III's minority government noted that Llywelyn had disinherited Gruffydd, and accepted Dafydd's claims; and two years later, Pope Honorius III confirmed their action. It was recorded that the leading figures of Wales renewed their recognition in 1226, and in the same year, Honorius III removed the stigma of bastardy from Dafydd's mother, Joan. Two years later, Henry III accepted Dafydd's homage for the lands and rights which would come to him when his father died, but the form of words used on that occasion was less precise than Llywelyn and Dafydd assumed. The culmination came in 1238 when Llywelyn called for the leading men of Wales to do homage to Dafydd. The English administration heard what was afoot and reacted quickly. In March, Llywelyn was reminded that Dafydd was not yet in a position to claim their homage, and that a number of them had already done homage to Henry III. The king would sanction only a more limited form of commitment. So, in October, at Strata Florida, the princes gave their fealty to Dafydd. His position was by no means as strong as his father had wished and, as with all negotiations, the undertakings could be ignored or rejected as circumstances suggested.

Gruffydd ap Llywelyn was not to share power, but he remained an important magnate and a potentially dangerous figure in Gwynedd. He was given land and authority in Meirionydd and Ardudwy, but in 1221 his father removed him for maladministration. Within two years he had been sent as his father's *penteulu* (military commander) on two separate forays against William Marshal in west Wales, but again, by the end of the decade his father had imprisoned him, and he was kept in custody for six years before his release in 1234. Recovery followed, for he was given land in Llŷn, and he had wide authority in southern Powys, holding Ceri, Cyfeiliog, Mawddwy, Mochnant and Caereinion. Whatever his motives, he had proved to be a problem for his father and might be a problem for his brother. In the last

years of Llywelyn's life tension between the two brothers was a
major factor in the politics of Gwynedd. Matthew Paris reported
that in 1237 Llywelyn, now in his mid-sixties, was weakened by a
stroke. Dafydd was certainly able to take the initiative though not, as
it seems, to supplant Llywelyn. In two stages, he was able to remove
Gruffydd from Powys and then to imprison him. When Llywelyn
died, Dafydd was geared to succeed him without challenge, but he
had miscalculated: perhaps he placed too much reliance on his
father's diplomatic agreements, but certainly he did not count on the
determination of Henry III to intervene in Wales.

After such long and careful preparation, Dafydd's short reign
(1240–6) was a sad anti-climax. His first years were marked by personal failure and serious losses. When, in 1244–5 he felt able to
attempt a serious campaign to restore the power of Gwynedd, time
was already running out for him. Within a month of his accession,
Dafydd joined Henry III at Gloucester where the king's council had
been summoned to meet. Writing at Tewkesbury, only 11 miles
away, the monastic annalist recorded it as a happy family occasion.
The king welcomed his nephew, knighted him and granted him all
the lands which his father had rightfully held. The prince wore his
'garland' or 'chaplet', the *talaith* which was the mark of his princely
status. Behind the public façade, matters of more serious import
were transacted. The new prince gave his homage to Henry III, and
the terms were incorporated in a formal agreement. The lands of
Gruffydd ap Gwenwynwyn and others of the king's barons in Wales
were to be subject to arbitration by a panel made up of Ottobuono,
the papal legate, the bishops of Worcester and Norwich, Richard,
earl of Cornwall, and John of Monmouth, with the bishop of St
Asaph, and two prominent administrators, Ednyfed Fychan and
Einion Fychan. The king reserved for himself the homage of all his
barons of Wales, and a range of judicial cases. Dafydd would have
been better advised not to seal so comprehensive and explicit a document for much of the theoretical basis of his power as prince of north
Wales and as overlord of other parts of Wales was seriously under-
mined. Arbitration was no mere threat, and the proceedings which
followed brought home to Dafydd the insecurity of his position.
Despite his own preparations in Gwynedd, his brother's claims to
land were not forgotten. With great skill, using terms for wrongful
dispossession well known in English courts, Gruffydd's wife,
Senena, presented her husband as a man deprived of his lawful
inheritance, and she agreed the terms on which the king should
secure justice for him. It was a small step for Henry III to let it be

known that, if Gruffydd were set free, he should have his share of Gwynedd. Among the lesser Welsh leaders there was enough sympathy for Gruffydd's claims to cause his brother real anxiety. None of this represents a sudden new departure in English policy. Both in England and Gwynedd influential figures had been watching events closely; in 1238, Henry and his ministers checked Dafydd's aspirations, and now in 1240 and 1241, they reacted quickly to events. In the summer of 1241 Henry moved an army from Chester into Tegeingl and westward as far as Rhuddlan. It was important that Dafydd should check their advance, but instead, he was out-manoeuvred and almost cut off from his base in Snowdonia. Before the end of August he had submitted.

This time, there were no pleasantries to disguise the hard realities. The terms were laid down at Gwern Eigron, and confirmed two days later at Rhuddlan; they were restated in London in the autumn. Dafydd promised to release Gruffydd and his son, Owain, into the king's keeping; he would submit to the judgement of the king's court as to what lands he and Gruffydd should hold; they would both hold their lands as tenants-in-chief of the king. In broader terms, the *status quo* of John's reign was accepted as a norm. Any land occupied since the war between John and Llywelyn ab Iorwerth should be handed back to the king. The homage of all those who used to give homage to John, and especially the homage of all Welshmen, was to be restored to the crown. There were careful arrangements for Dafydd to pay the expenses and damages incurred by the royal forces during the present campaign. Commentators have found it difficult to speak of these terms as anything other than an abject surrender of all that Llywelyn ab Iorwerth had achieved. It was, undoubtedly, a black moment for the prince of Gwynedd, but it would be a misreading of the course of Welsh history to see it as a moment of final or total defeat. Dafydd might be compared with a boxer who has survived a withering first round and whose primary task is to survive the onslaught and to build up a steady and persistent resistance to his opponent. For the next two and a half years, Dafydd seems to have been psychologically incapable of making that effort. He attached great importance, perhaps undue importance, to the role which Gruffydd might be called upon to play. Henry III had secured his release in 1241, but had transferred him to the Tower of London. He was too useful a pawn as a rival claimant for Gwynedd; both Henry and Dafydd knew that there was an undercurrent of support for his claims, and it appears that the threat immobilised the prince of Gwynedd. Then, on St David's day (1 March), 1244, Gruffydd made a bid for freedom; using an improvised rope, he climbed from his window, but the rope broke, and he plunged to his death. As if released from fear, Dafydd resumed the offensive in Wales, inflicting substantial losses on the English. Henry was slow to react, and the summer and autumn passed without a major campaign, but in 1245 he took up the challenge and brought an army as far as Degannwy. Slow and inadequate preparation, a badly organised commissariat, and an element of indecision, robbed the English army of any success in that campaigning season, but both sides were aware that the war must be resumed in the spring of 1246.

Before spring came, Dafydd was dead. He died, not in battle, but from natural causes in his *llys* at Aber, between Bangor and Penmaenmawr. For him, the task of reconstructing native power in north Wales was unfinished business.

In two respects, Dafydd displayed a flair which held promise. He made an attempt to put Gwynedd under papal protection. Matthew Paris laid out the essential features of this somewhat bizarre development asserting that Dafydd wished to 'free his neck from the yoke of fealty to the king' and that in 1244 'he took flight to the wings of papal protection, pretending that he held part of Wales from the pope directly'. The chronicler also noted that the pope favoured his case, and that Dafydd was committed to pay 500 marks (£333 6s. 8d.) a year. Matthew Paris' claim was not without foundation. In July 1244, Innocent IV instructed the abbots of Cymer and Aberconwy to act in a dispute between Dafydd, prince of north Wales, and King Henry. They were to call upon Henry to answer the charge that he had abandoned arbitration in Wales in favour of war. The citation asserted that Dafydd's parents had given him to the church as a vassal, but the king had forced him into taking oaths which went counter to this status. Within nine months Innocent had rescinded his instructions and would no longer sustain the role of feudal lord. A flurry of diplomatic activity, the unexpected payment of outstanding dues, and the promise of support for papal policy in Europe, seem to represent the reaction of the English court to this bid for independence and to explain the change of heart at the curia.

Dafydd's second move was of a different order: in the last months of his life he used the style 'prince of Wales', and the real danger of his approach to the papacy was that it involved recognition of his new standing. His predecessors had used the style 'prince of north Wales' until, in 1230, Llywelyn ab Iorwerth adopted the style 'prince of Aberffro and lord of Snowdon'. Dafydd preferred 'prince of north Wales', the title which best described the territorial base of his power. Hard pressed as he was by the English king, to call himself prince of Wales had no real meaning, and modern commentators find it difficult to interpret. Rees Davies sees it as defiant and incongruous, while Michael Richter considers it to be a kind of challenge, a title which reflected Dafydd's ambitions rather than his actual powers. Both the appearance of the title and the approach to the papacy belong to the period after the death of Gruffydd ap Llywelyn, and may properly be seen as part of the renewal of the conflict with Henry III once the 'pretender' was out of the way. If nothing else, they are a reminder that Dafydd was ready for a long struggle, and that he was not afraid to match Henry's powers as king and overlord with new claims which were certainly disconcerting, even if, in the short run, they were not very effective.

By 1245, in the east and in south and west Wales the influence of the prince of Gwynedd had been greatly reduced. In 1241 Gruffydd ap Gwenwynwyn's standing as a feudal vassal of Henry III was precisely defined and he was allowed to resume his proper place in southern Powys. There he was to enjoy sixteen years of authority, the longest period of unbroken rule he would experience. The uneasy peace in south Wales was threatened in 1242 when Maelgwn ap Maelgwn of Is Aeron, a comparatively minor figure in the dynasty of Deheubarth, built a new castle in Ceredigion. Open conflict broke out in 1246, and in the absence of any strong Welsh leader, local marcher lords were able to exploit the internal weaknesses of Deheubarth to their own advantage. Under pressure from the English king and the lords of the march, it appeared that chaos was to be encouraged and further weakness ensured.

With all the major decisions made by the princes of north Wales, the records emphasise their personal responsibility, and it is very difficult to gauge whether they acted alone, or whether they were aided by an *éminence grise*. The formalities of government are clear to see. A council of leading figures in Gwynedd was consulted by Llywelyn ab Iorwerth and used to give added weight to his decisions. Where judicial work was concerned men learned in the law were at hand to advise and assess, and to serve as arbitrators. When the prince did not take the field himself, he could call on the *penteulu*, the commander of his personal troops, to act for him on any particular foray or campaign. He was usually a close member of the family circle, and everything suggests that his expertise and advice would influence decisions. Llywelyn worked closely with his wife, Joan, in political matters, especially in his dealings with King John. His son, Dafydd, had wide responsibilities in Powys for many years, and so also, when he enjoyed his father's trust, did Gruffydd. The interplay of sound knowledge and useful policy must be assumed rather than established by any appeal to the evidence. These instances would compare with the great reliance which Henry III placed on close members of his own family circle, and especially on his brother, Richard, earl of Cornwall, and later his eldest son, Edward. Beyond the immediate family, Llywelyn and his successors could call upon a small coterie of powerful administrators. The outstanding figure was undoubtedly Ednyfed Fychan, who served from about 1212 to 1246 as *distain*, usually identified as steward or seneschal and occasionally equated with the English justiciar. Ednyfed was entrusted with the most crucial of negotiations as a diplomat and arbitrator. So, too, was his contemporary, Einion Fychan, who was probably the representative of an administrative family which had served the princes of Gwynedd since before 1170. These men could speak for the prince and commit him by their decisions; they would be involved in intimate and continual discussions about policy, and it is scarcely possible to think of them as passive agents. In English terms, they would compare with administrators like Hubert de Burgh, Peter des Roches, and Peter de Rivaux. Surviving records make it possible to watch Henry III's administrators at work and to analyse their influence in great detail, but the paucity of material bearing upon Welsh administration frustrates all attempts at a similar analysis for Wales.

One measure of the pre-eminence of Ednyfed Fychan, Einion Fychan and a very small group of their contemporaries is the importance which Henry III attached to them. Sometimes he wooed them; sometimes he threatened them. In 1235 Ednyfed was staying in London on a journey which would take him to the Holy Land, and King Henry ordered his treasurer, Hugh Pateshull, to find out where Ednyfed was lodging and to take him the gift of a silver cup. His son, Tudur, was taken as a hostage in 1245 and was effectively kept out of Welsh politics for twenty years. He was only released after five years of custody; he had then to do homage to King Henry and to hand over two sons as hostages, and while they were in the king's hand he himself was technically free but totally dependent on the king's good will. Royal generosity over the years 1246 to 1258 was a mark of Tudur's importance. He was allowed 22 marks (£16 13s. 4d.) to buy a horse, part of his own estates were restored and he was allowed to have the lands of his wife's inheritance. Provisional allowances were followed by a life-grant of one estate, and he was given the vill of Maenan. He had, however reluctantly, to be the king's man until his son, Heilyn, was set free in 1263; only then could he return to Gwynedd and resume his place in the prince's entourage. In Tudur's absence the family interest was maintained by his brothers; one, Gruffydd, succeeded Ednyfed as *distain*, serving Llywelyn ap Gruffydd, while the other, Goronwy, took service with Owain ap Gruffydd and his career faded as Owain's fortunes fell. Einion Fychan was himself a hostage between 1241 and 1246, and he too had to do homage to Henry III before he was released. He returned to Wales in 1247, but very little is known of his activities during the next decade. He lived to see his son, Dafydd, launched on a career which would span nearly thirty years as a leading adviser and administrator.

Ednyfed and Einion were important figures in a small corps of about twenty secular administrators who can be identified as men serving Llywelyn ab Iorwerth; rather fewer, about fourteen, can be identified from Dafydd's reign, and in the second half of the thirteenth century some thirty administrators who worked with Llywelyn ap Gruffydd can be traced. These were matched by clerical figures who worked with the princes of Gwynedd. Dafydd, archdeacon of St Asaph, was clearly a man of influence until the early 1240s, while Ystrwyth, Master Adam and Philip ab Ifor were clerks who built up a considerable expertise in Llywelyn ab Iorwerth's service. Compared with secular administrators, fewer clerics can be identified: the numbers are of the order of seven for Llywelyn ab Iorwerth, three or four for Dafydd, and as many as nineteen for Llywelyn ap Gruffydd. It is impossible to gauge what influence an individual administrator might have, but service for a long period of time and continuity may provide useful indices. Dafydd, archdeacon of St Asaph, Philip ab Ifor and five laymen who served Llywelyn ab Iorwerth continued to work for his successor, Dafydd, and Philip was still active twelve years after the accession of Llywelyn ap Gruffydd. At least six others of Dafydd's staff remained with him in the prince's service. For a small political unit, both the numbers and the continuity are significant elements, for they point to long-term memory, and to expertise, and both factors could influence diplomatic and political decisions. There is a dark side to record, for a number of leading administrators found it easy to transfer their loyalties to Edward I in the 1280s. 'Defect' is a modern verb with pejorative overtones: could it be applied to what happened in north Wales under pressure of conquest? These men of power had much to lose, and unless overriding loyalties prevented them they had to reassess personal and family interests and determine their future line of conduct. Did they make a quick decision (as men of power in England in 1066 did) and see the independence of north Wales already as a thing of the past? Or are the suggestions that Llywelyn ap Gruffydd was a difficult and suspicious master the explanation of their conduct? On a crucial issue, it is easier to ask the questions than to establish the answers.

All this was still in the future. When Dafydd died in 1246 with no son to succeed him, the claims to his territory passed to his nephews, all of them young and still lacking political experience and maturity, though already they had ambitions if not expectations. The initiative was taken by the oldest, Owain ap Gruffydd (Owain Goch), then living near Chester, who made all speed back to Gwynedd. His immediate bid for power was only partially successful, for he did not receive the full support of the men of influence. His brother, Llywelyn, had avoided the stigma of English patronage, and could be identified as one of the magnates of north Wales who had supported Dafydd in the last year of his life. It was agreed that the brothers should divide the territory between them. Their agreement was sanctioned by Henry III at the end of April 1247, but they were obliged to acknowledge that they held their lands of him, and they had to cede a wide range of territories to him. With two brothers sharing the inheritance, and with younger brothers, Rhodri and Dafydd, who might be anxious to establish themselves, the scene was set for a battle for supremacy which could prove costly for Gwynedd. Their uneasy partnership lasted for nine years until, in 1255, Owain, acting with his brother, Dafydd, attempted to oust Llywelyn who met their combined forces at Bryn Derwin, where they were defeated and taken prisoner. For Owain, the price of defeat was high; he remained in custody until 1277. Dafydd, on the other hand, was released after only a few months, and it is clear that Llywelyn was already building up the close relationship with him which would be a major factor in Welsh politics for a generation. For Llywelyn, the victory of 1255 marked a threshold, and despite all the signs of weakness and disruption, he was to emerge as the dominant figure in Wales. But the nature of the task which faced him was daunting in the extreme, for all the political gains of Llywelyn ab Iorwerth had been eroded, and the independence which had been built up had been compromised. Instead of building on inherited strength, Llywelyn ap Gruffydd had to reconstruct the fabric of Welsh power after fifteen years of weakness, and the language of politics which had served the prince of Gwynedd in the first half of the thirteenth century would no longer suffice for his purposes.

6

THE EDWARDIAN CONQUEST

Llywelyn ap Gruffydd came to power under distinctly unfavourable auspices. He shared power with his eldest brother, Owain Goch, as protégés of the English king. In the interest of re-establishing a strong, unitary kingdom of Gwynedd, he strove to disinherit his brothers. At one point, in 1267, he secured unprecedented recognition from Henry III as prince of Wales. In 1277 he was forced into a defeat which has been universally recognised as a humiliation, his princely standing was deliberately diminished and his power in Wales was truncated. Five years later in 1282, when his brother Dafydd rebelled against English domination, he had no choice but to join the revolt and make himself its leader. He died in a minor skirmish, and no one was able to salvage anything of the independence which he had achieved. Yet this bare record of strife, brief success and ultimate failure does not do full justice to the man. Much as he and the ambitions of his dynasty were feared by rival Welsh families, the force of his personality made its mark. The charm which, in Dafydd, was linked with bold speech and venturesome action, was yoked in him with cooler judgement and greater political acumen. His primary objective was to see Gwynedd strong and independent, but part of the means by which this was to be achieved was to subject other princely dynasties to himself. He was anxious to continue that process by which he might become the intermediary between Henry III and those Welsh leaders over whom he claimed the right of lordship. Where, between 1240 and 1246, Prince Dafydd ap Llewelyn had made his bid and failed, Llywelyn ap Gruffydd made his bid with open success. Two things, as it seems, were essential to give that success a real hope of permanence. One was to ensure a strong succession; the other was to persuade the English king that the power of the prince of Wales could be absorbed into the concepts of feudal, political and diplomatic relationships which prevailed in Britain in the thirteenth century. Neither of these prerequisites could be secured.

The beginning of the new reign was not marked immediately by any spectacular event. How Owain and Llywelyn had shared power in the years 1247 to 1255 remains something of a mystery. That power was exercised jointly is clear from the pledge which they issued in March, 1248, guaranteeing the loyalty of their brother, Rhodri, to Henry III, and by the pact drawn up in the autumn of 1251 between them and their 'dear and special kinsmen' from Deheubarth, Maredudd ap Rhys Gryg and Rhys Fychan. In the document which they issued on that occasion, Owain and Llywelyn did not claim any distinctive titles, but in keeping with the treaty of Woodstock, they were content to identify themselves as the sons of Gruffydd, son of Llywelyn the sometime prince and as the heirs of north Wales. Then, curiously, there is one agreement, drawn up in November 1250, between Llywelyn, acting alone, and Gruffydd Maelor ap Madog, lord of Bromfield. Should these documents be seen as indications that the brothers were building up a network of alliances for their joint advantage, or was Llywelyn making sure of an ally in his own interest? In both these pacts, no particular enemy is named, and no special purpose is defined, but it may be significant that any reference to loyalty to the English king is ignored in each text.

The trial of strength in 1255 was initiated by Owain and Dafydd, not by Llywelyn, but he was quick to profit from it. The chance to do so came, again, not from his own initiative, but from events beyond Gwynedd. Henry III was determined to establish his son, Edward, with lands and responsibilities, and in 1254 Bristol was made the administrative centre of his widespread possessions, which included lands in Gascony and Ireland as well as in England. There, apart from many estates scattered through the kingdom, he was made earl of Chester, and with that title he acquired lordships and lands in Wales: the Perfeddwlad, Montgomery, Builth, the honour of the three castles of Whitecastle, Grosmont and Skenfrith, Cardigan and Carmarthen, each with its separate shire, and the northern part of Ceredigion. There is little doubt that, in all his territories, Edward's agents were overzealous and harsh; complaints of their rigorous administration were voiced in Bedfordshire, where Dunstable priory suffered from their depredations. The annalist there recorded that similar harshness was experienced by the men of Edward's Welsh lordships. Geoffrey of Langley, the prince's chief agent, boasted cynically to the king and queen that he had the Welsh in the palm of his hand, but the annalist also knew that the Welsh were determined to do nothing for him in breach of their native law. In the summer of 1256, Edward made a formal visit to his possessions in north Wales, and that seems to have brought resentment and opposition to a head. Welsh magnates sought out Llywelyn ap Gruffydd, and confident of support, he moved against the English. With his ally from the south, Maredudd ap Rhys Gryg, he stormed the Perfeddwlad, and within a week he had secured the four *cantrefi* there. Meirionydd, northern Ceredigion, Builth, and then Roger Mortimer's lordship of Gwrtheyrnion fell quickly. For Edward, still a youth of seventeen, it was a bitter humiliation. Llywelyn continued his campaign in 1257, overrunning the greater part of southern Powys at the expense of Gruffydd ap Gwenwynwyn, and then moving into west Wales, and finally attacking the lordship of Glamorgan. The most notable feature of these campaigns was the speed with which Llywelyn restored the authority of the ruler of Gwynedd, and brought into one cohesive force the military resources of north, south and west Wales.

Early in 1258, this was given formal sanction when the Welsh leaders, as the *Brut y Tywysogyon* puts it, 'made a pact together, and they gave an oath to maintain loyalty and agreement together, under pain of excommunication upon whomsoever broke it'. An alternative version of the same source cast this in sharper terms, and claimed that the Welsh magnates gave an oath of allegiance to Llywelyn. In that year, Llywelyn began to use the title, prince of Wales. On 18 March, a group of Scottish magnates, nineteen of whom were named, met a similar group of Welsh leaders, twenty-one of whom were named, and they and their companions agreed not to make a separate peace with the English king. The first of the Welsh leaders was Llywelyn, prince of Wales. It was the first public acknowledgement of his title. They all authenticated the document with their seals: what legend did Llywelyn's bear – a mere name, or a princely title? After nine years of low-key activity, and perhaps stalemate, in Gwynedd, the speed with which Llywelyn ap Gruffydd moved from his successful response to the challenge posed by his brothers in 1255 to his assumption of the title of prince of Wales in 1258 is a striking testimony to his gifts and his growing political maturity. So was his insistence that all the lands claimed by Owain and Dafydd should come into his hands without reservation. To unite all the component parts of Gwynedd was a major step in the emergence of a powerful and undisputed prince in north Wales.

The apparent unity of 1258 concealed weakness as well as strength. On the one hand, Gruffydd Maelor ap Madog of northern Powys, viewing events from his lands bordering on Gwynedd, decided in 1257 to withdraw from his direct dependence on Henry III and to give his allegiance to Llywelyn ap Gruffydd. That was a valuable reinforcement of Llywelyn's power, and it made possible the renewal of an aggressive policy against southern Powys, leading to the exile of Gruffydd ap Gwenwynwyn. On the other hand, Welsh leaders in the south were not universally eager to submit to Llywelyn. To secure their estates in south-west Wales, Maredudd ap Rhys and his nephew, Rhys Fychan, could seek support from the king and his officials. In 1257, Rhys Fychan, with the king's leading official in south Wales, Stephen Bauzun, advanced together from Carmarthen to Dinefwr to recover his patrimony for Rhys. There they were outmanoeuvred by his kinsmen and rivals, Maredudd ap Rhys and Maredudd ab Owain, and once it was clear that their venture could not succeed, Rhys Fychan deemed it wiser to abandon his English allies. Stephen had to withdraw his forces under heavy attack, suffering such losses that the king was anxious to call out an army to avenge a major defeat. That did not prevent the king from taking Maredudd ap Rhys into his peace in the autumn, and confirming him in the possession of his lands. Maredudd was among those who gave their support to Llywelyn in 1258, with a solemn oath, but he was also the first Welsh leader to break his oath and to move away from Llywelyn before the year was out. For him, the ruler of Gwynedd was only one possible ally; his options were open, and he was not afraid to use them.

Further east, in Elfael, the adhesion of Owain ap Maredudd, the representative of a minor dynasty, followed Llywelyn's seizure of the lands entrusted by Prince Edward to Roger Mortimer, the lordship of Builth, in 1260. Two years later, with Llywelyn maintaining the pressure on Roger Mortimer, the leading Welshmen of the lordship of Brecknock gave him their homage. The most reluctant of all the Welsh magnates to compromise his direct links with the English crown and to come into Llywelyn's entourage was Gruffydd ap Gwenwynwyn of southern Powys, but late in 1263 he, too, submitted. The terms on which he was now to hold Powys, rehearsed at length, laid down that he was to give his homage and allegiance to

Llywelyn and to hold his lands in southern Powys from Llywelyn. In all these arrangements, Llywelyn's intentions were clear: the lines of dependence in Wales would emanate directly from himself and, like his grandfather, he would hold the homage of the leading Welshmen of his day. Where he differed from Llywelyn ab Iorwerth was in the greater precision of the terms of their dependence, and a sharper awareness of the need to replace the English king as the focus of Welsh loyalties.

It would be wrong to belittle the strength of Llywelyn's purpose and drive towards this political goal, but it must be said that the conditions which made for his success were largely created in England. From the late 1230s onwards, the power of Henry III was brought under critical survey and was being tested by his own military and diplomatic failures. Ideas of reform were in the air, and schemes for curbing the independent power of the king were under discussion by secular magnates and by leading ecclesiastics. Costly and unsuccessful undertakings in Gascony, and unpopular and potentially expensive involvement in papal plans to replace the Hohenstaufen dynasty in Sicily and southern Italy, forced Henry III into submission to his critics among the English baronage. Then, plans for checking the autocracy of the royal administration ceased to be matters of informed discussion and became matters of practical politics, and for a brief period, between 1258 and 1265, baronial attempts at reform were to dominate the English court and kingdom. Llywelyn read the signs of the times with skill, and his assumption of a new title was made at the moment when it was least likely to be challenged successfully by King Henry.

Part of Llywelyn's strength lay in the fact that he was given time to consolidate his hold on north and central Wales. That it was important to intervene in Wales and to subdue Llywelyn was fully recognised at the English court, where the king's young half-brother, William de Valence, who had acquired the earldom of Pembroke by marriage, was a vigorous and hawkish advocate of renewing the war in Wales. Henry III himself shared his sentiments and needed little persuasion. Political tensions in England made it expedient for William and his brothers to withdraw from the kingdom in July 1259, and the threat subsided; but the call for a militant approach to the Welsh problem remained a subsidiary theme of English politics during these critical years. In fact, Llywelyn was able to secure a series of truces which put off hostilities, and so delayed any direct challenge to his authority. They sustained peace, despite numerous infringements, and they ensured that Henry III and Llywelyn and their men should continue to have seisin of their lands and castles. For the Welsh prince, undisturbed possession was an undeniable advantage. For the English king, his capacity to provision and maintain his garrisons at the castles of Diserth and Degannwy depended upon the agreements he could make with Llywelyn. So, in 1258, it was agreed that the king might revictual these castles by sea, or, if weather conditions made that impossible, by using land routes under Llywelyn's protection.

A truce was, at best, a useful substitute for a treaty of peace, and Llywelyn was well aware of the value of a permanent agreement. He was able to exploit Henry III's weakness and to benefit from conflicting jealousies and ambitions in the Welsh marches. In August 1258, Henry was obliged to accept the restrictions on his own powers imposed through the Provisions of Oxford, and for the next five years there was a struggle as baronial leaders sought to impose these restrictions while Henry sought to escape from his promise to accept them. His opponents tried to establish a corporate leadership which had dubious constitutional standing and lacked any measure of permanence. The death, in July 1262, of Richard de Clare, earl of Gloucester and lord of Glamorgan, removed from the scene a wise and experienced magnate who exercised a strong influence on the marches and in the royal circle. Of all the king's opponents, none was more forceful, more bitter or more fiercely driven by personal motives than his brother-in-law, Simon de Montfort, earl of Leicester. But he was ill-fitted by nature to be part of an organised group, whether in government or in opposition: he was autocratic and arrogant, contemptuous of his fellow-barons and often capricious. In the autumn of 1261, when the king had largely re-established his authority, he withdrew from England, to return in April 1263, as the leader of a movement which was already degenerating into rebellion. His return, and the last stages of the story of his involvement in English politics, were closely linked with events in Wales and the marches.

The episode which was the occasion of his return centred on the Lord Edward and a number of younger barons of the march. In June 1262, Edward's steward, Roger Leyburn, found himself in grave trouble. There had been sharp differences of opinion between Roger and his lord, and Roger had aroused the hostility of Queen Eleanor, and there were deep resentments below the surface. Edward now accused him of a series of offences: there was apparently financial peculation; Roger had retained possession of Elham, in Kent, given to him by Edward, perhaps when the king's son was still too young to be considered capable of alienating royal estates. The implication is that he had taken advantage of his lord and had been less than scrupulous in dealing with Edward's affairs. For that he must answer in the appropriate courts. Edward's action reveals much about the future king. In early manhood, as in maturity, Edward was deeply concerned with the rights and privileges of lordship and resentful of any attempt to misuse or ignore them. When Roger's career as a courtier and administrator was threatened, he chose open defiance in preference to any appeal to law. The friends to whom he turned included a group of young men linked with Edward's household and with the march. Their long-term interests lay in continued association with Edward, and their reaction in 1262 was cause for surprise. They joined together in rebellion, and with others they invited Simon de Montfort to return to England as their leader. The estrangement between Edward and Roger Leyburn and his friends was short-lived and was soon resolved, largely through Earl Simon's influence. By August 1263, Roger was restored to favour and had been appointed a steward in the king's household, where he served for the remainder of Henry III's reign; and after 1270 he continued to be a loyal and influential figure in Edward's service.

Simon de Montfort's power rested on a very narrow basis, and in the last years of his life he came to depend heavily on Welsh support. There were personal and purely Welsh successes which demonstrated how valuable an ally Llywelyn might be. In the late autumn of 1262, local forces captured Roger Mortimer's castle at Cefnllys, and when Mortimer, with Humphrey de Bohun, earl of Essex and Hereford, counter-attacked to regain the castle, Llywelyn intervened, routed their forces and, with Maelienydd secure, moved south to receive the homage of the Welshmen of Brecknock. In the spring of 1263 he was threatening Abergavenny, where Peter de Montfort managed to hold out against him. Success, and even the freedom to campaign in this area, underlined the continuing weakness of the Lord Edward in the march. The summer saw successes in a different quarter: Diserth surrendered to Llywelyn in August, Degannwy in September. At this stage, he still saw these castles as a threat to Gwynedd, and not as strongholds which might be valuable for the defence of his territories, and they were both demolished. Edward's tenure of Chester was a permanent threat to Llywelyn's security. Edward could make use of his forces, and especially his mercenaries, working from Chester, where they represented a potential rather than a serious and immediate threat. He could also provide shelter for Llywelyn's brother, Dafydd, who defected to the English crown in April 1263. There were enterprises in which joint action produced success: in June 1263, baronial and Welsh forces were involved in an attack on Bridgnorth, and in February and March 1264, they co-operated at Radnor and Montgomery, and on the English side of the border at Worcester.

The trial of strength between Henry III and Simon de Montfort produced a series of crises, culminating in civil war. By August 1263, Henry had accepted the plain fact that he did not have the resources to stand against the earl, who used the opportunity to revive the policy of the Provisions. Each still hoped for a declaration of principle which would justify his position, and for a resolution of their conflict they sought the arbitration of Louis IX of France, who delivered his decisions in the *mise* of Amiens in January 1264. In political terms, it was a firm vindication of royal authority. The limitations imposed by Magna Carta were taken for granted, but the claims put forward and the experiments essayed by the baronial reformers were swept aside. For the king, it was a major diplomatic victory. For Earl Simon, it was a defeat which he was not content to accept as permanent. He sought instead the judgement of battle, and at Lewes, in May 1264, he routed the royalist army and took prisoner Henry III, Edward and a number of their leading supporters. Henry was reduced to the status of a puppet-king, giving formal authority to Simon's will. Edward was imprisoned. A rescue bid, in which a number of his young associates on the marches were involved, failed, but it demonstrated the need to keep him under close guard, and it confirmed that his political strength must be reduced. His castle at Bristol, and the earldom of Chester, were taken from him, with the promise of suitable lands in exchange for them, and three of his followers, Roger Mortimer, Roger Clifford and Roger Leyburn, were required to go to Ireland and to remain there for the next twelve months. The attempt to banish these magnates failed, while the redistribution of Edward's castles and estates produced jealousy and suspicion since Earl Simon's sons were the chief beneficiaries of the process. Once Edward had accepted these terms, and after formal negotiations, he was released, though he still remained under close guard. In these easier circumstances, a second attempt to rescue him was mounted on 28 May, with the active co-operation of the young earl of Gloucester, Gilbert de Clare, and his brother, Thomas; this time, it succeeded, and he was able to rally support in his father's cause. Events moved rapidly to a climax. Simon allowed himself to be cornered on the Welsh side of the Severn; on 2 August he managed to cross the river at a minor ford, slipped past the Lord Edward's troops concentrated at Worcester, and reached Evesham. There, on 4 August, he was attacked and defeated by the royalist forces, and he himself was killed. The battle marked the end of the period of baronial reform, and royal authority was soon re-established. De Montfort's immediate family, including his daughter, Eleanor, were proscribed and found refuge in France, while his supporters were given harsh justice and heavy punishment. Only a show of force by Gilbert, earl of Gloucester, persuaded Edward and the royalists to mitigate the severity with which the king's opponents were treated.

Against this background, Prince Llywelyn had to decide how much support he would give de Montfort, and what price he might exact for his aid; and after the battle of Evesham, he had to determine what attitude he should take towards the victorious royalists and what advantage he might gain from them. He acquitted himself with considerable skill. At Pipton-on-Wye, on 19 June 1265, he negotiated terms which were greatly to his advantage. His title as prince of Wales was recognised; the homage of the leading Welsh princes was to be his; lands and castles taken from him or from Dafydd ap Llywelyn were to be restored; he was to be given three castles for the extra security of his territories, Painscastle in the south, and Hawarden and Whittington in the north-east. These were concessions for which Llywelyn was ready to pay: he promised 30,000 marks (£20,000) over a period of ten years. The force behind the agreement was Earl Simon's, and his political weakness made the concessions necessary, but the negotiations were carried through in the king's name. Recognition and approval by Henry III were Llywelyn's objective, and that was what was promised at Pipton. It is a measure of Llywelyn's perception of the unstable political conditions in England that he hedged his own commitment and made it conditional on Henry's good faith. But that should not be taken as an indication that Llywelyn anticipated Earl Simon's failure at that stage. There were rumours, never firmly substantiated though justified by later events, that the two men had arranged a marriage alliance between Llywelyn and Simon's daughter, Eleanor. Since she was Henry III's niece, the match would have brought Llywelyn into the king's inner circle. With Earl Simon's death at Evesham, and with Eleanor in exile, the possibility of the marriage lapsed. In the 1270s Llywelyn revived the scheme, perhaps as an act of political provocation; Edward was quick to intervene and to delay the marriage, but in 1278, on 13 October, their wedding was celebrated formally under the king's patronage. With Simon's death, the agreement of Pipton also lapsed, and Llywelyn had to exercise patience and wait until Henry III, free to act in his own right, was ready to make concessions. Neither Henry nor Edward were inclined to give way, and their underlying hostility to the Welsh prince remained a strong emotional and political factor. The restoration of peaceful conditions in England after 1265 owed much to the papal legate, Ottobuono, working with the strong support of Pope Clement IV, and it was the legate who engineered a settlement with Llywelyn. The treaty of Montgomery, which acknowledged so much of what Llywelyn had claimed and achieved since 1258, was primarily his work.

By the treaty of Montgomery, Llywelyn ap Gruffydd was able to establish his standing in Wales on the most favourable terms ever to be extracted from the English crown. The two major issues which were agreed were that Llywelyn should hold the principality of Wales and be called the prince of Wales, and that, with one exception, he should have the homage of all the Welsh leaders. This was the position which the rulers of Gwynedd had been seeking since the beginning of the thirteenth century. (The exception was Maredudd ap Rhys Gryg of the house of Deheubarth, who as a reward for his consistent loyalty to Henry III was allowed to continue to give his homage directly to the king.) In terms of territory, Llywelyn received Perfeddwlad, Whittington, Ceri, Cydewain, Builth, Gwrtheyrnion and Brecknock. He had to accept limitations and make concessions: he must make provision for his brother Dafydd; Hawarden was to be restored to Robert de Montalt with the proviso that no castle was to be built there for thirty years. Some issues could not be settled in 1267. Llywelyn claimed Maelienydd, but here the Mortimers had strong claims. It was agreed that Roger Mortimer should be free to build a castle in the territory, but he must restore the land and the castle to Llywelyn if the prince proved his right to hold them. In financial terms there was a heavy price to pay for this agreement. Llywelyn committed himself to pay 25,000 marks on rigorous terms. The round figure can be converted into the somewhat clumsy value in sterling of £16,666. Of this, 1,000 marks had to be paid within a month, and 4,000 before Christmas, and then regular payments of 3,000 marks fell due each year. It was a heavy burden, but Llywelyn had paid some 12,750 marks before he suspended payments as a sign of dissatisfaction at the way in which the treaty was being carried out. From the beginning, the treaty embodied two dangerous weaknesses which the English king could exploit. The first was that the treaty was not couched as a recognition of rights but as a royal grant: Henry III gave Llywelyn his principality and his title. The treaty of Montgomery did not offer any escape from the irksome and dangerous lordship claimed and exercised by the kings of England. The second was that the treaty reiterated another cause of grave misgiving for the Welsh ruler. If there were any dispute about the lands assigned to Dafydd ap Gruffydd, it was to be settled by Welsh law, but Henry III could send one or two representatives to see that justice had been done. The integrity of Gwynedd was acknowledged, but the kingdom had little protection against the rights of lordship and the exercise of royal jurisdiction within Welsh territory.

The decade which followed drew out the weaknesses inherent in the treaty of Montgomery. From a Welsh standpoint, the relationship with England deteriorated as the balance of power shifted in favour of the English king and the marcher barons. Part, and perhaps much, of the responsibility lay with Llywelyn. He was pushing some of his contemporaries close to the limits of their tolerance. One key issue centred on his plans for a new castle on a fine hill-top site at Dolforwyn, with a small borough at Abermule. Work started in 1273, and these foundations were a clear sign of Llywelyn's confidence in the future. The castle had considerable strategic importance, and the borough was intended to attract a substantial local trade. (The same factors would lead at a later date to the foundation of a borough at Newtown, 3 miles further up the river Severn, but Llywelyn did not have sufficient time to develop Abermule, and Newtown was always a stunted growth.) Dolforwyn aroused anger and resentment. Since it gave Llywelyn an advanced post, controlling routes into Rhayader and the lordships of Gwrtheyrnion and Builth, it was a direct threat to Mortimer interests in central Wales. It also threatened the great border stronghold of Montgomery, and Edward I reacted strongly, issuing peremptory orders to forbid the building of the new castle and borough.

One Welsh leader was especially affected by the new castle. Gruffydd ap Gwenwynwyn saw that the value of his own castle and borough at Welshpool would suffer directly from Llywelyn's new developments. Like other Welsh magnates, he had been hard pressed by the prince of Wales, and 1274 was the year which saw him driven beyond the limits of his endurance. While Llywelyn was inspecting the progress of work at Dolforwyn in the spring, he summoned Gruffydd to him, charged him with infidelity and deceit, deprived him of lands within his own territory of southern Powys and demanded his eldest son, Owain, as a hostage. Resentment bred retaliation. When Llywelyn's agents were visiting Welshpool in the autumn, Gruffydd entertained them with all the outward display of friendship, but covertly he called up the royal garrison from Shrewsbury to capture and imprison them. Llywelyn mounted a full-scale campaign to rescue his men. These clashes help to explain a conspiracy to assassinate Llywelyn. The leading figures were Llywelyn's brother, Dafydd, and Gruffydd ap Gwenwynwyn with his wife and his son, Owain. All of them had much to gain from Llywelyn's death. The scheme was hammered out at Welshpool, and when it was discovered Gruffydd and Dafydd fled to England where Edward I gave them protection. Their plot was the most ominous event in Welsh domestic politics for a generation; it pointed to the discontent caused by the stern discipline by which Llywelyn sought to hold his Welsh supporters, and to the delicate balance of loyalty and treachery on which his rule, not to say his very survival, depended.

On the marches, English magnates were finding a new confidence, though it was not always matched by military success. In Glamorgan, Gilbert de Clare, nicknamed the Red, who succeeded his father in 1262, had made his mark in English politics, and was strengthening his hold on his Welsh lordships. The upland territories, in Welsh hands, were brought under closer control; Gruffydd ap Rhys, ruler of Senghennydd, was captured and imprisoned in the earl's Irish castle at Kilkenny. The power of independent action by Welsh leaders was curtailed. In the neighbouring Clare lordships of Gwynllŵg and Caerleon, the Welsh dynasties were curbed, and the power of the English lord was enhanced. Earl Gilbert tried, somewhat tentatively at first, to limit Llywelyn's freedom to intervene in Glamorgan. In 1268 he began to build the castle at Caerphilly which he intended to be the major northern defence for the lordship. Llywelyn was equal to the challenge, and in 1270 his forces captured the castle, then only in its initial stages of construction. Within a year, Gilbert's constable had retaken Caerphilly, and the earl began the task of remodelling and rebuilding the concentric stronghold, with its formidable water defences, which remains one of the most impressive of the castles to be built in Wales in the thirteenth century. Brecknock, once the centre of power of the great marcher dynasty of Braose, passed in 1230 to Humphrey de Bohun, earl of Hereford, husband of one of the four co-heiresses of William de Braose. The Bohun tenure of Brecknock was challenged by Llywelyn ab Iorwerth and, more effectively, by Llywelyn ap Gruffydd, who swept through the lordship in 1262. As one consequence of the conflict between Henry III and the baronial opposition, Brecknock was given in 1264 to Roger Mortimer, lord of the neighbouring territories of Maelienydd, Radnor and Gwrtheyrnion, but to capture it and hold it against Llywelyn was beyond even his powers, and in the treaty of Montgomery Brecknock was recognised as part of Llywelyn's possessions. Despite his reverse there, Roger Mortimer was a most dangerous enemy until his death in October 1282; he was one of Edward I's trusted commanders in the final conflict with Llywelyn, and his successors were to become, under royal patronage, dominant figures in the marches in the late thirteenth and early fourteenth centuries.

By 1275, Llywelyn had reactivated the plan to marry Simon de Montfort's daughter Eleanor. The *Brut y Tywysogyon* betrays uncertainty about their union, asserting that the prince had married Eleanor through words uttered by proxy. The *Annals* of Dunstable priory echo these words. That may be a reference to an earlier betrothal; it may be, as J. E. Lloyd believed, that Llywelyn's agents carried through some form of undertaking on his behalf before she left France, though that would stretch the chroniclers' words to their limits. The proposal has all the appearance of a decision intended to annoy Edward I; it could easily be seen as an attempt to raise the spectre of disorder and defiance in England. It was singularly offensive to Edward I because, as recently as March 1271, Eleanor's brother, Guy de Montfort, had murdered the king's cousin, Henry of Almain, in Viterbo. Travelling through Italy on his return from his crusade, Edward had been anxious to hunt down Guy and to punish him for his crime. So Llywelyn's marriage was not merely a reminder of the troubles of the previous decade, but rather of a recent and much resented personal vendetta. The marriage, which may no longer have been dangerous in political terms, was unacceptable on personal grounds. Late in 1275, Eleanor and her brother, Amauri, set out from France for Gwynedd, but their ship was intercepted and they were taken as prisoners to England. Not until Llywelyn had been humbled and reconciled would Edward sanction the marriage which was finally celebrated on 12 October 1278. Llywelyn was then probably approaching fifty. If, as is not unlikely, he considered himself committed to marriage with Eleanor since 1265, when he was still a man in his prime, his late marriage is capable of reasonable explanation. The few years of life which they shared show Eleanor as a useful intermediary with the English court, arguing her husband's case with force. Her death in childbirth in June 1282 removed

from the scene a tragic figure; her father and husband, both men of
high ideals, were hounded down and destroyed largely through the
tenacity and determination of Edward I.

The critical issue was that of homage. Llywelyn consistently
refused to do homage to Edward I after his accession as king, plain
though the obligation was. At the outset, he was obdurate, if not
sullen; he failed to do homage in 1273 soon after the king's return to
England, and he deliberately absented himself from Edward's
coronation in August, 1274. That must surely account for the
demand that he renew his homage at the end of the year, but again he
would not concede. In the autumn of that year, the full details of the
conspiracy to assassinate Llywelyn became known, and Gruffydd ap
Gwenwynwyn and Dafydd ap Gruffydd fled to England and were
given shelter by Edward I. That affected the plans made for 1275. It
was agreed that Edward and Llywelyn should travel to Chester
where the ceremony of homage would take place. But Llywelyn's
council advised him that he should not do homage while the king
was giving protection to his enemies, and he withdrew from the
arrangement and refused to go to Chester. There is no means of
establishing whether he reacted to their advice, or whether they gave
him the opinion he wanted to hear. The affront made Edward bitter
and angry, but he proceeded by strict protocol, summoning
Llywelyn on three successive occasions. Each time, Llywelyn
refused to obey the summons, and the last occasion, on 26 April
1276, left Edward free to wage open war to bring a recalcitrant vassal
to heel. It is difficult to see what Llywelyn hoped to gain from this
consistent refusal to accept his obligation and give homage to the
new king. To refuse what was due under the terms of the treaty of
Montgomery was clearly an error of political judgement. Llywelyn
had gained much from the treaty; to refuse to pay the price was to put
his gains in hazard. Taken with other factors, his exploitation of
Dolforwyn and Abermule, and above all his marriage with Eleanor
de Montfort, withholding homage could be seen as part of a deliberate and hostile policy towards the English king; it suggested that
Llywelyn was seeking confrontation.

The campaign of 1276–7 demonstrated the underlying weakness
of Llywelyn's position. The war was Edward's war, but it was
undertaken with the full approval of the council: the king and his
magnates were of one mind. There was little hope of support for the
Welsh prince on the marches. He had alienated the lord of
Glamorgan, Gilbert, earl of Gloucester, by his attack on the new
castle at Caerphilly and by the fact that he was then strong enough to

impose a conditional settlement upon the earl. When war came, the earl of Hereford was glad of the chance to regain control of Brecknock, and John Giffard, lord of Clifford, saw it as the means of reclaiming Llandovery and the lordship of Cantref Bychan. Other lords of the march were ready for active service, as the lords of Gower, Llanstephan and Laugharne mobilised their forces to support the royal army. Carmarthen was one of three bases used by Edward I, and there his commander was Payn de Chaworth, lord of Kidwelly. By April 1277, he had subdued the leading figures in south Wales and secured the major castle at Dinefwr, and he was able to take over much of Ceredigion. Llywelyn ap Gruffydd would find no support from the old Welsh dynasty of Deheubarth. This could be matched from the middle march and the north where the marcher lords were active well before the royal armies were ready to move. In north Wales, Llywelyn's brother, Dafydd, as lord of Hope, con-tributed substantially to the English forces in the field. The military, strategic and financial aspects of Edward's Welsh wars are best con-sidered in relation to the campaigns of 1282–3, but for the war of 1276–7, two particular aspects of his policy should be emphasised. The first is that he saw the major campaign against Gwynedd as a problem of logistics; the second is that he regarded Anglesey as the key to success. Llywelyn had been contained in Gwynedd by August 1277. To invade his stronghold Edward called in the pioneers who were commissioned to create easy and open access through the forest and woodland between the Dee and the Conwy. They took ten days to clear the way to Flint, where they spent three weeks preparing a well-defended base; the extension to Rhuddlan was a less demanding task, and they needed nine days to open up the route from Rhuddlan to Degannwy. Armies and supplies could be moved without fear of ambush. A frontal assault was not necessary, for Edward had sent a separate force to take Anglesey and to deny Llywelyn the vital corn supplies from the island. Early in November, Llywelyn submitted and the war was over.

Llywelyn's humiliation was given effect through the treaty of Aberconwy. There were two major financial penalties which, had they been implemented, would have been crippling: a fine of £50,000 to buy the king's grace and mercy, and an annual payment of 1,000 marks (£666 13s. 4d.) for Anglesey. These, Edward could remit without difficulty, but the fine, in particular, set the tone for the treaty. Llywelyn was to do homage: he must join the king at Rhuddlan and do homage there, and he must in due course travel to London where the ceremony would be repeated. He must release his brother Owain Goch and make proper provision for him and for their brother Rhodri; that settlement must be approved by Edward. He must provide ten hostages from Gwynedd, and arrange for twenty men from every *cantref* left under his control to swear each year that they would uphold the treaty and that they would oblige Llywelyn to honour its terms. There were minor penalties – an insistence that Llywelyn should resume and complete the payments due under the terms of the treaty of Montgomery. There was a major loss of territory. The four *cantrefi* – the Perfeddwlad – were to be handed over to Edward, with other territories taken by the king during his campaign. Anglesey was to be held in future from King Edward on narrowly defined terms.

Against these punitive clauses must be set the concessions which Edward was ready to make. Llywelyn's title as prince of Wales was not challenged; it was used punctiliously in all the documents which passed during these critical days. Llywelyn was to have the homage of five Welsh magnates, of princely stock. It is possible to express this in language which is contemptuous and critical, as an empty title, conceded and maintained in mockery. That does not fit easily with Edward's character and habit. Llywelyn was a prince and a vassal: he had offended as a vassal, and for that he would pay heavily. Then the terms on which he would continue to hold title and lands could be settled. It is much more in accord with Edward's liking for legality and orderliness that he should leave Llywelyn with the homage of a small number of magnates as an outward sign of his princely status. In the nature of things, they could not be very powerful or very distinguished: the accident of birth and survival, partible inheritance, and the steady erosion over two generations of the power and trappings of princely authority in Powys, Deheubarth and the southern lordships of Wales had all contributed to create a group of petty rulers. But these were the men with whom Llywelyn had surrounded himself in his days of power.

Another feature of the treaty demonstrates Edward's feel for propriety. Llywelyn was to make proper provision in Gwynedd for his brother, Dafydd, but Edward was prepared to grant to Llywelyn all the land which Dafydd might have claimed in Gwynedd, and he would provide proper compensation for Dafydd from his own estates. Dafydd had been living in England, a traitor to his brother and a valuable pawn and ally for the king. Edward seems to have had scruples about imposing upon Llywelyn both the renegade and the obligation to give him a share of Gwynedd. As a last concession, Edward undertook that disputes should be settled by the law of the march for those things which might occur in the march, and by the law of Wales for those things which might occur in Wales.

Although his power had been savagely reduced, Llywelyn could hold Gwynedd with some security. Edward remitted the fine of £50,000 and the annual payment for Anglesey. Since these were accounting figures rather than actual income, it was an easy gesture. Royal pressure ensured that Llywelyn's brothers should be treated

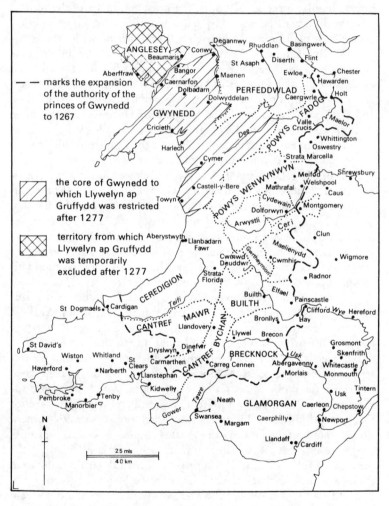

Map 2   Political changes in Wales in the thirteenth century

equitably, though none of them was allowed to become a threat to Llywelyn's position. After two decades as a political prisoner, Owain Goch was given lands in Llŷn where he enjoyed a few years of freedom until his death at some date before the final crisis of 1282. Rhodri had already abandoned any claims to a patrimony in Gwynedd. As early as 1272 he was prepared to accept a promise of 1,000 marks (£666 13s.4d.) in lieu of his estates, and his concern after Llywelyn's submission was to ensure that the money was paid to him at regular intervals. Rhodri, the most enigmatic of the sons of Gruffydd, never displayed any flair for military action or political power, but made a life for himself as a member of the local aristocracy of Cheshire, and Llywelyn was fortunate that he did not take any share of Gwynedd. King Edward provided for Dafydd and established him as a powerful magnate in the north-eastern borderlands, giving him two of the long-disputed four *cantrefi*, Rhufoniog and Dyffryn Clwyd, with the lordship of Hope. The three main strongholds of this area, Denbigh, Ruthin and Caergwrle, made an important contribution to the defence of the English border and to the process of containing Llywelyn's influence

It would be easy to dwell on Llywelyn's losses in 1277; his principality was reduced to the territory which Dafydd passed on to his successors in 1246. But the prince still controlled Gwynedd, the land on which the true strength of his dynasty rested. What he most needed was time and a successor; with those assets, the future might still be bright. The indications are that he read the auguries in that sense, and that over the next five years he was content to rebuild his personal power and to wait for the right opportunity. He does not appear to have seen the events of 1277 as a final and irrevocable defeat. In October 1278, Edward signalled his approval of Llywelyn's attitude by sanctioning the long-delayed marriage between the prince of Wales and Eleanor de Montfort.

Between 1277 and 1282 the issues which produced the greatest strains in Wales were issues of jurisdiction. Edward was concerned to extend the range of activities of his judges, with little regard for the niceties of Welsh law or marcher custom, and with no regard for the susceptibilities of Llywelyn and other prominent Welshmen. Llywelyn, though certainly the greatest figure in Wales, was only one of a number of Welsh magnates who felt and resented the pressure of Edward's forceful approach. What Edward was doing in Wales was not uncharacteristic; he could be just as aggressive and demanding towards those who were his friends and allies. Therein lay real danger, for among those who were angered and embittered by the king's demands was Dafydd ap Gruffydd, enriched by Edward as lord of Hope.

The final disaster was triggered by Dafydd who launched an attack on Hawarden castle towards the end of March, 1282, inflicting heavy losses and wounding and capturing the English commander, Roger of Clifford. Had this been an isolated attack it could have meant only that Dafydd had precipitated a struggle for which his brother was not ready. But there were risings elsewhere along the borders of Gwynedd, and it may be that Llywelyn's forces were already co-ordinated. Llywelyn did not attempt to disguise the fact that he had not been involved in, or even aware of, Dafydd's attack, but he joined forces with his brother soon after the capture of Hawarden. It was expedient, if not inevitable, that he should do so. Here was a chance to reverse the humiliation of 1277. The alternative was to compromise Dafydd's rebellion and his own standing as ruler of Gwynedd. Llywelyn could scarcely remain neutral; apart from the loss of reputation which that would involve, he would have surrendered to his brother any claim to lead the Welsh against Edward I and his administrators. There was another choice: that he should remain loyal to Edward as his overlord and play an active part in bringing Dafydd to heel. There is no hint that Llywelyn had any problem in making his decision. Dafydd's attack on Hawarden was followed by assaults on Rhuddlan and Flint, and Llywelyn joined in these attacks. From that point the two brothers worked in close harmony to develop the campaign. But it has to be said that Llywelyn had reacted to events, just as he had done in his younger days; he committed himself to war, as J. G. Edwards put it, 'at the twelfth hour'. He could not claim the advantage of choosing his moment to challenge Edward I. The king seems to have been deeply and genuinely surprised and shocked at the renewal of violence in Wales, and the note of anger at being betrayed by the two brothers continued right through to the savage execution of Dafydd in 1283. Outrage formed part of the rhetoric which was a by-product of the war, and which found expression in letters, and in negotiations conducted by Archbishop Pecham late in 1282. He believed that his experience of the Welsh equipped him to be an acceptable and, as he hoped, a successful intermediary. He received many complaints against the arbitrary and ruthless approach of Edward's administrators; one clear sign of the scale of the revolt of 1282 lay in the range and number of Welsh leaders from whom they emanated. Pecham was impressed and tried to persuade Edward to take these complaints seriously, but Edward was intent on obtaining submission without conditions, and the chances of compromise and settlement were very slight. Even so, when he visited Llywelyn in Gwynedd, Pecham had the basis for a settlement which, however improbable, represented what Edward regarded as generosity. North Wales was to be at the king's disposal, with Llywelyn and Dafydd removed from the scene. For Llywelyn there was the prospect of an earldom in England worth £1,000 a year with a limited and guarded suggestion that, should he have a son in the future, the earldom might pass to him. For Dafydd there was nothing more than the prospect of exile. He was to go on crusade and to remain abroad. There was one ominous note: Edward would provide for Llywelyn's infant daughter, Gwenllian, and for Dafydd's sons, Llywelyn and Owain. The terms were unacceptable, and the brothers rejected them, Llywelyn in measured terms, and Dafydd with open and contemptuous defiance. At that stage, in November 1282, no one could say whether that hard and uncompromising attitude would be reflected in any ultimate peace terms which might be negotiated at the end of the struggle.

Dafydd had surprised and captured Hawarden on 21 March. Edward received the news of his insurrection on 25 March and acted swiftly. He appointed three commanders to begin their preparations, and he summoned a council to meet at Devizes on 5 April. There, practical steps were taken to mobilise forces. Forty ships were required from the Cinque Ports, and the first steps were taken to raise money; agents were ordered to leave for Ireland and Scotland, and for Ponthieu and Gascony to recruit mercenaries, and especially to raise a force of 40 crossbowmen from Gascony. There were to be further requests for as many as 1,500 crossbowmen from the duchy as the summer and autumn progressed. The immediate response was slow, but numbers began to build up in the autumn, and by the end of January 1283, there were 40 knights and 1,523 crossbowmen – 210 mounted and 1,313 foot-soldiers – at the king's disposal. It was an expensive business. Imbert de Monte Regali, a veteran of 1277, served the king with 40 mounted crossbowmen for a year in the new campaign, and he and his well-trained unit were paid £979.

As in 1277, the royalist forces operated from three main centres and their first task was to contain local opposition so that Llywelyn could be isolated in Gwynedd. In August, Edward repeated the tactical move which had proved so valuable in the earlier campaign, and sent a force to invade Anglesey. There, his commander, Luke de Tany, secured the island and was ordered to build a pontoon bridge across the Menai Strait in readiness for a full-scale invasion of Bangor and the mainland. Edward was anxious to co-ordinate all his forces in the north, but de Tany was impatient and launched an attack on his own initiative while Archbishop Pecham was in Gwynedd seeking to establish conditions for peace. It was an attempt to cut short the campaign by an act of open treachery, but the surprise failed, de Tany was killed, and his force routed. Speed and flair stood the Welsh commanders in good stead, but they would need greater resources and a major victory to check King Edward's advance.

In Snowdonia, Llywelyn and Dafydd were under heavy pressure from the English forces. To create a major diversion, and to bring Welsh forces from mid-Wales and south Wales into the conflict was a strategy which offered many advantages. The brothers divided their responsibilities. Dafydd remained in the north to continue the active conflict with Edward's armies. Llywelyn travelled south with a sizeable body of men. Contemporary writers hinted at motives which could not then, and cannot now, be established. It may be that he saw in the lordships of Brecknock and Builth the prospects of new and dangerous activity against the English, and that he was anxious to rally supporters in this crucial area of the marches. It may be that he was caught up in an elaborate charade of treachery. It was said that he had been betrayed in north Wales 'in the belfries of Bangor'. He may have been persuaded to think that on the death of Roger Mortimer in October 1282 the young Mortimers were ready to rebel against Edward I, and that together they might make common cause against the king. There was, at least, a suspicion that by such double-dealing he had been drawn away from Gwynedd. Whatever may be made of that, he and his army were at Llanganten, near Builth, and he dispatched a large part of his force to Brecon. While the Welsh were deploying on the Welsh side of the Wye, the English forces were ready for action on the opposite bank, and were on the move. There is much confusion about the actual sequence of events. Llywelyn, as it seems, had with him only a small band of retainers, perhaps as few as a dozen-and-a-half men. On the river Irfon they encountered an English contingent commanded by Stephen Frankton who was credited with striking down the Welsh leader. Llywelyn was mortally wounded. Later, his body was identified and the head was cut off and sent to Edward I at Rhuddlan. The body was buried by the monks of the abbey at Cwmhir. So, in a sad and con-fused anti-climax, the balance of power in Wales was drastically altered. Welsh chroniclers were almost laconic in their reports of his death. They did not accord him even the briefest of appraisals, and it was left to court poets to celebrate his work and lament his death. Narrative accounts in English chronicles provide more detailed notices of what happened – or what the writers understood to have happened. A long and distinguished reign was over; a dedicated and tenacious prince was dead.

Perhaps his greatest assets were buoyancy and a confidence which was rarely shaken. He was able to make use of opportunities created by others and to reap a rich harvest. He lacked the charisma which was so obviously part of the appeal of Llywelyn ab Iorwerth. Where persuasion and common interest failed to win support, he was prepared to rely on discipline and coercion. He could be ruthless, as his brothers had good cause to remember. Though he could bring unity to his people and win recognition for his title as prince of Wales, he could not provide for the succession. The skill with which Llywelyn ab Iorwerth used his son, Dafydd, and (within the limits of his loyalty) his elder son, Gruffydd, was a lesson which he might well have taken to heart. To live so long unmarried and without an heir, was a dangerous way of playing politics, and it is scarcely an adequate explanation to suggest that if he had no sons he avoided the perennial problems of partible inheritance and disputed succession. In the middle decades of the thirteenth century, Gwynedd needed a clear succession, just as a centralised monarchy needed a dynasty rather than a single individual if it was to grow and to survive. Llywelyn seems to have placed too much reliance on Dafydd as his heir, despite ample evidence that he was untrustworthy and self-seeking. Prince Llywelyn has been seen as a man beset by suspicion and distrust, an impression which springs partly from the tone of his letters and partly, perhaps, from his truculence in dealing with Edward I. He could yield and give ground, but not lose major issues of principle. He could work fast and work with discretion; his activities have sometimes to be inferred from their sequel.

Between 1255 and 1258, he had made rapid progress symbolised by the assumption of the title of prince of Wales. Between 1278 and 1282, he had repaired much of the damage inflicted on Gwynedd by Edward I, and he was surprisingly well placed to take advantage of Dafydd's rebellion. Some traits were consistent features of his character throughout his life. All told, he had formidable gifts, and while a man of his courage and resilience lived there was hope for his principality. How Edward I might have dealt with him, and with Gwynedd, had he survived to make terms with the king, must be a matter of guesswork, though Edward had already provided a scale of values: for Llywelyn, an honourable status as an English earl, but for

Dafydd, exile. In the king's eyes in 1282, Llywelyn was not a traitor to be hounded to death. As long as Llywelyn lived, Gwynedd had the hope of survival: when he died at Irfon Bridge, more was lost than one man's life.

It remained to be seen whether Edward I would seek, or accept, peace with Llywelyn's heir and successor. From long experience, Dafydd knew that one of the few permanent elements in a career of treachery was forgiveness, but this time, there was to be no forgiveness and no reconciliation. In the first weeks of 1283, Edward and his forces made steady advances into Gwynedd. His troops captured Dolwyddelan; the king himself moved from Conwy, while his army from Anglesey crossed the Menai Strait to establish a firm hold on the northern coastal territories. Slowly, Dafydd was driven from Snowdonia towards Cader Idris, and to the stronghold of Castell-y-Bere. From the safety of that castle he was driven to the greater insecurity of the open countryside. The castle was captured on 25 April, and he himself was taken by Welsh compatriots and handed over to King Edward. His wife and sons were captured in the same way. Dafydd was condemned at Shrewsbury as a treacherous vassal, and there he was hanged, drawn and quartered. His sons were kept in close custody at Bristol castle. One, Llywelyn, died in 1288, while as late as 1305 the king was issuing instructions that the conditions of imprisonment of the other, Owain, should be made even more rigorous. How long he survived is not known. There remained one other sad victim of this disaster, Gwenllian, daughter of Llywelyn ap Gruffydd. Her mother died when she was born, and she herself was taken into the king's hand, to be consigned in due course to the nunnery of Sempringham for a gentler, but no less final, sentence of a life shut off from the secular world.

Throughout the thirteenth century it was accepted that strong castles, some of which must be royal fortresses, were an essential military requirement if the power of Gwynedd were to be contained. Hawarden, Rhuddlan and Degannwy were critical defences for the northern coastal route from Chester to the river Conwy. In or soon after 1241, Henry III commissioned the hill-top castle at Diserth, intended to be an additional defence for the northern march-lands and a threat to Gwynedd itself. In 1277, and on a greatly increased scale in 1282, Edward I linked the advance of his armies with the establishment of new castles. Builth was refashioned in contemporary style in 1277 to safeguard the vital crossing of the Wye, and on the west coast Aberystwyth was redesigned and rebuilt at the same

time. Edward's advance from Chester was marked by his new concentric castles at Flint and Rhuddlan. With the renewal of hostilities
in 1282 and the need for another major campaign to put down the
Welsh insurgents, Edward redoubled his castle building. Conwy
was built on the west side of the estuary to fill the function hitherto
assigned to the hill-top castle at Degannwy. Harlech and Caernarfon
were fortified during the course of the same campaign. Twice, in
1277 and 1282, Edward's forces took Anglesey, and the need for a
castle to defend the vulnerable south-eastern shore of the island led to
the building of Beaumaris where work started in 1295. In all this,
Edward drew deeply on his experience of the duchy of Gascony
where an intricate and dangerous combination of forces threatened
ducal authority. The local nobility were volatile and often unwilling
to accept the control of a central administration. There was always
the threat of intervention by the French king, intervention which had
produced spectacular advances for Louis VIII and Louis IX earlier in
the century. Local trade needed encouragement and protection, and
a combination of strong castles and bastides – fortified towns –
proved highly successful, both for the French and the English in their
attempts to control different areas of the old duchy of Aquitaine.
Edward himself, closely associated with the duchy both as prince
and king, was well aware of the bastides founded under his energetic
seneschal, John de Grilly, and the list of foundations grew steadily
during his reign, from Beaumont in 1272 to Monpazier in 1281. The
strategies and techniques which had proved valuable in Gascony
were applied in Wales, and administrators who had proved their
worth in the duchy were widely employed in Wales. For his principal architect, Edward went to the lordship of Savoy, where he
engaged the count's architect-builder, James de St Georges
d'Esperanche.

Flint, the earliest of the Edwardian castles in north Wales, demonstrates a number of these elements. Edward, established nearby at
Basingwerk, commissioned the new castle, and work began on
25 July 1277, when a large force of 950 'dykers' were at work. Before
the end of August, there were 1,800 at work, digging the ditches and
throwing up the defensive banks which were the basis of the castle
and the whole site. A new planned borough was laid out, with its
defences, as the castle was being built. Flint was a concentric castle,
and in its finished state it had extensive outerworks beyond which
the borough was built. The main castle had three corner towers
linked by formidable curtain walling. The fourth corner was treated
differently; here a *donjon*, much larger in scale than the other towers,

was built as a separate unit within its own moat. It is unique in the Edwardian castles, but it resembled one particular bastide with its fortifications which Edward had seen for himself in southern France. In 1270, he had sailed on crusade from Louis IX's magnificent bastide at Aigues-Mortes which was defended by a detached *donjon* of great strength, the Tour de Constance. Edward's second castle was commissioned at Rhuddlan, where a concentric castle and a new bastide-type town replaced the old Norman castle and borough. Work began here in September 1277, with signs of the same large work-force and feverish speed. Both castles owed much to the work of James of St George who was chief master mason at the two sites from 1278 until 1283. Flint seems to have been completed by 1280, and Rhuddlan by 1281, though minor works and repairs carried out over the next few years make precision difficult.

The king believed that the campaign of 1277 was a final solution to the problems posed by the prince of Wales; the military dangers had been overcome and the political power of Llywelyn ap Gruffydd had been drastically reduced. Although Gwynedd was not at that stage encircled by royal castles, Builth, Aberystwyth, Flint and Rhuddlan were key strongholds from which, as it seemed, the Welsh could be held in check. When war broke out again in 1282, Edward had to revise his views and increase his investment in castles and garrisons. This second phase of castle building indicated a much harsher approach to the problem. As he moved from Chester towards Gwynedd in 1282, he ensured that castles which guarded the English frontiers were sound. From 1277, Dafydd ap Gruffydd had held a lordship dominated by three strongholds. One was the natural fortress site of Denbigh where the style, and even the siting, of his castle has been obliterated by later developments. The others, Caergwrle (Hope) and Ruthin, were massively built stone castles. As the revolt of 1282 unfolded, Dafydd fell back on Gwynedd, abandoning his castles; Caergwrle was slighted sufficiently to make it of little immediate use to the English, but Dafydd did not count on the speed and energy with which Edward would have the castle repaired and brought back into commission. During the next few years, James of St George was concerned with the redevelopment of Ruthin and Caergwrle, though how much was extension and how much was radical new design is impossible to determine. Denbigh was fortified by its new lord, Henry de Lacy, earl of Lincoln, who was responsible for the first stage of redesigning the defences of the castle and borough as a single unit. This was a site put onto a war footing during a campaign, and at a later stage, between 1295 and 1309, the king's architect, James of St George, was at work completing the circuit of the castle by cutting off the castle-defences from the town, and, in particular, building the remarkable gatehouse protected by twin towers in orthodox fashion but dominated by a third, larger tower constructed within the enceinte itself. Meanwhile, at Holt, another magnate, John de Warenne, earl of Surrey, was building a new castle, and here again, James of St George may have been involved. He was one of a number of master builders at work on the Edwardian castles: Richard of Chester and Manasser de Vaucoulers were involved at an early date, and Walter of Hereford, William of Drogheda, Henry of Oxford, and Laurence of Canterbury were among those who occur in later stages of the building operations.

The castles which were to enclose Gwynedd in an iron grip were commissioned during the course of the campaign of 1282 and brought to completion over the next few years. The key event was the capture in January 1283 of Llywelyn's castle at Dolwyddelan, on which the prince's control of the defences and communications of Gwynedd largely depended. This was followed over the next few months by the fall of Dolbadarn, Castell-y-Bere and Cricieth. The loss of these strongholds and the creation of the new Edwardian castles totally changed the balance between English and Welsh and created the conditions for Edward's armies to control the whole of the north. Work at Conwy began in the spring of 1283, with Richard of Chester responsible for the initial stages and James of St George for the castle itself. It was a mark of Edward's determination that he ordered the removal of the monks of Aberconwy abbey to a new site at Maenan in order to clear the way for his new castle and borough. It took some four and a half years to build Conwy castle and the town defences, at a cost of about £15,000. Edward appears to have envisaged this castle as a major administrative centre for north Wales. At the western end of the Menai Strait, Caernarfon, the second major castle was built. The earthworks were created in 1283 and the greater part of the stonework was built between 1284 and 1286, while a further building season was needed in 1287 to fit the castle out and make it habitable. From the start, Edward intended Caernarfon to be much more than a military fortress. This castle suffered great damage in the revolt of Madog ap Llywelyn in 1294, and over the next six years the castle and borough were rebuilt at great cost; the height of the castle walls was raised, and on the town side was provided with defences as strong as those of the exposed western walls along the river bank. It was a basic and costly error to have built them initially so that they were capable of being breached and stormed. Estimates of the cost of Caernarfon's defences vary: the first castle is thought to have cost some £12,000, and the repairs and rebuilding after 1294 certainly equalled, and may have exceeded, this figure. At Harlech, the castle was first planned in 1283, and it was built largely between 1285 and 1287. It was one of the most dramatic of James of St George's designs, and it matches very closely the castle which he built at Villandraut (Gironde) for Pope Clement V in 1305. It was a mark of James' standing that he was appointed constable of Harlech. Dolwyddelan and Dolbadarn were not discarded, though they no longer had a critical role to play. Cricieth was kept in good repair and strengthened at minimal cost, and it became an important castle on the western flank of Gwynedd. Beaumaris, the last and most beautifully proportioned of Edward's Welsh castles, was begun in April 1295 under the direction of James of St George; ten months later only ten of the outer towers and four of the inner towers had been completed. The work was carried on slowly until the death of James of St George in 1309, and his successor, Nicholas of Durnford, continued building until 1331, but the grandiose scale of the original conception was never realised, and parts of the building, and even of the defensive towers, were never completed. All these new castles had direct access to the sea, and if control of the land-routes were lost, they could still be supplied, or relieved, by the king's ships.

Three features of this massive building programme deserve special attention. The first is that Edward I planned to build the mainland castles while his campaign to break the power of the prince of Wales was still in progress. They were not an afterthought but, rather, an indication of the intensity with which he pursued his policy to have done with Llywelyn and Dafydd as untrustworthy vassals. The second is that after 1283 Gwynedd was to be held in a tight circle of royal castles and garrisons. Any future outbreak of hostility to the king would be contained. The third is that they represented a great drain on the royal finances, for they involved an outlay of something like £90,000. A clean balance sheet for the Welsh wars is not easily achieved, though the figures adduced by J. E. Morris deserve great respect. The cost of troops for 1277 can be calculated, in round figures, at £20,000, and for 1282–3 the comparable figure would be £60,000. One attempt made in the Exchequer to draw up a statement of income for that year, and to show that it would cover the cost of the year's fighting and building, had so many hidden weaknesses that the clerk discounted the total by 15 per cent to make it more realistic. Despite his sanguine approach, there were heavy debts to be cleared. The campaigns of 1277 and 1282–3 and the Edwardian castles required an outlay of some £170,000, and the final figure was perhaps closer to £175,000. Of that, the £90,000 spent on castles can be seen, from a contemporary English point of view, as a sound investment, if only because it made a third Welsh war virtually impossible.

7

UNDER THE HEEL: WALES IN THE FOURTEENTH CENTURY

·

The framework of the Edwardian settlement was provided by the statute of Rhuddlan, issued on 19 March 1284, barely six months after the execution of Dafydd ap Gruffydd. To issue a major and definitive document after a period of strife was not uncommon in England. The early conflicts of Henry III's reign, and especially the social problems revealed by the work of the leading judges, produced the reforms loosely known as the statute of Merton in 1236. After the constitutional struggles of the years 1258–64, the social reforms which had been expressed in the Provisions of Oxford in 1259 were preserved and promulgated in the statute of Marlborough of 1267. Each was an important and lasting statement of principles. The statute of Rhuddlan belongs in the same category, but since it was designed to do two very different things, it was, and has remained, a contentious and controversial document. The statute was a political affirmation: it proclaimed the annexation of Wales. Beyond that, the statute extended to Wales, with significant emendations and exceptions, the legal system which prevailed in England. For legal historians, the importance and attraction of the statute lie in the precision and detail with which this system of law was defined. Rhuddlan is partly a statement of legal principles, partly a register of writs, and partly a commentary on legal procedure. After 1284, no working lawyer or administrator in Wales could afford to be without it, or could fail to benefit from its guidance.

The outward sign of conquest was the conversion of Welsh territory into shires on the English pattern: in north Wales, Flintshire,

Anglesey, Caernarfonshire and Merionethshire were formally created; and in central and south-west Wales, Cardiganshire and Carmarthenshire, were recognised, and the offices of sheriff, coroner and bailiff (of a commote) were established. By 1284, English justice depended upon a highly developed system of courts, staffed by professional judges; apart from the courts which sat regularly at Westminster, commissions of judges travelled around differ-

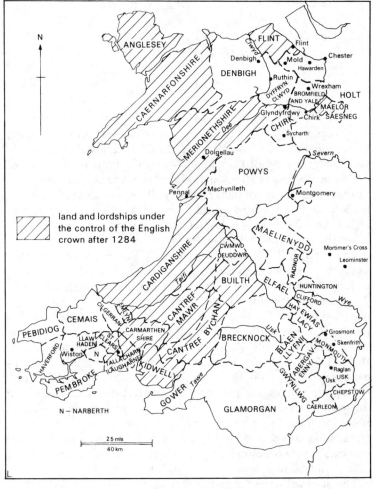

Map 3   The marcher lordships

ent areas of the kingdom, carrying with them the full weight of the king's authority. They dealt with a wide range of criminal offences and breaches of the king's peace. They also heard and decided a large number of civil cases, many of them arising from the increasing complexities of land tenure, ranging from major disputes to the normal business of property conveyancing. While some commissions covered the whole spectrum of criminal and civil matters, others were dispatched for particular and limited purposes. Lawlessness and violence could be held in check and the normal business of a rural society could be expedited. By appointing a justiciar for Wales to oversee the keeping of the king's peace in his new territories, Edward began the process of introducing this system into the lands he held in Wales. That lies behind the common description of this document as the statute of Wales.

The law administered in England was much valued. Some basic principles survived from Anglo-Saxon times, and many more evolved during the twelfth century. In the area of crimes of violence, although a wronged individual could seek justice by bringing an accusation in person, through the appeal, the state assumed the responsibility for initiating cases through a local jury of presentment. Where land was concerned, no man could be required to answer for his freehold except in a suit initiated by a royal writ; possession of property and rights was under royal protection, and a series of possessory assizes offered the means of bringing disputes before the royal judges for decision. In Henry III's reign the judges were keenly aware of social grievances and were anxious to make the law an instrument of reform. The professionals took pride in the fact that a writ could be devised for any circumstance, and by the early decades of the thirteenth century, they had standardised writs 'of course', each of which would cover a problem likely to recur in the courts. The law book ascribed to Glanvill, and the *Treatise* compiled by Bracton demonstrate the value which legal administrators placed on the system they were helping to produce, and the volume of work which faced the justices itinerant shows plainly the popularity of the royal courts. Edward I's contemporaries would have found it hard to think of the English legal system as repressive, or to see its introduction into Wales as an instrument of authoritarian rule. What Edward did was to take this system of law and legal procedure and to adapt it for use in his Welsh territories. From his point of view, it was modified to the direct advantage of the Welsh.

The statute provided in detail for cases which would now be classified as civil actions; cases initiated by writs, cases settled under the assizes and various types of pleas. A number of writs were selected for discussion. Rhuddlan does not provide a comprehensive record of all the writs which could be obtained as a matter of course from the royal chancery. In that, it differs sharply from the method by which English law was introduced into Ireland in 1227; then, a register of sixty writs was sent to Ireland. In 1284, seven forms of action were covered in a register of eighteen documents. For someone who had been deprived of his freehold, the writ of *novel disseisin* was provided with three variant forms: one was for land, another for the particular problem of the loss of common of pasture – especially relevant in a Welsh setting – and the third for an act which had created a nuisance. It was made clear that these were examples, and that 'the forms of the writ shall be changed according to the diversity of cases'. A second area of dispute arose when land and rights were lost at the point of inheritance, and the writ of *mort d'ancestor* was provided, with detailed instructions to cover a variety of circumstances. One was directly related to Welsh experience: the rights of co-heirs in different generations and different degrees of kinship were carefully safeguarded. To cover other instances of wrongful dispossession, a general writ of *disseisin* was provided in two forms, one to cover questions of right and the other to cover questions of possession. A royal official, a litigant, or a working lawyer, using this section of the statute would have at hand the material necessary for him to decide which expedient covered his particular case. There followed writs of dower, and of debt (whether in money or in goods withheld), and of covenants. With these there were writs ordering that a case be brought to court (*pone*), that justice be done (*justicies*), that attorneys should be appointed, and that a coroner should be appointed. This section of the statute is very practical and severely limited. It provides a short *formulare*, with the standard form of documents and a recurrent insistence that the details must be changed to suit the circumstances. The writ of covenants brings out the principle very clearly: contracts and covenants are infinite, and it would be difficult to make mention of each kind in particular, but the statute lays down that every circumstance can be put to trial, and the writ must be drafted accordingly. Here, and in pleadings, the objective is to arrive at the truth, and the courts must not work 'following that hard rule, "He who fails in a syllable, fails in the whole cause"'.

With some repetition the statute lays out the cases which must be settled before the king's justiciar under the assizes of *novel disseisin* and *mort d'ancestor*, with the judge receiving the facts from a local jury and forming his judgement on the basis of their information. It emphasises the very limited range of delays and excuses (*essoins*) which are to be allowed. It points to a series of defences which might be possible, and one in particular was stressed. A man claims that he has been deprived of land which he should hold by inheritance: one defence would be that he was a bastard, and could not therefore inherit. That defence, if it were established, must stand, and the claim must fail. In a Welsh context that limited a long-standing practice; it gave great offence to clerics and lawyers from England that, in Wales, the bastard son should share the right of inheritance with the son born in wedlock. The statute was drafted to put a stop to that. The Edwardian legislators objected to another feature of Welsh life: in Wales widows could not claim any dower land, and whatever provision was made for them was limited to movable goods. In England the feudal practice prevailed that a widow was entitled to hold land, usually one third of her husband's estates, as dower while she lived. By including a writ of dower and detailed instructions on this issue, the statute introduced the concept of dower land into Wales. These were changes which would affect substantial landholders in the new Edwardian shires, and the consequences of dower would be widely felt in every generation. There was some misgiving that the descent of lands passed only to male co-heirs, and the statute provided that, in default of male heirs, female co-heiresses could have their shares of land and pass them on to their own heirs.

In several important respects the statute of Rhuddlan incorporated Welsh custom into the law which was promulgated in 1284. Edward did not attempt to interfere with the principle of partible inheritance: because inheritance is, and has been from time immemorial, partible, the king will not have that custom abrogated but wills that inheritance shall remain partible among like heirs as it has always been. (Here, Edward made the critical proviso that bastards should not share in the inheritance.) It was accepted that, in dealing with lands and tenements, good and lawful men should be chosen with the consent of the parties to a dispute, and they should establish the facts: they would be men who knew the disputants and were aware of the niceties of local custom. The principle was stated plainly that judgement must be based upon the facts established by a jury since other methods, traditional in England, trial by battle and recourse to the grand assize, were not available in Wales. Contracts and debts and other similar matters had traditionally been arranged in the presence of neighbours who saw and heard what had been transacted and who could speak to what they had witnessed. It was agreed that this

method of ensuring the authenticity of an agreement should be continued. A minor detail may have made for great convenience: fines
for default were to be paid in accordance with Welsh law, and the
customary payment of three cows or their value was to be the norm.

Those who drafted the statute saw no need to deal at length with
criminal law. It was laid down that the evidence of those who had
seen and heard transactions should not be extended to felonies –
theft, larceny, arson, murder, manslaughter and notorious robbery:
these were to be heard and judged by English law, with no concessions to Welsh practice.

If it is possible to view a code of law imposed upon a conquered
people dispassionately, the statute of Rhuddlan was a fine piece of
work. It achieved Edward's intentions, and it incorporated important elements of Welsh custom. From a Welsh point of view it was
impossible to divorce the political aspect of the statute from the legal,
or to reconcile the unfamiliar law imposed upon tribal society with
the loss of so much of the familiar custom which had been taken for
granted for so long. There is, too, a dark side to the story: there was
a sharp contrast between the idealism of the legal theory which produced the statute and the application of the law by local officers.
What the statute provided and what the people experienced were not
always the same thing.

The settlement owed much to Edward's administration of his
lands in the marches. From 1254 he was directly concerned with
Carmarthen, Cardigan, Builth and the three castles of Gwent,
Whitecastle, Skenfrith and Grosmont, in addition to his lands in the
north. In 1265, when his energies were much needed in England, he
relinquished Carmarthen, Cardigan and the three castles to his
brother, Edmund, and it was only after the defeat of Llywelyn ap
Gruffydd that, in 1278, he resumed part of these southern lordships.
The three castles were left in Edmund's possession and descended to
his successors as part of the honour of Lancaster. Carmarthen and
Cardigan were handed back to Edward I in exchange for two Derby-
shire manors. These shires formed the basis of the king's possessions
in south Wales, but they were augmented by castles and lands taken
from Welsh magnates. Rhys Fychan died at Dinefwr in 1271, and six
years later his successor surrendered the castle to Edward, together
with the neighbouring castle of Carreg Cennen on its imposing
escarpment and with the second major castle held by Rhys, at
Llandovery. By 1279, John of Penrice, the royal bailiff, was super-
vising the repair of both castles. Dryslwyn, only a few miles below
Dinefwr, did not come into the king's possession until 1287.

Elsewhere, Edward's officers could exercise power for a limited period of time. The succession of a fitz Alan minor gave the king control of Clun and Oswestry in the middle march. Abergavenny was in Edward's hands during the minority of George de Cantilupe from 1263 until 1273. That Edward's officials were active in these areas is not open to doubt. The king's directives in the years 1278–82 indicate very clearly his own interest in what they were doing, and his determination that the Welsh territory in his hands should be firmly administered.

Apart from the steady flow of writs and letters, and the occasional boasting of efficient but unfeeling senior officials, the king's determination can best be seen in terms of judicial authority. In 1278, Edward set in motion two judicial commissions, one for Builth, Montgomery, the royal lands in Powys, and the Perfeddwlad, and the other for west Wales, identified in somewhat ominous terms as the lands of the Welsh and the marcher lords of the south-west. Snowdonia, and the two largest lordships in the south-east, Brecknock and Glamorgan, were exempt from the judges' activities. The southern commission was made up of Payn de Chaworth, of Kidwelly, and a royal clerk, Henry de Bray, and when Payn died later in 1279 the commission effectively lapsed. The northern commission was led by Walter Hopton, of Shropshire, and was made up of English and Welsh judges. Hywel ap Meurig, a prominent Welsh tenant of Roger Mortimer, Rhys ap Gruffydd ab Ednyfed, and Goronwy ap Heilyn were appointed to deal with Welsh cases. For Llywelyn ap Gruffydd himself and for Gruffydd ap Gwenwynwyn, as well as for leading marcher lords, the commission was an innovation which might prove an asset or a threat, but in its early stages it was welcomed and many Welshmen turned to it to solve problems of land tenure. Even Llywelyn saw it as a possible means of securing swift justice. Speed, however, was one thing which the royal judges could not offer, for there were too many disputed points of law which required definition, and adjournments and postponements served only to produce frustration.

Through his judges, Edward hoped to impose the judicial aspects of the treaty of Aberconwy and that added political overtones to reactions to their activities. They could consult him for guidance and decision on sensitive matters, and this produced not only delays but resentment that inquiry and decision should be necessary. There was ample room for dispute as to whether a case should be heard within Llywelyn's jurisdiction or the king's. Welshmen holding lands in both royal territory and in the principality were caught in a conflict of obligation. Gruffydd ap Madog of northern Powys held Iâl (more obviously identified as the lordship of Yale) of King Edward, and had lands in Edeirnion within Llywelyn's territory. When the widow of his brother, Madog of Bromfield, was in dispute with him about estates in Edeirnion, should she seek justice from Llywelyn as lord of the commote, or from Edward as Gruffydd's lord in Yale? Understandably, she tried both, and caused confusion and uncertainty in the process. When that conflict of jurisdiction was brought to Edward to be resolved, he decided in favour of the prince of Wales and the issues were referred to him for settlement. Closely linked with the problem of rival jurisdictions was the equally contentious problem of alternative systems of law: should English law or Welsh law prevail? This came to a head in a dispute over the tenure of Arwystli, an area of southern Powys which had been a cause of dispute between Gwynedd and Powys since at least the second half of the eleventh century. In 1278, Llywelyn happily made use of the royal judges to establish his own rights in this area, but while he asserted that the matter should be settled in Arwystli by Welsh law, his opponent, Gruffydd ap Gwenwynwyn, asserted that Arwystli was a barony which he held from the king as a lord of the march, and he was determined that any litigation should be settled by English law. The delays and the pleadings in this cause rankled with Llywelyn, and he singled them out as a major factor in his final break with Edward. What had started with promise ended in recriminations. Apart from such big issues, the royal judges at work between 1278 and 1280 were hampered by the sheer weight of cases to be heard and decided. Unpopular judgements in some suits and long delays in many others created bitterness and bad feeling. Even the ultimate loyalties of the judges themselves were open to question. One of them, Rhys ap Gruffydd ab Ednyfed, was a magnate close to Llywelyn until, in 1277, he went over to the king and remained a valuable royal agent working in Edward's interest until his death in 1284. Another, Goronwy ap Heilyn, served Edward I, but in 1282, in the last days before the final revolt, he joined Dafydd ap Gruffydd and stood against the king.

The victory of 1277 reduced Llywelyn ap Gruffydd's power to a minimum and offered Edward I the prospect of sound government in those parts of Wales which he had regained and of firm control over Gwynedd through the treaty of Aberconwy. The result, which fell far short of his expectations, was untidy and only partly effective. After his victory of 1283 he was able to design and impose a settlement with a greater promise of success. Since land tenure and rival claims were a major social problem, the possessory assizes offered a chance of clean and swift justice: they depended upon simple and neat definitions of the wrongs to be put right and they did not allow excuses and delays. With the statute of Rhuddlan, as with others of the Edwardian statutes, the king and his advisers wanted specific remedies for specific problems; they thought deeply and worked hard, drafting, revising and emending until they were satisfied with their final version. It was meant to last.

What law did this settlement challenge and, in large measure, replace? Welsh law in the thirteenth century was essentially community law, archaic in form, and retaining much detail in concepts and procedures which were already obsolete, though at the same time there were signs of development and of dynamic qualities. It was a system of laws which depended upon the memory and support of the kindred and the neighbourhood, and in its primitive form it did not expect, or require, a strong princely authority. It was preserved and imposed by specialists, semi-professional lawmen. The view which now holds the field is that manuscripts containing material on certain aspects of law and procedure, short tractates on limited themes, were being produced during the twelfth century, and that they (or some of them) were brought together in a single volume in south Wales under the patronage of Rhys ap Gruffydd (the Lord Rhys) before 1197. Legal manuscripts multiplied in the thirteenth century and continued to be produced throughout the later middle ages and well into the modern period. About forty medieval manuscripts survive, six of them with Latin texts of Welsh laws and the remainder containing Welsh texts. They share one characteristic: those who study Welsh law must work from late manuscripts presenting the laws in their fully developed form. They cannot, as students of early Irish law can, work on early texts and glosses, nor do they have the sequence of early codes which are available for the study of Anglo-Saxon law. The manuscripts of Welsh law fall into distinct, though never completely exclusive, groups. In 1841 Aneurin Owen distinguished them geographically as emanating from north Wales (his Venedotian group), south Wales (his Dimetian group) and south-east Wales (his Gwentian group). Later generations of scholars have preferred to use personal names rather than geographical associations, though the 'families' of manuscripts are very similar. The prologues of two groups of manuscripts mention Blegywryd and Morgeneu and Cyfnerth, and the law books have been identified as *Llyfr Blegywryd* (*The Book of Blegywryd*) and *Llyfr Cyfnerth* (*The Book of Cyfnerth*). It was assumed in the prologues that both men were jurists who were contemporaries of Hywel Dda in the tenth century. The third 'family' of manuscripts is known as *Llyfr Iorwerth* (*The Book of Iorwerth*), which was made up of seven tractates. Iorwerth ap Madog was a thirteenth-century jurist, and the last four tractates, which make up about one third of the *Llyfr Iorwerth*, were attributed to him. *Llyfr Iorwerth* equates with Owen's Venedotian group, *Llyfr Blegywryd* with his Dimetian group, and *Llyfr Cyfnerth* with his Gwentian group. There are hybrid documents which incorporate material from more than one tradition.

Issues of principle and forms of procedure provided a simple framework. Crucial to an aristocratic society were the ideas of status and the protection of status. The king (*brenin*), the prince (*tywysog* or *arglwydd*) and the man of standing or the nobleman (*bonheddig*, *uchelwr*) each had his status (*braint*) which affected the status of his wife, family and entourage. Any insult or slight must be put right, and the law provided for compensation for an insult (*sarhad*). Any damage or loss was significant in itself, but the fact of the insult was more significant. A man's standing would affect the scale of payments due for any damage to his property. So, for example, the laws distinguished the relative scale of values for damage to a kiln: of the king, six score pence; of a *breyr* (ruler of a lesser kingdom), three score pence; of a king's bondman, thirty pence; and of the bondman of a *breyr*, twenty-four pence. Men of all ranks could bring others under their protection (*nawdd*) and if that protection were violated compensation was due. The importance of the kindred was a fundamental concept. The compensation for killing a man (*galanas*) was a heavy payment to be shared by the immediate and more distant members of the kindred, extending to fifth cousins. In certain circumstances, women might be included among those liable to contribute to this payment. Inheritance, carefully defined, was confined to a smaller kindred unit, extending to second cousins; it could affect those who claimed a common great-grandfather. Property must be held for four generations before the kindred lost any claim to share the inheritance. Land passed in the first instance to sons, then to first cousins, and finally to second cousins, and surviving members of older generations had clear claims. Marriage produced a complex system of gifts and payments which included gifts or support from the bride's family and a gift which might be made by the husband at the time of marriage (*cowyll*). Partible inheritance created many problems; to define each share of land, and to verify the standing of every claimant, were essential in any dispute. The permanent interest of the kindred in property meant that the outright alienation of land was difficult to achieve. With grants to religious houses, for example, it was necessary to cover the claims which might be made by a wide range of the kindred; the parallels with the need, in a feudal society, to secure the assent of a widow, an immediate heir, the lord of the fee and the crown, are obvious. Useful techniques for creating short-term leases and tenures were gradually evolved, and the short-term mortgage or *prid* (which should more accurately be described as a *vifgage*) allowed a measure of flexibility. One application of particular importance for Welsh society in the thirteenth and fourteenth centuries was the use of *prid* as the means of conveying to Welshmen burgages and property in towns, even where military precautions and nervous legislation in parliament sought to debar such tenures.

The role of the community was always important, and in its earliest forms the law was to be supervised and imposed by the community. It is not surprising that Welsh law was much valued by Welsh communities in the marcher lordships. There, more than in the Welsh principalities, the archaic basis of the law had a continuing attraction. Increasingly in the twelfth and thirteenth centuries, the patronage and protection of the prince became more important. Cases could be settled in his courts, whether at his *llys*, one of his principal residences, or in local courts in different commotes. When Edward I imposed his settlement by royal authority, that was an extension of a process already clearly marked before 1282. It is a curious feature of the Edwardian conquest that Edward was at pains to preserve some of the *llysau* of the princes of north Wales, and in some instances to transport them physically into his castles. Is it possible that that may have been intended to make his own royal courts more easily recognisable or acceptable after 1282–3?

The Edwardian settlement was maintained by a well-organised bureaucracy. The justiciar, responsible for north Wales, had oversight of all that might affect the king's peace and controlled the whole administration virtually as a vicegerent. His authority was limited by the special provision that the county of Flint should be associated closely with Chester, and the justiciar of Chester exercised great influence there. This link was strengthened when, in 1301, the principality of Wales was conferred on Edward of Caernarfon. South Wales was the sphere of a second justiciar, standing for the king, though it was common practice to appoint the same magnate to the office in both north and south Wales. This overall responsibility was entrusted to a well-tried curial figure, and, as the fourteenth century advanced, to one of the greater English magnates. The first justiciar in the north was Otto de Grandson, a well-born Savoyard, one of Edward's small circle of intimate friends, who had worked with him in Gascony and who was given control of Anglesey at a critical moment in 1282. He served as justiciar until 1295 and was succeeded by his deputy, John of Havering, an Essex man who had made a successful career in Edward's service. In the early fourteenth century, three prominent marcher lords were among those who held the office, Roger Mortimer of Chirk, Edmund fitz Alan, earl of Arundel and lord of Bromfield and Yale, and Roger Mortimer, earl of March. In the south, where royal administration already had a long history, Edward brought together the royal estates of west Wales, first on an informal basis under Roger Mortimer, and then in 1280 under Bogo de Knovill as justiciar. Bogo was a career administrator, sometime sheriff of Shropshire and bailiff of Montgomery, and in his brief tenure of the justiciarship he caused deep resentment. It has been said that he used in local administration the procedure associated in England with cases heard *coram rege*: a direct summons to the parties to appear before him, wherever he might be, so that justice could be done. In 1281 he was replaced by one of Edward's close associates, Robert Tibetot, a veteran of Gascon administration and of Edward's crusade. He was justiciar, with custody of all the royal castles in south Wales, from 1281 until 1298.

The combination of the justiciarship of north and south Wales in the hands of John of Havering, Roger Mortimer of Chirk, Edmund fitz Alan, and Roger Mortimer, earl of March, made for a consistent approach to administrative problems. Among these English magnates one Welshman, Rhys ap Hywel, was justiciar of south Wales very briefly in 1326–7. He had made a career in the service of Edward II and then of two marcher lords, Roger Mortimer of Wigmore and Humphrey de Bohun, earl of Hereford. He was an active deputy-justiciar when Roger Mortimer of Chirk held office, and in the first decade of the fourteenth century he acquired estates in Pontesbury, in Shropshire, and Talgarth and Bronllys, in the lordship of Brecknock. The years of crisis at the end of Edward II's reign gave him the chance to hold the justiciarship. His career overlapped with that of another active, and generally successful, Welsh administrator, Rhys ap Gruffydd, whose great-grandfather had been Ednyfed Fychan, an outstanding administrator in the service of Llywelyn ab Iorwerth. Rhys was a distinguished deputy-justiciar, but he could not aspire to be justiciar. Deputy-justiciars might hold office for a period of time, and the name could be used to describe those commissioned to act for the justiciar on a particular occasion. They were, predominantly, of English or marcher stock. So, too, were the chamberlains, responsible for financial administration, and the castellans of the major royal strongholds. Sheriffs were drawn from the royal service and from marcher families, and men of Welsh blood found the opportunity to work at this level of local government. In Carmarthenshire, John Yweyn was sheriff in 1319–20, John ap Llywelyn in 1349–50 and John Iorwerth, who served in 1378–9, was followed by six Welshmen in the remaining years of the century. Between 1378 and 1400, seven Welsh sheriffs served in Cardiganshire. In north Wales one Welshman was quickly given large military responsibilities; Gruffydd ap Tewdwr was put in charge of Dolwyddelan castle when it was taken in 1282, and in the following year he was appointed constable for life. His contemporary, Gruffydd Llwyd, grandson of Ednyfed Fychan, found even greater opportunities in royal service. His loyalty to Edward I was the basis on which his career was built. He served successively in the households of the queen, of Edward I from 1283, and of Edward of Caernarfon from 1301. In that year he was knighted. From 1297 to 1314 he was the king's commissioner of array to raise troops in north Wales, and between 1301 and 1327 he served as sheriff for fifteen years, in Caernarfonshire (1301–5 and 1308–10), Anglesey (1305–6) and Merionethshire (1314–16 and 1321–7).

Local officers who had to deal directly with people were drawn from, and were part of, the local community. The settlement pattern of Carmarthenshire meant that these could be recruited from English or Welsh: some 30 per cent of senior officials were English, and 70 per cent Welsh. Below that level, with the lesser offices of local bailiff, beadle, constable and forester, the proportion of Welsh officials may have been as high as 85 per cent. Move north to Cardiganshire, where the settlement pattern was very different, and the proportion of Welsh administrators may have been of the order of 90 per cent at all levels. At best, such estimates can only be a very rough guide, but two tendencies deserve attention: officials held office for more than one spell of duty, and could work in more than one administrative area; and successive members of the same family can often be traced holding the same office. Overall, the picture is clear: in the most responsible offices the appointment of a Welshman was rare; in the median grades there was a career structure for Welshmen of ability and education; and at grass-roots level everything depended upon local Welsh families to keep the machinery of government working smoothly. The detailed analysis which would make the structure of local administration in the lands of conquest equally clear has yet to be completed, but the general trend would be the same, with Welshmen heavily committed to holding office in their community, working with and for the senior officials of the royal administration.

Was the massive investment in castles and garrisons in Wales justified? On two occasions they were challenged and tested before the end of the thirteenth century. The first appeal to arms was made in south-west Wales, and it was put down with comparative ease. It was an act of defiance from a magnate whom the English regarded as an unlikely rebel, Rhys ap Maredudd, of Dryslwyn, who had succeeded his father in 1271. They had both been consistently loyal to the English crown, though Maredudd was eventually drawn into the circle of Llywelyn ap Gruffydd, and had given his homage to the prince of Wales as late as 1270. In the crisis of 1276–7, Rhys confirmed his loyalty to Edward I in what was effectively a treaty drawn up by the king's agent, Payn de Chaworth. The castle of Dryslwyn and his own share of the family inheritance were not at issue when the agreement was drawn up, but Rhys ap Maredudd's kinsmen, Rhys Wyndod and his three brothers, were deeply committed to Llywelyn ap Gruffydd, and their lands were at the king's disposal. Rhys ap Maredudd acquired the castle of Dinefwr, and his tenure of four commotes (Maenordeilo, Mallaen, Caeo and Mabelfyw), all in Cantref Mawr, was confirmed. There were also two commotes in northern Cardigan, Gwynionydd and Mabwynion, which he was to continue to hold on limited conditions. The most important privilege which Payn was commissioned to grant was that Rhys should never in future be removed from the king's homage. Some parts of these arrangements were, at best, tentative, and events would prove that they would not all be sustained when peace was restored. In 1277, with Prince Llywelyn defeated and subdued, Edward took possession of Dinefwr castle, and a few years later he reclaimed Maenordeilo, but the grant of a fair and market at Dryslwyn in 1281 pointed to the fact that hostility was not the keynote and that Rhys was not being penalised. When war broke out in 1282, Rhys, unlike his kinsmen, had no intention of joining Gwynedd, and Edward singled him out as the only leader of any substance in west Wales to support him and was quick to reward him. Rhys was to have the lands which Rhys Wyndod – now an enemy and a rebel – held in Caeo and Mallaen. The greater rewards came in Cardigan; not only were the commotes of Gwynionydd and Mabwynion confirmed to Rhys, but for the first time he was to be given seisin of them and his tenure was the more secure. He was, beyond question, the leading figure in the dynasty of Deheubarth; his gains were small scale and local, but he was building up a compact lordship. However, there were problems. He was required to give up any formal claims to Dinefwr castle, and he had to surrender lands intended for the young Llywelyn ab Owain when he came of age. He had been given a writ to deliver to Robert Tibetot who would put him in seisin of his lands, and this technical but important step he had ignored. Instead he took possession of his lands without proper formality. It was in character that Edward should be angered because the legal niceties had not been observed. He declared Rhys to have forfeited his lands and summoned him to appear at the royal council to answer for his offence. Once the action had been condemned, Edward restored the lands and ordered seisin to be given in proper form. Rhys also had ambitions beyond Ystrad Tywi, for he was anxious to secure two commotes in Cantref Bychan, Hirfryn and Perfedd, long associated with his dynasty and recently held by Rhys Wyndod. Here, his ambitions clashed with the interests of John Giffard who was given the whole of Cantref Bychan, and Rhys was left aggrieved and disappointed. Against these checks must be set small signs of royal favour, the grant of a fair and market at Lampeter in 1285 and in the next year a guarantee that, while he was in England, his lands, rents and possessions would be under the king's protection and he would be free from answering a wide range of pleas. Above all, there was his marriage in 1285 to Ada, sister of John de Hastings of Abergavenny, with a substantial marriage settlement. All the signs are that Edward considered Rhys to be a sound ally who had won great advantages through his loyalty and who was still receiving clear marks of royal favour. For Rhys, the losses and failures in the record were much more significant; they led to frustration and disappointment of which the king and his officers remained in ignorance.

In June 1287, Rhys rebelled and the king mustered a force of 22,000 men to meet the danger which at that stage might have been the prelude to widespread revolt. In fact, Rhys' defiance was personal and local, and by September his castle of Dryslwyn had been captured. In November he renewed the struggle, moving to Cardiganshire and capturing the castle at Emlyn as part of his wife's estates. There he held out against the royalist forces until January

1288, when the castle was taken; even then, he did not seek peace, but remained a rebel and an outlaw, finding shelter within the narrow confines of his own territory. In 1289 a group of hostages at Dryslwyn were given a stark choice: find Rhys and bring him to the castellan, Alan de Plukenet, by Palm Sunday, or face execution. Rhys remained at large until 1292, when he was betrayed by his own people in the commote of Mallaen, taken to York, and executed. It is difficult not to see in Rhys ap Maredudd the same feature which was so marked in Llywelyn ap Gruffydd in north Wales, a sense of personal humiliation which was a more powerful motive than any consideration of political wisdom or territorial gains.

The second, and much more serious, challenge to the Edwardian settlement was mounted in 1294. It was more difficult and more costly to put down, and it tested the defences of north and south Wales very severely, but in the end it lacked co-ordination and leadership. The principal figure was Madog ap Llywelyn who was so loosely identified by contemporaries that as recently as seventy years ago he was thought to be an illegitimate son of Llywelyn ap Gruffydd. He was, in fact, descended from a junior line of the ruling dynasty of Gwynedd. He and Llywelyn ap Gruffydd shared a common ancestor in Owain Gwynedd who had died in 1170, but they were cousins in the fifth degree, and Madog was in no sense an outsider. His family had maintained claims to Meirionydd where they established themselves somewhat fitfully. They had been ousted by Llywelyn ab Iorwerth by 1202, and were reinstated, perhaps as early as 1221; as part of his efforts to diminish the standing of Dafydd ap Gruffydd in 1240–1, Henry III confirmed their tenure of the *cantref*. Llywelyn ap Gruffydd secured their overthrow and exile in 1255, and Madog and his father found a refuge in England under the benevolent patronage of Henry III. Madog was one of the prominent Welshmen who sought to use the Hopton commission for their own advantage, putting forward his claim to Meirionydd and impleading the prince of Wales in his attempt to be re-established there. After 1282 he was back in Wales, apparently with a base in Anglesey. In 1294 he thought of himself as the successor of Prince Llywelyn, and he adopted the style prince of Wales.

His associates were lesser men with purely local aims. In Glamorgan, the leading figure was a Morgan, who was almost certainly Morgan ap Maredudd, son of the last Welsh lord of Caerleon. His enemy was the earl of Gloucester, and his ambition was to make personal and local gains at the earl's expense. In west Wales the leader of the rising was Maelgwn ap Rhys Fychan, of the line of that Maelgwn, son of the Lord Rhys, who had played a leading part in the affairs of south Wales. By 1294, as lord of Glenau'r-glyn, a single commote in northern Cardiganshire, he was a minor landholder of high lineage. The same must be assumed of Cynan, identified as the leader of disaffection in Brecknock.

The primary cause of the revolt was the heavy and insensitive attitude of the English administrators, aggravated by the taxation levied in 1291, when a tax of one fifteenth was demanded. The opportunity for revolt was a by-product of Edward I's policy in Gascony. By September 1294, the king had raised a large force for operations in southern France, much of it recruited from Wales. Leading administrators were deeply committed to raising troops, Reginald Grey in Flintshire, Robert de Staundon, sheriff of Merionethshire, in north Wales, and Walter of Petherton and Geoffrey Clement in the marches. The garrisons of royal castles were cut down drastically. John Giffard withdrew so many men from Builth that he compromised his chances of defending the castle effectively once war broke out. A number of castellans were withdrawn for active service, and the justiciar of south Wales, Robert Tibetot, was appointed to command the expeditionary force. The date fixed for levies to muster at Shrewsbury was 30 September, and on that day the rebellion began. Maelgwn attacked royalist forces at Cardigan, killing Geoffrey Clement, and besieging Aberystwyth castle, while elsewhere attacks were launched on Builth, Castell-y-Bere, Denbigh, Cricieth, Harlech, Caernarfon and Morlais. Reginald Grey, drawing on his long experience, recognised the dangers and acted with speed, reinforcing the depleted garrisons of Flint and Rhuddlan and ordering emergency work to strengthen the defences. Builth was under siege for six weeks, and John Giffard made five attempts to break through and relieve the castle before he could claim success in mid-November. Madog's most devastating attack was directed against Caernarfon where he overran the defences of the borough and broke through into the castle. The castellan, Roger de Puleston, was killed, and the castle and borough so severely damaged that they had to be rebuilt.

Edward's reaction was characteristic: his campaign in Gascony was suspended, and he began the task of diverting his troops to Wales. He used the well-tried expedient of operating from three local bases. In south Wales Earl William de Valence and Roger Bigod, earl of Norfolk, were given charge; de Valence worked with a group of local magnates which included Alan de Plukenet, Nicholas of Carew and John of Cogan, while Norfolk's support group included Thomas and Maurice de Berkeley from Gloucestershire. The defence of the middle march from Brecknock to Montgomery was entrusted to the earl of Hereford and John Giffard, backed up by Roger Lestrange and Edmund Mortimer. John Havering dealt with Merionethshire, and Henry de Lacy, earl of Lincoln, and Reginald Grey were to hold the Perfeddwlad. Meanwhile, Edward ordered three armies to muster at Chester, Montgomery and Gloucester, the base from which forces could be deployed in south-east Wales. He himself secured Ruthin and Denbigh and moved to Conwy. Then, whether through haste or misjudgement, he attempted a swift advance to Bangor, but his baggage train was attacked and destroyed and he was obliged to return in disarray to Conwy and to wait there for the winter months to pass. It was a difficult period, for without effective use of shipping the major coastal castles could not have been provisioned. The king's discomfiture was matched by a military disaster in which Madog and his forces were overwhelmed. In February, Madog moved into Powys, venturing within 10 miles of Montgomery where English troops were commanded by William Beauchamp, earl of Warwick. On 5 March the earl surprised Madog in open country at Maes Madog in a night attack and the Welsh were routed. It was a decisive encounter, for although Madog escaped there was no second chance to repair the damage and at the end of July he surrendered. How the king dealt with him is not recorded, but his son was taken into the royal service and joined the growing band of Welshmen loyal to the crown. Edward set out on a long journey around the central massif of Wales visiting the major strongholds, from Caernarfon to Cricieth and Harlech, and then to Aberystwyth and Cardigan. He cut across through Emlyn to Carmarthen and moved eastwards through Dryslwyn to Brecon. After a brief diversion to Morlais, in the lordship of Glamorgan, he made his way to Montgomery, Welshpool, Oswestry and Chirk, and so back to Conwy. At one point he allowed old hostilities to come to the fore, taking Glamorgan into his own hands, pardoning Morgan ap Maredudd, and receiving the rebels there into his peace in defiance of the earl of Gloucester's interests. Madog's revolt was a serious threat, and Edward overcame it partly by heavy investment in men and fortifications, and partly by the military skills and successes of his commanders. Once it was over he showed little animosity towards the Welsh leaders and he set in motion a thorough investigation into the underlying causes of complaint and unrest. The English grip on Wales was perceptibly tightened, with the network of castles strengthened: Caernarfon was rebuilt, Beaumaris commissioned and the Lacy castle at Denbigh was refashioned. The administration was modified if only because the leading officials devoted more time to their duties in Wales. Where the revolt might have sharpened divisions, it seems rather to have created a sense of common interest between the king and the Welsh elite, and increasingly Welsh magnates showed that they were prepared to give their loyalty to the king and, especially, to Edward of Caernarfon as prince of Wales.

The Edwardian boroughs, designed as indispensable adjuncts of the castles which now dominated the north, brought a new prosperity to north Wales. The speed with which they could be built owed much to the king's earlier experience and to his ruthlessness. In 1277, at Flint, his builders were working on a new site; earlier, the obvious centres of English influence in the immediate vicinity were Basingwerk, with its abbey, and Bagillt, defended by its castle motte. The new castle and borough might have damaged local interests but did not cause disruption. At Aberystwyth, also fortified in 1277, the site of the castle and borough was already occupied, and a small Welsh community – farmers, not townsmen – were moved to an alternative site, more suitable for grazing than for arable farming, some 10 miles further up the valley of the Rheidol. That was characteristic of the larger number of Edwardian boroughs. There were castles, but not organised communities, at Harlech and Cricieth before Edward I made use of these sites. At Conwy there was the Cistercian abbey of Aberconwy, together with 'the abbot's borough'. To be consistent with Cistercian principles, the abbey should have been isolated, and to see a borough outside its walls would be very unusual. That has led some historians to suggest that the abbot's borough lay on the opposite side of the Conwy estuary, at Degannwy, though it is not easy to conceive of a private borough built up around a royal stronghold. Aberconwy was closely associated with the ruling dynasty of Gwynedd, and was very much like a royal *eigenkirche* – a proprietary church – and it may be that a small community grew up around the monastic buildings. To clear the ground for his new castle and town, Edward moved the monks to Maenan, further up the valley. The monks were consulted about the choice of a new site, and they received 580 marks (£386 13s. 4d.) by way of compensation. There is no hint of bitterness in their reactions to the king's policy; instead, they spoke with some warmth of his patronage and his concern for them in their new house. He was scrupulous to recompense those landholders who were deprived of their lands to make way for the new abbey. On the old site, the conventual buildings were used as a headquarters while Conwy castle was being built, and the abbey church was converted into the parish church of the new borough, even though the alignment of the church and churchyard did not fit happily into the grid-system.

At Caernarfon there was already a royal residence and a town, and although Llywelyn ap Gruffydd did not treat it as a particularly favoured *llys* he enjoyed the profits of justice of the town court, perhaps already recognisable in formal terms as a borough court (*curia burgi*). All this was swept aside to make way for the new castle and borough. The foundation of Caernarfon demonstrates the ruthlessness with which Edward could resolve a dilemma. The last of the Edwardian castles, Beaumaris, was commissioned in the wake of the great scare produced by Madog ap Llywelyn's revolt of 1294. On the obvious site, at Cerrig-y-Gwyddyl, was a small Welsh community. Llanfaes, little more than a mile away, was a large and prosperous Welsh borough which had grown under the patronage of Llywelyn ab Iorwerth and Llywelyn ap Gruffydd to a town of about 120 tenements. The only borough under Welsh control which could match it was Welshpool which had grown to more than 170 tenements by the beginning of the fourteenth century. In 1294, Llanfaes was burnt by Madog, and Edward and his advisers had to decide how to protect Anglesey, and how to control the flourishing trade built up by the merchants and sailors from Llanfaes. Their answer was to plan the new castle and borough at Beaumaris, where building work started in April 1295. The Welsh community at Cerrig-y-Gwyddyl was uprooted to make way for the new complex, and what remained of Llanfaes was demolished, and the site used as a base for the army of workmen required to build Beaumaris. Some of the men of Llanfaes moved into Beaumaris, but the majority were resettled elsewhere. By way of compensation, the whole community of Llanfaes was given 90½ acres in Rhosfair, on the western coast of the island, and there the town of Newborough was established. On the face of it, the new Welsh borough had limited prospects, but trade flourished, a royal charter was issued in 1303 and already burgage rents were being paid. Within the next year or two, Newborough was paying the same amount in borough rents as Llanfaes had formerly paid (£8 8s. 6d.), and in the early fourteenth century the town was growing in wealth and importance. But already, drifting sand was a threat in the whole of the Malltraeth and

Llanddwyn area, and in the long run it was this change in the environment which destroyed the prosperity of the borough.

The garrison towns were a curious phenomenon, for two contradictory principles were at work. One was to ensure the military effectiveness of the castle-borough complex, which demanded an immigrant population. The other was to control and attract trade, and this led to the insistence that Welshmen should come into the town to trade. There were several factors at work which were socially corrosive. The Welsh castle shared features common to garrisons the world over. The troops and immigrant settlers formed a minority in the area, and permanent hostility and a ghetto mentality were not, in military or political terms, productive. Racial tension and racial hatred could erupt in times of crisis, but there were long periods of quiescence. The immigrant population itself was not stable: it was not uncommon for burghal families to last for only three or four generations. Burgages could be seen as investments, not as an element in a system of defence; property in Conwy was particularly attractive for burgesses of other towns. There was a fluid property market; over eleven years, 1295 to 1306, between one third and one half of the burgages in Conwy changed hands.

In the immediate aftermath of conquest burgesses were required to contribute much to defence. Their presence guaranteed an immediate force to supplement the castle garrison in the event of an attack, and they could play a regular part in the defence of the whole complex. At Caernarfon, in the fourteenth century, the holder of a burgage was expected to do watch seven times a year, and the fact that prominent citizens were building up multiple holdings was recognised as a potential source of military weakness. In the late 1280s and 1290s, administrators and construction workers held burgages and became part of the new community of the borough. The troops, craftsmen and burgesses were drawn from England, and especially from Cheshire and the border counties, as well as from Gascony and Aquitaine, and occasionally from Ireland. They were aliens holding Wales by force and reaping the benefits of conquest.

Garrisons demanded services and generated wealth, and the Edwardian castles were no exception. The boroughs of north Wales attracted craftsmen, traders and a number of lesser agents like tavern-keepers, and the burgesses and castle staff also attracted servants and attendants. At Caernarfon, to take one example, properties were let and sub-let, and it is possible to see the substructure of a complex society, such as that which could be identified in any English town like Chester, Bristol, Norwich or Lincoln. Even where burgage tenure might prove difficult, Welsh people were moving into, and settling in, boroughs throughout north Wales. An upwardly mobile element was clearly discernible in the fourteenth century and it can be identified in stronger terms in the fifteenth century. To look for a uniform pattern would be a mistake. Caernarfon has been identified as the most conservative of the Edwardian boroughs, though indications of change are clearly to be seen there. It is revealing to move elsewhere and to judge from a wider spectrum of towns the pace of social change. At Carmarthen, with a long history of urban development, Welsh settlers were secure in the 1260s, and one of their number, Meilyr Fychan, became reeve at some point after 1280; then, after the Edwardian conquest of the north, there was a slight but perceptible shift towards English settlement. Throughout the fourteenth century, men of English or marcher stock were preferred as reeve or mayor, and only seven Welshmen served in that office. There were indications of hostility to Welsh infiltration in another old town, at Cardigan, and the administration of that borough remained in English hands: only a quarter of the leading officials who can be identified were Welsh. The most extreme form of an English plantation was to be found in the lordship of Denbigh, where the earl of Lincoln attracted and endowed a large immigrant population in the lordship and in his borough of Denbigh. The merchants of that town thought of themselves as insecure settlers in a hostile country, where danger lay not far beyond the protection of the castle. Time softened these rigorous conditions of the years of conquest, and by about 1330 the racial mix in the lordship had changed markedly. The most successful attempts at integration seem to have been at Aberystwyth and Ruthin. From the beginning, Aberystwyth sought to avoid language and legislation which would limit or exclude Welsh burgesses, already numerous before the death of Edward I. Privileges which would mark out the burgesses against others who lived in the town were deliberately avoided. Again, by 1330, about half of the burgesses of Aberystwyth were Welsh. Ruthin developed in quite remarkable fashion as an integrated community. In 1324, forty out of seventy burgesses were Welsh and all the signs are that the two peoples lived amicably together. There was a heavy concentration of Welsh burgesses in Welsh Street; of the twenty-seven who are known to have had houses there, five were English and the rest Welsh. There was heavy concentration of English burgesses in Castle Street, linking the castle gatehouse with the market and church. That may perhaps reflect the defensive attitude of the years in which Ruthin was transferred from Dafydd ap Gruffydd to Reginald Grey. The market in property was open, with houses passing from Welsh to English or from English to Welsh ownership. If there is one feature which distinguishes the two races in Ruthin it is that the Welsh tended to remain in the borough for many years while a number of the English stayed for short periods and moved away. Even at Beaumaris, despite the clearance of Welsh farmers and townsmen in 1295, half the burgesses were Welsh by 1330. Prosperity made a *modus vivendi* well worth seeking, but resentment was never far below the surface. A cause and a leader could release that resentment with explosive force.

The conquest brought about widespread social upheaval. Those who were defeated paid a heavy price for failure, and there can be little doubt that many Welshmen were deprived of their lands and of the security of their old communities. Many had to make do with inadequate compensation on marginal land or more remote pastures and grazing land. Many were reduced to subservience, living under the patronage of immigrant settlers. For a minority, conquest produced new opportunities and a new-found prosperity. Not all the social changes can be measured in the crude terms of English gains and Welsh losses.

The settlement of 1277 and the revolt of 1282 resulted in major changes in land tenure in north-east Wales. The Four Cantreds of the Perfeddwlad were firmly in English hands from 1277; the king kept Rhos with its key posts at Rhuddlan and Degannwy in his own hands, while the Montalt family remained at Hawarden in Tegeingl. Rhufoniog and Dyffryn Clwyd were given to Dafydd ap Gruffydd together with the lordship of Hope where his principal castle of Caergwrle (at Hope itself) and the strongholds of Ruthin and Denbigh formed a valuable part of the defences of the frontier. The creation of these new lordships foreshadowed the future settlement of the northern march. So, too, did the expansion of the possessions of Roger Mortimer of Wigmore. With Llywelyn ap Gruffydd in eclipse, Maelienydd, Gwrtheyrnion and Cwmwd Deuddwr were restored to him. Builth was retained by the crown but in 1270 Roger was given the border territories of Ceri and Cydewain, with the castle of Dolforwyn. To set up or to strengthen a marcher lord was the traditional way of building up a power bloc in the marches. In 1282, Edward used this as the basis of his settlement of the north-east. The Welsh magnates of Powys Fadog were deemed to have forfeited their lands by joining Llywelyn ap Gruffydd, and Dafydd lost his lordship of Hope. With some slight reshuffling Edward made fresh arrangements for the Perfeddwlad: Dyffryn Clwyd was given to Reginald Grey, justiciar of Chester, and Rhos and Rhufoniog to Henry de Lacy, earl of Lincoln, whose lordship took its name from his castle of Denbigh. The northern section of Powys Fadog went to the earl of Surrey, John de Warenne, to become the lordship of Bromfield and Yale, and the southern section passed to Roger, the second son of Roger Mortimer of Wigmore, with its principal castle at Chirk. Each large defensive unit made a valuable contribution to the security of the frontier. So, in south Wales, did Cantref Bychan, given to John Giffard. Southern Powys survived with minimal losses in the hands of the ageing Gruffydd ap Gwenwynwyn, whose sons called themselves de la Pole and identified themselves closely with their English neighbours.

The stability of this system of new lordships depended upon a firm political loyalty and a secure succession, but in the fourteenth century neither of these could be guaranteed. Roger Mortimer of Chirk joined the earl of Lancaster and Bartholomew Badlesmere in open opposition to Edward II in 1322 and after the king's victory he was imprisoned and deprived of his lands. The chief beneficiary of his fall was Edmund fitz Alan, earl of Arundel, who was given custody of his lands in Chirk, a limited tenure converted into a permanent possession by his son. The fitz Alans already held Clun and Oswestry and by marriage and negotiation they acquired Holt, making themselves key figures in the middle and northern march. With the accession of Edward III, Roger Mortimer of Wigmore (made earl of March in 1328) was able to recover from his own political disaster of the 1320s, and he and his successors built up a formidable body of lordships in the marches: they already held a run of territory from Wigmore through Radnor to Maelienydd, Gwrtheyrnion, Cwmwd Deuddwr, Ceri and Cydewain; they regained Builth, and they acquired Ewyas Lacy, Clifford, Blaenllyfni and Pencelli (in Brecknock), Denbigh and smaller holdings in west Wales. The opportunities for expansion for the fitz Alans and Mortimers, as well as for new families like the Beauchamps and the Despensers, came through failure of male heirs in families which had once been powerful, the Clares of Glamorgan, the Lacys of Denbigh and, at a later date, the Warennes and the Bohuns. The spectacular rise of the Despensers was the result of shrewd exploitation of their brief political ascendancy. Gilbert de Clare, earl of Gloucester, was killed at Bannockburn in 1314 and his ultimate heiresses were his three sisters whose claims were recognised in 1317: Eleanor was given in marriage to Hugh Despenser, with the lordship of Glamorgan, Margaret, the widow of Piers Gaveston, to Hugh Audley, with Gwynllŵg and its castle and borough of Newport, and Elizabeth Clare to Roger Damory, with Usk. Despite the major setback of 1321–2, Hugh secured Dryslwyn and Cantref Mawr, Gower, Brecknock and Blaenllyfni, Goodrich, and as a share of Cantref Bychan the commote of Iscennen; he ousted the Clare coparceners from Usk and Gwynllŵg, and he gained temporary control over Emlyn, Cilgerran and Pembroke in the west and Abergavenny in the east. His father, concerned more for his dynasty than for himself, made smaller gains, but he acquired the lordship of Denbigh. When Edward II was overthrown in 1326, the younger Despenser was captured and executed, and his spoils were redistributed. Some, like Abergavenny and Pembroke, were secure in the Hastings family, Brecknock now returned to the Bohuns and Blaenllyfni passed to the Mortimers and later to the Staffords. Others again would become part of the duchy of Lancaster in due course. But not everything was lost as the Clare interests survived. Elizabeth, married three times before she was twenty-seven, preferred to use the name of her first husband, John de Burgh, and from 1322 until her death she held Usk and administered the extensive dower lands which were the product of her three alliances. Through her grand-daughter, Elizabeth, her lands passed to Lionel, duke of Clarence. Eleanor passed on to her son, Hugh Despenser, the lordship of Glamorgan which he held until his death in 1349 when the lordship passed to a nephew. Gwynllŵg remained in the hands of Margaret and her husband, Hugh Audley, and their daughter and heiress brought the lordship to her husband, Ralph, who became earl of Stafford in 1351. Marcher society was flexible and volatile.

When the evidence becomes comparatively plentiful in the fourteenth century it is clear that English and Welsh administrators could work in harmony. Senior officials, stewards and constables could be drawn from the feudal tenants of a lordship, or from the tenants of English honours held by marcher lords. They were their lord's familiars, sharing his business and his leisure. Financial administration could be entrusted to prominent burgesses, grown wise in long experience of local trade and in the affairs of their borough, or in some cases a leading cleric might serve. Lesser offices could be filled, as in the administration of the king's lands, by English or Welsh according to the nature and racial make-up of the area. The affairs of Welsh communities tended to be handled by the leading family, and the English magnate could deal exclusively with the Welsh leader within his lordship. There was a small number of influential Welshmen who served in posts of responsibility. As early as 1277, Hywel ap Gruffydd was serving the king as bailiff in Rhos and Rhufoniog, and he could be matched in the neighbouring lordship by Cynwrig Sais, a professional soldier who had served Henry III, and who was castellan of Hawarden. Hywel ap Meurig was constable of the Mortimer castle at Cefnllys, and he served as steward for the Bohuns as well as for the Mortimers; he was one of the judges on the Hopton commission after 1278. When Builth was restored to Roger Mortimer in 1279, Hywel was appointed castellan and supervised the building of the new castle there. In Brecknock, one family was especially prominent in administration. Einion Sais and his successors were at the centre of affairs, often serving as sheriffs, in the late thirteenth century and throughout the fourteenth century. As with other Welshmen identified as Sais (Englishman), the name may not have been complimentary. Einion and his heirs, like the two brothers who served the Lacy lord of Denbigh, Iorwerth ap Llywarch and Cynwrig ap Llywarch, could commit themselves wholeheartedly to their lords or live in obscurity. The number of Welshmen who served in the most responsible offices was small, but they were trusted and efficient. Presumably they enjoyed their responsibilities enough to compensate for their unpopularity, and certainly they enjoyed the wealth which accrued from office.

8

RESURGENCE AND DECLINE:
THE FIFTEENTH CENTURY

———— • ————

That claims to the principality of Wales were regarded as dangerous can be seen from the career of Owain Lawgoch – Owain of the Red Hand. He was the grandson of Rhodri, brother of Llywelyn ap Gruffydd, and so of impeccable lineage, but his family had been settled in England for two generations. He was born and grew up there and had no direct association with Wales. As a young man he had opted for a military career in France and he built up a formidable reputation as a mercenary captain, serving in Spain, France, Alsace and the Swiss cantons. His force was made up partly of Welsh expatriates. The mercenary bands active in France in the fourteenth century had an unsavoury reputation, but the Breton, Bertrand du Guesclin, constable of France, and Louis, duke of Anjou, the son of King John II, made use of him and admired his qualities. His career, as Yvain de Galles, passed into legend. He returned to England briefly in 1365–6 to secure his inheritance, but left for France as soon as the formalities were completed. Like all mercenary captains, he found the changing pattern of war and peace a threat to his fortunes. In 1369 he was deprived of his English estates for being in league with the king's enemies, and the authorities kept his activities under review: an Anglesey man was charged and condemned in 1370 for being in touch with him, but whether he was a potential recruit or a potential opponent to English rule in Wales is not known. In these circumstances he acquired a political value as a claimant to Wales, a pretender very similar to those claimants to the English throne who caused so many problems in the fifteenth century. To finance a fleet for an attack on Wales he borrowed from the French king, Charles V, and in May 1372 he sailed from Harfleur. At Guernsey he was recalled to the king's service and diverted from his purpose. Five years passed before the prospect of a second attempt was raised. To prevent it, John Lamb, a Scot in English pay, was sent to assassinate Owain, and in July 1378, at the siege of Mortagne-sur-mer (Poitou), having ingratiated himself with the Welsh mercenary, he killed him. It was a sad end to a flamboyant career, but it demonstrated how seriously the English regarded the threat to Wales. Owain Lawgoch's career also demonstrated that the restoration of princely authority in north Wales was scarcely a matter of practical politics. His claims had a nuisance value which the French king could exploit as long as it suited his purpose, but no one was prepared to commit money or men on a sufficient scale to mount a serious invasion of Wales.

In fact, the restoration of princely authority had already ceased to be a practical possibility with the failure of Rhys ap Maredudd and Madog ap Llywelyn to break the English hold on Wales. Until the last years of the thirteenth century there was a firm link between princely achievements and the praises lavished upon individual princes by their bards. The praise might be exaggerated and inflated, and the lament which marked the passing of a particular ruler might overstate his qualities and his role, but the literary work was still linked with reality. In the fourteenth century there was a divorce between poetry and politics. Poets and scholars looked back and re-echoed old strains of prophecy. They admired their patrons and sought compliments and flattery which might please them but, constrained by circumstances, they could only write about domestic virtues, praise hospitality, exalt the virtues of lineage and recall a glorious past. To look for a glorious future was to hope for, or to prophesy, a complete break with a lack-lustre present. The bards performed a limited function for the clan, the sept or the immediate family. Did they introduce a note of romanticism as they spoke of potential leaders who might restore ancient glories? That is a central issue in the story of Owain Glyn Dŵr, the last champion of Welsh independence. In the literary record his prospects and his capacity as soldier and leader were, by well-known convention, overstated. Did the poets lead him and his partisans to offer more in political terms than they could deliver? Have the poets led historians to expect too much, and perhaps to attribute too much to the Glyn Dŵr revolt?

Owain's great-grandfather had ruled the easternmost areas of northern Powys, Maelor Gymraeg and Maelor Saesneg, and had clearly held estates elsewhere in Powys, but all these were forfeited in 1282. The family was able to retrieve two estates: one was the lordship of Glyndyfrdwy in Merionethshire, some 6 miles east of Llangollen, and the other a lordship in Cynllaith, some 15 miles to the south-east, centred in the parish of Llansilin, in the lordship of Chirk. There, at Sycharth, was the family's principal residence of which the impressive earthworks still remain. Owain took his name, not from Sycharth, but from Glyndyfrdwy; the name means the glen of the water of Dee (Glyn-dyfr-dwy), and the first two elements (with the second in an alternative form) supply his name Glyn Dŵr, anglicised as Glendower. His mother was descended from the princes of Deheubarth, and in addition to her lineage she brought the family valuable possessions in Cardiganshire. Owain was a gentleman, a squire, comfortably well off and able to enjoy a high standard of living. His wife was Margaret, daughter of David Hanmer who served Edward III as a judge, but whose roots in Wales were comparatively recent. Thomas of Macclesfield, David's great-grandfather, served Edward I in Wales and settled on the borders in Maelor Saesneg at the end of the thirteenth century, and there he married a Welsh girl. In the next four generations his successors married into local Welsh families, and by blood and sentiment they became more Welsh than English. Hanmer followed in this tradition: his wife, Angharad, was Welsh, his daughter married Owain Glyn Dŵr and his son married into the Tudor family. The intriguing problem would be to discover how he viewed himself at the end of his career, as Welsh or English, as Dafydd or David.

As a young man Owain studied in London at the Inns of Court, acquired some expertise as a soldier and was attached to noble retinues, of Henry Bolingbroke and Richard fitz Alan, earl of Arundel. He saw action in Scottish campaigns and elsewhere. As he matured he was educated, trained and equipped to settle as a landowner and squire. At the end of Richard II's reign he was a man of forty or forty-five with a growing family. He ran foul of his neighbour, Lord Grey of Ruthin, and their claims to disputed land were put to the test in the royal courts. While Richard II reigned Grey could not win royal support and overawe his opponent, but in 1400, after Henry IV's successful usurpation, he was in a stronger position and the land was adjudged to him. Resentment was the immediate cause of Glyn Dŵr's rebellion. On 16 September at Glyndyfrdwy he met with a small group, his brother Tudur, his son Gruffydd, his brothers-in-law Gruffydd and Philip Hanmer and Robert Puleston, the dean of St Asaph, a bard identified as a prophet, and a few friends.

In this domestic setting and modest assembly Owain was proclaimed prince of Wales. An attack on Ruthin was the obvious first
consequence and it demonstrated the measure of support for the new
prince. His army was small, with a handful of local landowners who
had much to lose, but it was drawn from his own lordship of
Glyndyfrdwy and from Yale, Edeirnion, Denbigh and Dyffryn
Clwyd. They did not waste time; a series of targets were attacked,
Denbigh, Rhuddlan, Flint, Hawarden, Holt, Oswestry and Welshpool. There they were checked, and the new administration had to
determine whether the revolt was merely a flash in the pan or a
prelude to more serious trouble. They had to gauge whether a local
quarrel between neighbouring landowners was sufficient to bring
about a widespread rejection of English rule, and whether it was the
only occasion for protest.

The support for Owain Glyn Dŵr reflected social unrest and discontent, much of which was due to economic factors. The violent
impact of the plague, with its especially heavy mortality in the Black
Death of 1348–9, can be identified clearly in the lowland areas and
towns, but the effects in upland areas of Europe are less easily traced.
Loss of manpower and shrinking markets affected the pastoral
economy; so, too, did the problems of producing sufficient cereal
crops for basic necessities. If nothing else, there was little money
available. Townsmen and burgesses, shaken by the shrinking population and declining trade, turned defensive and looked for protection for their trade and privileges. In Wales, that meant a sharper
emphasis on the exclusive trading privileges of the boroughs and on
the racial structure of the borough community. Prosperous Welsh
burgesses inspired envy and there were renewed demands that the
penal legislation of an age of conquest, designed to keep the
boroughs English, should be reissued and enforced. Expensive
foreign commitments, the need to maintain a large army and to
ensure internal security in the face of increasingly bitter political
discord made demands for heavy taxation unavoidable. The social
discontent and resentment caused by this financial burden was not
limited to Wales, but here they were exacerbated by the legacy of
conquest and settlement and by the added problem of racial tension.
    North Wales was also much affected by the constitutional
upheavals of the years 1397–9. Richard fitz Alan, earl of Arundel,
was one of the lords appellant opposed to the king in 1388, and when
at length the king was able to take vengeance on his enemies Earl
Richard paid the price of his action. He was arraigned in 1397, and

sentenced to death; no amount of pleading would move the king and on 21 September he was executed and his lands were forfeited. That involved the loss of the fitz Alan lordships of Chirk and Holt in north Wales and the neighbouring lordship of Oswestry, and the balance of power was materially altered. As his fortunes declined, Richard II attached more significance to his tenure of the earldom of Chester, and in 1397 he combined Chester with these fitz Alan lordships to create the principality of Chester as a royal *apanage* to be attached to the crown. If only as a source of fighting men it was valuable for the king and dangerous for his opponents, and for the next few months he found a kind of security with the forces of both the principalities of Wales and Chester behind him. He launched an ill-judged expedition to Ireland in 1399 and that gave Henry Bolingbroke, duke of Hereford, the opportunity to make a bid for power. In his attempt to counter this bid the king recognised that Chester and north Wales were crucial to his survival. At the end of July he commissioned John de Montague, earl of Salisbury, to go from Ireland to north Wales with a body of troops and to raise reinforcements while he himself sailed to Haverfordwest and then made for the north. He was forestalled by Bolingbroke who seized Chester, and he had to be content with Conwy as a base for operations. He was sadly let down by Salisbury who arrived at Conwy, not with an army, but with a force of about 100 men, and his hopes of putting down Bolingbroke's insurrection were dashed. Instead, he was ambushed at Flint, and taken to Chester on the journey which would lead to deposition and death.

The process by which Bolingbroke's usurpation was legalised had been completed by 30 September 1399, and was confirmed by his coronation in mid-October, but the early years of his reign were to be marked by insurrections and rebellions. The first challenge came in January 1400, and its outcome was to affect the course of events in Wales. A group of disaffected magnates tried to capture the king and his heir at Windsor, and although they took the castle, Henry and his son had already escaped. The revolt was quickly put down, and a number of the leading conspirators were lynched, the earls of Kent and Salisbury at Cirencester, Lord Thomas Despenser at Bristol and the earl of Huntingdon in Essex.

Glyn Dŵr's rebellion in the autumn might have been equally short-lived. He defied the king at Glyndyfrdwy on 16 September, and after his initial successes his force was checked, and effectively dispersed, by the king's commander, Hugh Burnell, with the levies which had been raised from Shropshire, Staffordshire and Warwick-

shire. Had Glyn Dŵr been acting in isolation, his show of force
might have ended there, but in Anglesey his kinsmen, Rhys and
Gwilym ap Tudur, were restive and eager to challenge the king, and
with their intervention the revolt continued. Henry IV intervened in
person and the presence of a royal army was enough to pacify north
Wales. As in England, the king was more anxious to placate than to
punish, and he used Henry Percy, son of the earl of Northumberland, as his representative. Many local men were pardoned and
reconciled to the crown, though Owain, Rhys and Gwilym were
excluded. At the same time, the king was urged very strongly to use
harsher methods in Wales and government pressure was perceptibly
increased in two ways: royal judges and tax collectors were active in
the north and, in the new year, legislation was re-enacted to exclude
Welshmen as property owners and burgesses not only from the
Welsh boroughs but from a number of border towns ranging from
Chester to Hereford and Worcester. The harsh reaction bred
resistance; Rhys and Gwilym ap Tudur seized Conwy castle and
Owain carried rebellion into southern Powys, and Henry IV eventually responded with a sweep into west Wales. Despite the posturing,
there was a prospect of a settlement; Owain was in touch with the
earl of Northumberland who was ready to be his friend at court, but
the chance of peace depended upon Owain submitting uncondition-
ally to the king with Northumberland's good will as his only hope of
pardon. At that point Owain recalled the fate of the earls earlier in the
year, and was not prepared to run the risk of submission. It was a
major turning point.

With a quick solution now ruled out, three characteristics of the
revolt became increasingly important. In the first place, the revolt
turned into a long guerrilla war which brought out Glyn Dŵr's flair
as a military commander. Secondly, an issue critical for success was
the search for allies, among the English nobility, and in Ireland,
Scotland and France. The third, and in many ways the most
intriguing feature, is that a long war gave Owain and his leading
advisers the opportunity to do some fundamental thinking about the
structure of a future Welsh state. The conduct of the war and the
search for alliances were closely interlinked. From 1402 to 1405
Owain Glyn Dŵr enjoyed a run of major successes, though decisive
victories eluded him. In 1402 he attacked Ruthin and captured
Reginald Grey, and then carried the war south with a very effective
campaign in Maelienydd. At Bryn Glas, near Pilleth, Welsh archers
serving with the English forces turned against their leaders and contributed substantially to his victory. The capture of one marcher

lord, Edmund Mortimer, was a valuable bonus. During August, in a limited sweep south, Glyn Dŵr attacked the strongholds of Usk, Caerleon, Newport and Cardiff, a clear signal that he was a threat to the security of the southern marchlands. Henry IV responded vigorously, but September produced appalling weather conditions and his armies were totally frustrated. Despite the king's efforts Owain was not seriously threatened. He emerged, in fact, with a political advantage which could be used to good effect in the following year. Henry IV negotiated with him the release of Grey for a ransom of 10,000 marks (£6,666 13*s*. 4*d*.), but Mortimer was left a prisoner. There were already suspicions that his loyalty to Henry IV was half-hearted, and very quickly he made alliance with Glyn Dŵr and married his daughter, Catherine. The ultimate prize for Mortimer was to secure the English throne for his nephew, the earl of March, Richard II's nearest legitimate heir. Mortimer, dangerous in his own right, had powerful connections; his brother-in-law was Henry Percy – Hotspur – heir of the earl of Northumberland who were both men of high political ambition. In 1403 they were building up a justification for rebellion against the king, and one element in their case was that Henry IV had made no attempt to ransom Mortimer. In July, the earl and his son rebelled and planned a quick coup: Henry Percy, with an army of about 14,000 men made for Shrewsbury where Henry, prince of Wales, was based. King Henry forestalled them, joined his son at Shrewsbury, and then took the bold decision to seek battle rather than await an attack. It was a long and costly engagement, with some 6,000 men dead in the final count, among them Henry Percy himself. His father was soon brought to submission. All this happened at such speed that Glyn Dŵr could play no part, but the defeat of Percy at Shrewsbury marked the end of Owain's first attempt to build on the strength of an alliance with English magnates. He himself had a year of considerable success in south Wales where his forces took Dryslwyn, Llanstephan, Emlyn and Carreg Cennen. They gained temporary control of Carmarthen.

He scored greater success in the late spring of 1404 when he took Harlech and Aberystwyth. In the summer he made a formal alliance with France. Squadrons of French ships had been deployed in the previous October to attack Kidwelly and Caernarfon; now he wanted to call on greater resources. The alliance displayed Owain's powers as prince of Wales as no other event had so far done. He summoned assemblies, parliaments at which policy could be approved or publicised, first at Machynlleth and later at Dolgellau; he dispatched ambassadors, his brother-in-law, John Hanmer, and his chancellor, Gruffydd Young, the most brilliant cleric in his entourage, to arrange the terms of alliance with France. If his actions suggested a supreme confidence, so did his title, for he used the style 'prince of Wales by the grace of God', and the arms blazoned on his seal were the royal arms of the princes of Gwynedd. He had firm control of north-west Wales and he was acknowledged by the bishops of Bangor and St Asaph, and the revival of the influence of Gwynedd was certainly well advanced.

He still needed recognition in England and in 1405 Owain made two attempts to secure that. The first came with a renewal of his alliance with Northumberland and Mortimer. In February the earl of Northumberland, Edmund Mortimer and Glyn Dŵr agreed in a formal document, the tripartite indenture, that England should be divided. Part of the border counties were to be incorporated into Wales under Owain's rule; his authority would extend to Chester, Shrewsbury and Worcester. Northumberland was to have northern England and the midlands, and the Mortimer share was to be the Thames valley and southern England. It is a curious farrago, part nonsense, part dream and, perhaps, part prophecy, but it seems to have been taken seriously by the three magnates. Owain's second attempt came through his French alliance which was carefully planned and discussed in advance at a parliament held at Harlech early in August. A show of force was to be mounted by Welsh and French in alliance, and it was believed that that would persuade the English king to make peace with the allies who had already agreed not to make a separate peace with him. Their combined strength would ensure advantageous terms for Owain as prince of Wales. Here was a promising scheme, by no means divorced from reality, save perhaps in one basic respect: Henry IV was not easily frightened. A fleet of 140 French ships arrived at Milford Haven early in August, with an army of 2,600 troops commanded by Jean de Rieux. The core was made up of 800 men at arms and 600 cross-bowmen under their *maître*, Jean de Hangest, a formidable combination in the hands of a good general. Owain was said to have 10,000 men from Wales. After useful local victories at Haverfordwest and Carmarthen, the joint force travelled through south Wales into England, penetrating to Worcester, which was plundered, and then inexplicably taking up a defensive position on Woodbury Hill, 10 miles north-west of the city. There, his army did nothing and achieved nothing. To have the chance of success Owain had to keep up his momentum and, if possible, bring the king to battle; instead he turned back to Wales. Henry took the initiative and carried the struggle into Wales, but there he found once more that the weather was his worst enemy and, as his army retreated, the baggage train was raided and looted.

The main thrust of the year produced stalemate, but elsewhere Owain had to face setbacks. In March a Welsh force attacked Grosmont and they were in the process of plundering when a royalist army under Prince Henry surprised them. In the town and in battle outside Grosmont they suffered heavy casualties of between 800 and 1,000 men. Only a few weeks later Owain's forces attacked Usk castle and were repulsed in disarray by a surprise sally. They were pursued to the banks of the Pwll Melyn, just outside the defences of the borough, where they were trying to regroup, and there they were defeated with heavy loss. The dead included Owain's brother, Tudur, and his son, Gruffydd, was captured and spent the rest of his life as a prisoner in the Tower of London. Henry IV sensed that this might be the moment for a decisive campaign and was poised to attack south Wales when rebellion broke out in northern England, with Archbishop Scrope as the leading figure, and the king's resources had to be used to deal with that. Even so, popular estimates of Glyn Dŵr's chances of success were changing, and the king began to win back the loyalty of many Welshmen, especially in Anglesey and south Wales and, with more reservations, in Brecknock. In 1408 Northumberland, deeply implicated in the northern rising, was defeated and killed at Bramham Moor, and Owain lost a discredited but still useful ally. Scotland also ceased to be a problem for Henry IV when the Scottish king's brother, the duke of Albany, seized power. The elderly king, Robert III, was said to be 'powerless and decrepit', and in 1402 he condoned the arrest and imprisonment of his eldest son who died in suspicious circumstances. His second son, James, was sent to France for his own safety; no safe conduct had been secured from Henry IV, who was almost certainly alerted by Albany, and on the voyage the boy was captured. The news hastened his father's death, and Henry found himself with the Scottish king as his prisoner, while Albany was governor of the realm of Scotland. James remained in custody for eighteen years, and Scotland was effectively neutralised. That, and the eclipse of the power of the earl of Northumberland, removed the hope of the diversions which had so often brought relief to Owain Glyn Dŵr.

For Owain, 1408 was a sad year. Aberystwyth and Harlech were recaptured, and at Harlech his wife, Margaret, their daughter, Catherine Mortimer, with her son and daughters, were all captured and taken to the Tower of London. They were there when Owain's son, Gruffydd, died in 1411, and Catherine and her two daughters all died there in 1413. Owain's principality had disintegrated. He would attempt a raid in Shropshire in 1410 and cause a stir by taking prisoner Dafydd Gam from Brecknock in 1412, but by then he was an old man without hope. Henry V could safely offer him a pardon in 1415. He refused it, but the tradition – if it has any truth in it – that he spent his last years in Herefordshire with his son-in-law and daughter, John and Alice Scudamore, assumes a tacit acceptance of the king's good will and a deliberate policy of leaving him undisturbed at Monnington Straddel. Despite these years of decline, the record of his career is very impressive. He claimed princely authority in 1400, made it effective in 1402 and maintained it until 1408; he remained a threat, however slight, to the English authorities until 1415. Bards might prophesy great things for him, but no prophet could have forecast that record of success and survival.

During his years of power Owain fostered the idea of a Welsh 'state'; to use 'principality' would imply a sharper definition than was possible in practice. There were handicaps, for it had no frontiers and no natural defences. His own homes at Glyndyfrdwy and Sycharth (with other properties) were burned and destroyed by Prince Henry in 1403. He never secured the whole of Gwynedd from Llŷn to Conwy. Harlech castle became his principal residence and the centre of his court. There he was crowned, and to his court at Harlech came enough representatives to reflect his princely dignity. The records suggest that Glyn Dŵr had a sense of style, and he knew the value of the outward trappings of power, but the limitations of his power were all too easily identifiable.

Administration was rudimentary; the tradition of administrative service as it had been in the thirteenth century had long since been broken, though there was some compensation from those with experience in the English administrative system or in the church. Rhys ap Gruffydd ap Llywelyn – Rhys Ddu – the constable of Aberystwyth castle came from a family of local officials; he had worked with the English government in the 1380s and was sheriff of Cardiganshire. Henry Dwnn had served in Ireland and Gascony; he was one of a prominent burgess family from Kidwelly, well experienced in the affairs of his borough. John Trevor, bishop of St Asaph, and Glyn Dŵr's appointee to Bangor, Llywelyn Bifort (anglicised in formal records as Lewis Biford) together with his friend and chancellor, Gruffydd Young, provided a valuable stiffening from their experience in the church. There was no effective financial administration. The area of north-west Wales which was secure could not provide money enough to maintain the court or to finance an army. What came from other parts of Wales was collected spasmodically and could not be estimated in advance. Plunder and thinly disguised extortion provided short-term supplies but left a legacy of bitterness. The persistent complaints of royal officials that arms, horses and supplies were being smuggled into Wales from the border counties point to the spending power which Owain could command. Behind the trappings of power was the practical approach of the seasoned guerrilla leader finding troops and resources as and where he could. There is, too, a curious disparity between the contemporary claim that Welsh support for Owain was overwhelming, and the steady record of those men of influence who held back or refused their support. Welsh sheriffs served in Carmarthenshire throughout the period of the Glyn Dŵr revolt, and there was no dramatic change in Cardiganshire where a Welsh sheriff served before Glyn Dŵr took possession of Aberystwyth and another local man, Thomas Roubury, was sheriff immediately after the castle and town were recovered by the English in 1408. Roubury had been deputy-justiciar in Richard II's reign and he occurred later as a burgess of Aberystwyth. It is ironic that Owain's last captive was the representative of a distinguished family from Brecknock. Dafydd ap Llywelyn ap Hywel was a man of high ancestry belied by his unprepossessing appearance and his unflattering nickname, Dafydd Gam – Dafydd with the squint. Like his predecessors, he was consistently loyal to the English lords of Brecknock; he served with Henry V and was killed fighting at Agincourt. The picture of Owain Glyn Dŵr with Wales firmly behind him confronting an adversary bedevilled by indiscipline and rebellion is an oversimplification which will not stand.

There was a view, perhaps a vision, of a larger principality with bolder and less regional ambitions. Owain Glyn Dŵr gathered around himself a group of able clerics; they formed the core of the equivalent of a modern think-tank, providing Owain with ideas and plans for the future. They all shared strong Welsh loyalties coupled with a sense of personal disappointment. One whose career had achieved some distinction was Ieuan ap Llywelyn, better known in a European setting as John Trevor. Serving in an international church, he found it simpler to identify himself from his home village. He was a legist, and by 1386 he had begun his advance in the hierarchy with an appointment as precentor of Bath and Wells. In 1389 he was elected bishop of St Asaph and he travelled to Rome to

secure papal confirmation. It was withheld, and Trevor remained in
Rome working in the papal curia. Five years later, by the more
secure means of papal provision, he was again appointed to St
Asaph, and this time there was no bar. He served Richard II as an
ambassador to Scotland, and could be identified as a minor
administrator-bishop, a royal agent with valuable experience of the
papal court. In 1399 he played politics and switched his support to
Bolingbroke; he was appointed to the commission to depose
Richard II, and read out the commission's sentence in parliament.
His adherence to Henry IV made his cathedral and diocese targets for
Glyn Dŵr's forces and his church and estates suffered at their hands.
It was not until late in 1404 that this able but not very attractive
character abandoned Henry IV for Glyn Dŵr. For the next few years
his legal expertise and diplomatic experience was available for
Owain to use. He was outmatched in ability by Gruffydd Young,
another cleric who served both Richard II and Henry IV. He was
illegitimate, and his career was overshadowed by bastardy.
Rewarded with the benefice of Llanbadarn and the archdeaconry of
Merioneth, he seemed to have reached his peak. After his defection
Glyn Dŵr made him his chancellor and he was closely associated
with the prince in forming and executing policy.

   The French alliance brought obligations as well as advantages, and
the Welsh delegates to the French court were persuaded to support
the claims of the Avignon pope against his rival at Rome. In 1406, at
Pennal, near Machynlleth, this promise was fulfilled. Owain Glyn
Dŵr undertook to support Benedict XIII, but at the same time a
radical new policy for the Welsh church was presented and the
French king was asked to use his influence with the pope to see it
accepted. Wales was to have an archbishopric at St David's; that
would restore the dignity of the church as it had been in the time of
St David. The province of this archbishopric was not confined to
Wales, but was to include five English dioceses, Exeter, Bath,
Hereford, Worcester and Coventry and Lichfield. Within the four
Welsh dioceses all the bishops and clergy were to be Welsh speaking.
The pope was to revoke all grants of Welsh churches to English
monasteries and colleges, and one of the major consequences of the
Norman invasions and settlements was thus to be negated. That
sweeping break with the past could be stated very simply: it was
much more difficult to envisage how the rights of presentation
might be restored to what were called the 'true patrons', but the
intention was plainly to have patrons in Wales presenting candidates
for institution to Welsh churches. The last feature of this policy state-

ment was to ask for two universities to be founded, one in north Wales and the other in the south. That would make Wales independent of England (or of continental Europe) where education was concerned, and the men of ability intended for royal administration or for the church in Wales could be trained at home. Although many commentators would like to claim these ideas for Owain himself they go far beyond the more limited aims for which he fought. They bear the mark of a zealot and reformer, and that was almost certainly Gruffydd Young. At last he could see the rewards of his services. In 1407 Benedict XIII appointed him to Bangor; Lewis Biford could not accept the rejection of the Roman allegiance and he was eased out of the way. Very quickly Young laid claim to St David's; it is hard to escape the conviction that he hoped to guide the province he wished to create and saw himself as a future archbishop of St David's. It was a vain hope. The crown did not wait for Owain Glyn Dŵr to disappear from the scene before Young's plans were frustrated. Henry Chichele was appointed to St David's in 1408 with the special commission to reconcile schismatics with the Roman papacy. For Young there was no political reconciliation and his career lay in future outside the sphere of English influence. In 1418, after Scotland had accepted Martin V as the true pope, he was provided to the Scottish bishopric of Ross, and five years later he was made titular bishop of Hippo and lived in exile in France.

In one important sense the Pennal scheme was well based and realistic: an independent Welsh church was a sound political ambition. A literate class, loyal to the prince, was an essential part of the pattern, and the prince would need a wide range of patronage from which to reward his servants. The insistence that clerics should have Welsh was a double safeguard: it ensured pastoral care for the people and it excluded the influence of the English king, of the marcher lords and of English clerics. In another sense, a plan which looked beyond the boundaries of Wales and envisaged five English dioceses as part of a Welsh province was very seriously handicapped. It implied a capacity to inflict a massive defeat on the English king which was far beyond Glyn Dŵr's resources.

The seventy years which separated the eclipse of Owain Glyn Dŵr (1415) from the succession of Henry VII (1485) were years of sad decline for Wales. In the short term, the campaigns in France of Henry V and the English military commanders who maintained the war and occupation there under Henry VI provided a welcome relief. Men who had fought for and against Owain Glyn Dŵr found

occupation, and often rewards, as soldiers and administrators in
France. John Scudamore, Glyn Dŵr's son-in-law, was captain of
Harfleur in 1416, and six years later he was responsible for the
security of the port there. Maredudd ab Owain, Glyn Dŵr's son,
served Henry VI in France after his reconciliation with the crown.
Dafydd Gam of Brecknock and his son-in-law, Roger Vaughan of
Bredwardine, both loyal to the Lancastrian kings, fought and died at
Agincourt. About 4,700 men served in Normandy alone, and there
was ample opportunity for Welsh contingents to join them. A succession of Welsh captains, often served by large numbers of Welsh
soldiers, were active in northern France. Richard Gethin, originally
from Builth, was captain of Mantes and in the 1430s he had made
enough money to be able to lend the duke of York £1,000. Gruffydd
Dwnn of Kidwelly served in France for some thirty years, fighting
at Agincourt in 1415, and continuing in France until he was taken
prisoner at Dieppe in 1445. Among his responsibilities was the command of troops at Tancarville. He acquired at least five lordships in
Normandy, including Alençon (Orne) and Fervaques (Calvados).
David Howell, from Pembrokeshire, was given the barony of Briars
and the lordship of Aufreville in 1437 and gained more estates in later
years. Perhaps the best known and most successful Welsh commander in these years was Matthew Goch, whose nickname was
anglicised as Gough. The son of Owain Goch, bailiff of the manor of
Hanmer in Maelor Saesneg, he moved into the king's service. He
fought at Cravant in 1423 and in the critical battle of Verneuil in
1424, and he was given command of a number of key towns and
castles during the course of his service, Laval, St-Denis, Le Mans,
Bellême and Bayeux. He was taken prisoner in 1432 but his release
was arranged and he continued in active service until the battle of
Formigny. His service brought rewards in eastern Normandy, with
estates at Rouen, Gisors, Caux, Evreux and Harcourt. When the
English withdrew from France, he was entrusted with the surrender
of Anjou and Maine to the French, planned in 1446–7 and, after some
delay, carried through in 1448, and within two years he had returned
to England where, as a reward, he was given a share of the responsibility for the Tower of London. He was killed in 1450 defending
London Bridge against the insurgents in Jack Cade's rebellion.

During these years political conditions in England were deterio-
rating steadily. Henry V's brothers, John, duke of Bedford, and
Humphrey, duke of Gloucester, had been given an ambiguous and
uneasy responsibility. Bedford's principal duties were seen to be in
Normandy and, if the duke of Burgundy would not act as regent, in

France. Gloucester was intended to be a regent acting for the king in England, but from the outset he and the king's council could not agree on the terms of reference by which he should discharge that duty. Until his death in 1435, Bedford was an effective commander-in-chief in France, and at times an influential figure in English politics. Gloucester, acknowledged as the king's protector, was to be the principal figure in the king's council unless Bedford himself was present. He survived until 1447, but he was never free from powerful enemies at the court and in the council. Henry Beaufort, bishop of Winchester, was constantly at odds with him, and in the later years of his life, William de la Pole, earl of Suffolk – from 1444, marquis of Suffolk – was his principal enemy. Suffolk found support from Henry VI's young wife, Margaret of Anjou, and he deliberately planned the overthrow of Duke Humphrey. First, Gloucester's wife, Eleanor Cobham, was accused of witchcraft, and then the duke was arrested and kept in close confinement at Bury St Edmunds. The shock apparently induced a stroke, and within three days the duke was dead. Suffolk had built up a dangerous edifice of power which included the offices of justiciar of north Wales and of Chester. In 1448 he was made duke of Suffolk. With a small coterie, and especially with Adam Moleyns, bishop of Chichester, and William Ayscough, bishop of Salisbury, he had manipulated the power of the crown to his own advantage and to the detriment of his personal opponents. So great was the cry for his blood that Henry VI banished him for five years, using his prerogative powers to circumvent the wishes of the council. As he sailed from East Anglia to France, his ship was waylaid and he was murdered. His closest colleagues also died by violence, the bishop of Chichester a few weeks before the duke, and the bishop of Salisbury less than two months after Suffolk's murder. Suffolk was not alone in the search for power. Edmund Beaufort, successively earl and marquis of Dorset and earl and duke of Somerset, had the king's confidence and may be said to have worked in collusion with Suffolk before the association became dangerous.

In the background during these critical years was a magnate closely associated with Wales, Richard, duke of York. He was a great-grandson of Edward III. In 1425 he inherited the lands of his uncle, Edmund Mortimer, though he was made to wait seven years before he received formal livery of these estates. York illustrates the major problem of this period. During the fourteenth century, lands and titles had been concentrated in the hands of a small group of magnates. The marriage alliances which Edward III had arranged for his family brought a number of great inheritances into his immediate family circle, but there was a price to pay: each of these families acquired royal blood and at least the basis for a claim to the throne. The usurpation of Henry IV left the Lancastrian dynasty with a flawed title, and political weakness might invite a direct challenge for the crown. The duke of York might be content to be recognised as protector of the king and as his eventual heir, but once a son was born to Henry VI and Margaret of Anjou in October 1453, the duke's political ambitions must change. Conflict between Lancaster and York, with the throne as the prize, was increasingly a possibility, and in May 1455, with the first battle of St Albans, that conflict became a reality.

Wales was divided between the two protagonists and their supporters. The Lancastrian dynasty controlled Chester, Flintshire, Anglesey, Caernarfonshire, Merionethshire, Cardiganshire and Carmarthenshire; they also held the lordships of Cantref Bychan, Cilgerran, Kidwelly, Monmouth and the three castles. Their supporters were scattered all along the marches, and they were especially strong in the south-west; the fitz Alan earls of Arundel in Oswestry, Chirk, Caus and Clun; the Stafford dukes of Buckingham in Gwynllŵg and Brecknock; the Audleys in Cemais; the Devereux in Weobley (just over the border in Herefordshire) and Narberth; the earls of Wiltshire in Tallacharn (Laugharne); the Talbots at Goodrich; and the earls of Pembroke at Emlyn and Pembroke itself. The duke of York, with his rich Mortimer inheritance, held Denbigh, Montgomery, Cydewain, Ceri, Maelienydd, Gwrtheyrnion, Cwmwd Deuddwr, Cleobury Mortimer, Wigmore, Ludlow (on the English side of the border), Radnor, Ewyas Lacy, Blaenllyfni, Caerleon and Usk. His supporters were well endowed: Grey held Ruthin; Norfolk held Bromfield and Yale and Chepstow; Henry Gray, Lord Powys, whose father had married the heiress of Edward Charlton, held Powys Wenwynwyn; the Nevills were established at Abergavenny; and the earl of Warwick held Glamorgan and Elfael. Whatever happened in an English contest would affect Wales very markedly.

In a curious way, the marcher lords were more divorced from Wales and Welsh interests than at any time in the past. They were much preoccupied in France or England; they tended to make rare visits to their Welsh estates, and these visits became formal progresses at which they received generous gifts from their tenants. Local affairs and local administration were left in the hands of deputies and agents. The income from their lordships had been greatly reduced during the period of Glyn Dŵr's dominance, perhaps by as much as 66 per cent, and recovery was slow and limited. It has been estimated that, in Henry VI's reign, the profits of judicial lordship fell to about 40 per cent of the peak level of the four-teenth century, and even after the accession of Edward IV there was only a slight improvement. Redemption fines to buy off judicial eyres remained the most profitable alternative for the great lords of the march. To avoid the Great Sessions in Brecknock could still pro-duce a payment of 2,000 marks (£1,333 6s. 8d.) in 1418–19 and the same figure was being paid as late as 1503: that represents a decline of about 25 per cent on the yield in the last quarter of the fourteenth cen-tury. The king's agents were not slow to use the same device in Wales. At Carmarthen, over some sixty years, only twelve of fifty-two sessions were allowed to run their full course, while the remainder produced substantial payments in lieu of the fines and profits which might accrue from the normal course of justice. The practice might mean a safe income; it certainly avoided the time and expense of collecting fines: but it also prevented any serious attempt to put down lawlessness. Attempts made in the fifteenth century to check this method of raising money produced little result, but only in the sixteenth century were efforts made to limit and finally to forbid the practice. In 1526 the council of Princess Mary banned the practice in Wales, and in 1542, with the establishment of the court of Great Sessions, the maintenance of law and order was given its full priority.

Under Henry VI, the highest offices of royal administration were given to the greatest of the English magnates: Humphrey, duke of Gloucester, and Richard Nevill, earl of Warwick, both served as justiciar of south Wales; Henry Stafford, duke of Buckingham, held the same post from 1483, but he combined with it the tenure of the office of chamberlain for south Wales, and of constable of the castles of Carmarthen, Cardigan and Aberystwyth. He also held the major offices in north Wales. He might have exercised almost absolute power, but he did not attempt to carry out any of his duties in person. The consequence of this was that, for much of the fifteenth century, Wales was administered by prominent Welshmen acting for absentee officers. No single example is more striking than the career of Gruffydd ap Nicholas and the extension of his power to his sons. When he first appears in the record it is as the king's approver for the lordship of Dinefwr in 1425; eleven years later he was sheriff of Carmarthenshire, but the care of the lordship of Dinefwr remained an important element in his duties and his income. He held judicial sessions for Duke Humphrey, and he is found in charge of the castle of Carreg Cennen. His most profitable office was that of deputy-justiciar; although he never held a higher office, and could never claim direct responsibility for government, he was effectively ruler of south Wales, He could ignore instructions from the justiciar; he could link his three sons in local offices with himself. When men of his standing chose to use force, or to employ armed retainers, justice was no more likely to be obtained in Wales than in many regions of England where power and a strong personal retinue could influence decisions. The ultimate beneficiary of Gruffydd's steady advance in Welsh administration was his grandson, Sir Rhys ap Thomas, who became chamberlain and justiciar for south Wales, exercising in his own right the office which Gruffydd ap Nicholas had exercised as a deputy. There were hazards and casualties, not least perhaps because Gruffydd could be ruthless in his treatment of other Welshmen working in the administration. In Cardiganshire, Gruffydd ap Dafydd was employed by Sir Edward Stradling as deputy-chamberlain in the 1430s. Gruffydd ap Nicholas, his son, Thomas, and others of their following, tried to move into Cardiganshire and to build up their influence there. For three years they ignored all attempts to uncover their activities and to discipline them. When a commission finally sat in judgement on them in 1442, they escaped with small fines, but the deputy-chamberlain was exposed as the culpable royal official who was either involved with them or duped by them, and he was fined 1,000 marks (£666 13s. 4d.). He did not, as it appears, choose his company or his enterprises with sufficient care, and he was continually in trouble and sometimes in prison over the next fifteen years. It was only in 1458 that he was given a pardon for his offences.

The era of government by deputy was broken by the appointment of William Herbert as justiciar for south Wales in May 1461. He was a Welshman, firmly rooted in south-east Wales as a leading tenant and steward of the duke of York in his lordship of Usk. His mother was the daughter of Dafydd Gam, a strong Lancastrian. In his youth he had served in France under Matthew Gough, and in 1450 he was taken prisoner at the battle of Formigny, and his services in Normandy were rewarded with a knighthood at the end of that year. Politically he was in some difficulty as a reliable supporter of the Lancastrians and as a member of York's entourage. At different times, each party saw him as a desirable ally and agent in Wales, and he himself was not unshaken in his loyalties. In 1456 he was involved in a major attack on the Lancastrians in Wales, leading an armed force

against young Edmund, earl of Richmond, and capturing Carmarthen. Edmund was imprisoned and although he was soon released,
he died within a few weeks, perhaps from a disease which he had
picked up while he was in custody. The decisive influence at that
point was that of Margaret of Anjou, who won Herbert over,
secured his pardon and kept him loyal to Henry VI. In those circumstances he was given estates forfeited by York and Warwick in 1459.
The revival of Yorkist fortunes in the 1460s made him a valuable
recruit, and largely, as it seems, through Warwick's influence he was
won over to the new dynasty. Hence his appointment as justiciar in
1461, the grant of a peerage as Lord Herbert of Raglan at Edward
IV's coronation, and the appointment as a knight of the Garter in
1462.

Herbert was intended to hold Wales for the Yorkists, and he
achieved this end by assuming direct responsibility for government
and administration. He presided in person over the Great Sessions
held in 1462 and 1463, and again from 1465 to 1468; to be present for
six sessions was unprecedented. He contained the activities of the
Lancastrians in Wales and, in 1468, in a most striking symbolic
action, he secured the capture of Harlech castle, which had held out
against all attempts to take it from 1461. The earldom of Pembroke
was his reward for that achievement. He was effectively Edward
IV's viceroy in Wales. It may not have been easy for one wooed so
assiduously by both sides in the internal conflict to maintain his
political judgement unimpaired. Herbert seems to have underrated
the influence of Warwick at Edward's court, and to have run the
dangerous risk of giving him offence. In 1466 he secured for his son,
the younger William Herbert, the title of Lord Dunster, and this
enhancement of his family roused Warwick's jealousy. Nemesis
came in 1469. Pembroke was summoned by Edward IV to join
forces with the earl of Devon and to check a group of malcontents
from Yorkshire. The two leaders quarrelled and Devon withdrew
his forces on the night before the battle. When Pembroke's forces
were fully committed at Edgecote, near Banbury, they found themselves opposed by the earl of Warwick with a large army. They were
defeated with heavy loss; nearly 200 Welsh gentry were killed, with
at least 2,000 soldiers. For a country with a small population, it was
a grievous loss to bear. The earl of Pembroke and his brother,
Richard Herbert, were executed next day. Their tragedy was that
they were acting on the king's behalf, and they were the victims of
Warwick's jealous spite.

The struggle for power and the occasional resort to battle provide

the framework for William Herbert's career. The Yorkists did not
lack good leadership. In Richard, duke of York, they had a vigorous
though not very perceptive leader. His son, Edward, earl of March,
growing to manhood in the years of conflict, promised continuity
and displayed greater maturity of judgement than his father. The
Lancastrians were sadly handicapped by the personality of Henry VI,
always weak and ineffective, and at times deranged. All the strength
of his cause lay in his wife, Margaret of Anjou. Neither Yorkist nor
Lancastrian were free from the danger of overmighty subjects
anxious to impose their own will on policy, with Somerset and
Warwick as the two most prominent and dangerous figures in the
conflict. In terms of land and resources the Lancastrians were strong
in Wales, but they were weak in terms of leadership, and in the 1450s
the pressing question was to determine who should lead their cause
in Wales. The promise of strength lay in Henry VI's young half-
brothers, Edmund and Jasper. In 1449 the king knighted them, and
in 1453 he made Edmund earl of Richmond and Jasper earl of
Pembroke. While Edmund was cast as the leader in Wales, Jasper's
earldom was a reminder that the royal dynasty did not ignore the
claims of their house to lands and authority in west Wales. Edmund
was to have four years of activity before his death at the beginning of
November 1456. He began the task of holding in check Gruffydd ap
Nicholas and his sons, but it needed more time than he would have
to wrest their power from them. He was still a young man in his
mid-twenties when he died. At that point, the influence of Margaret
of Anjou was critical, and she gave her full support to his brother,
Jasper. He proved himself devoted to Henry VI's interests, and,
whatever the odds, he maintained a steady pressure on the Yorkists
in Wales. He could not weaken the appeal which Duke Richard, and
even more, his son, Edward, earl of March, could make in Wales.
Their success in winning support among the Welsh gentry and in
recruiting Welsh soldiers played a major part in their ultimate
triumph. The decisive events took place in England. In 1460
Warwick defeated Henry VI's army at Northampton and took the
king prisoner. Margaret of Anjou fled to Harlech, then to Pembroke
and finally to Scotland. Heartened by success, the duke of York,
who was in Ireland, returned to England explicitly to claim the
crown, but he could not persuade the lords of the council to accede,
and he had to be content with the role of protector and heir-apparent
(despite the claims of Edward, prince of Wales). He set off for the
north and in December at Wakefield he was persuaded to leave the
comparative safety of the town and to give battle to an army raised

by Somerset and Northumberland. There he was defeated and killed, and when his body was identified he was beheaded, and his head was set up at York on public display. In mockery of his ambition to be king, it was crowned with a paper crown.

York's son, the earl of March, was the residual legatee of these events. Queen Margaret threw away the advantages of Wakefield when, through indiscipline, her troops plundered St Albans. By no means would the chief citizens of London allow her army to enter the capital to perpetrate the same offence there. Meanwhile, Edward, earl of March, was concerned for the defence of the western border of his kingdom. A Welsh army, led by Jasper, earl of Pembroke, joined forces with an invasion force commanded by the earl of Wiltshire, and as they marched towards the English border Edward moved to check them. They met at Mortimer's Cross, some 6 miles from Leominster, and there Edward routed them. As with the battle of Edgecote, the losses suffered by commanders and men from a particular region were very heavy, and the battle lingers in Welsh memory for that reason. Earl Jasper and the earl of Wiltshire were among those who made their escape from the débâcle, but one elderly champion of the Lancastrian cause was captured, Owain – the anglicised form, Owen, would be more appropriate – second husband of Henry V's queen, Catherine, and father of Edmund and Jasper. He was executed in the market place at Hereford. To the last, he did not believe that execution was possible, but he died with quiet dignity. There is, inevitably, a touch of distortion about Welsh influence in the course of the dynastic struggle. In the events which led to the overthrow of Edward IV, the restoration of Henry VI, the death of Warwick at the battle of Barnet and the final eclipse of the Lancastrians at Tewkesbury in 1471, Wales and Welshmen played little part. There remains one comment: in all that has been said about Edmund, earl of Richmond, and Jasper, earl of Pembroke, and their father, Owen, one simple word has so far been omitted, the word – Tudor.

9

A NEW DAWN?
THE COMING OF THE TUDORS

The Tudors, distant descendants of Ednyfed Fychan, the administrator who had served Llywelyn ap Gruffydd and, after his death, Edward I, were substantial landholders in Anglesey and strong supporters of Richard II, under whom they acquired a series of local offices which added to their wealth and influence. Their hostility to Henry IV and the Lancastrians led them into open rebellion and their activities complemented the early phases of the revolt of Owain Glyn Dŵr. They were penalised heavily. Rhys ap Tudur was captured and executed in 1412; his brother, Gwilym, was pardoned in the following year; some of the forfeited Tudor estates passed into the hands of their niece, Morfudd, and her husband, Gwilym ap Gruffydd. Maredudd ap Tudur, who may have been the youngest of his generation, kept his share of the family's lands, and his son, Owen – the anglicised form has to be used in this context – found employment in the royal service as an officer in the household of Henry V's queen, Catherine. After Henry V's death, leading politicians were anxious that his widow should not remarry, though Cardinal Beaufort saw her as a valuable alliance for one of his young kinsmen. To prevent that, a statute was passed in 1427–8 requiring the king's permission for any future marriage and providing heavy penalties for anyone who ignored the statute. The queen and her Welsh esquire formed a strong attachment and perhaps as early as 1431–2 they were married in defiance of the statute. It might be expected that Owen ap Maredudd would use Maredudd as a convenient surname, but for some reason his grandfather's name,

Tudor, was used instead. Over the next five years, they had four children, but open acknowledgement of the marriage and the family was delayed until after Catherine's death in 1437. The immediate penalties imposed on Owen were severe but they were soon mitigated. Of their children, a daughter died in childhood, and one son, Owen, became a monk at Westminster, and lived until 1502. Henry VII paid his funeral expenses. Two other boys, Edmund and Jasper, were cared for at the nunnery of Barking for some five years after their mother's death. Then they were brought into Henry VI's immediate circle and grew up as part of his family. They could give him companionship and, in their adult years, advice, but they were not likely to be a source of political danger for him; though they could claim a king of France as a grandfather, they had no dynastic connection with the Lancastrians. A critical moment came in the family's history when Edmund Tudor married Margaret Beaufort, daughter and heiress of John Beaufort, duke of Somerset. John of Gaunt's children by his mistress and second wife, Katherine Swynford, were legitimised in 1397, and the eldest of them, John, was Margaret's grandfather. They were not intended to be contestants for the English crown, but that was a difficult ban to enforce. Margaret's inheritance and shadowy claim were powerful inducements; that was part of the attraction which made her a valuable bride. Her first marriage was to John de la Pole, son of the ambitious marquis of Suffolk, a marriage annulled in 1453. Two years later she was married to Edmund Tudor. They had one son, Henry, born at Pembroke three months after Earl Edmund's death. Whatever claim he had to the English throne came to him through his mother. Margaret Beaufort did not remain a widow for long. Within a matter of months she had married Henry Stafford, brother of the duke of Buckingham, who lived until 1471; her fourth husband was Thomas, Lord Stanley, to whom Henry VII gave the earldom of Derby a few days before his coronation in October 1485.

Jasper Tudor showed all the qualities of a fully committed political leader who could never gain anything of substance for himself. He was devoted to the interests of Margaret Beaufort and her son, the young earl of Richmond. The accession of Edward IV marked Jasper's eclipse; he had been staunch in his support for Henry VI during the years of civil strife; now for a decade he was a vigorous advocate of the claims of Henry VI, as an ambassador, conspirator and active military commander. He appeared in arms at Bamborough and in north-west Wales; he was at times the pensioner of Louis XI of France; he maintained a cordial relationship with the duke of Brittany. He had to watch many of his estates, and in 1468, his earldom of Pembroke, given to Herbert. He played a part in the diplomacy which led to the coup of October 1470 and the restoration of Henry VI, but Edward IV's successes at Barnet and Tewkesbury soon ended that brief episode. Then the death of Prince Edward at Tewkesbury and the murder of Henry VI radically changed the political prospects for the surviving heirs of the Lancastrian dynasty. From that time until 1485 Jasper, with his nephew, Henry, were exiles, dependent upon the generosity of Duke Francis of Brittany and upon the changes of alliance in France. At times, they were kept in custody, not always in the same castle; there was no doubt that Edward IV was anxious to have them back in England under his own surveillance. Edward's death in 1483 and the accession of his son, Edward V, promised little change for them. Then Richard, duke of Gloucester, made his bid for power and took the crown for himself, and the prospect of a renewal of the struggle for the throne was reopened. There were too many claimants for comfort, though only two were adults: apart from Richard III, Henry, duke of Buckingham represented the line of Thomas of Woodstock, and Henry Tudor represented the Beaufort claim. Two boys also had strong claims: Edward Stafford, son of the duke of Buckingham, and John de la Pole, nephew of Edward IV.

Both attempts to overthrow Richard III had strong Welsh associations. Buckingham moved first. He had been given striking evidence of Richard's confidence in him. In addition to wide powers in western England he was made justiciar of north and south Wales, and the greater castles and lordships of Wales were entrusted to him. It was convenient that Wales should be in the hands of a viceroy. What may not have been seen at the time was that Buckingham's personal influence was limited largely to Brecknock: beyond that there was a big gap between nominal authority and real power. As Richard was making a formal progress through the midlands and the north in the summer of 1483, Buckingham left him and turned aside to his lordship of Brecknock. At Brecon castle, Bishop Morton of Ely was held in custody, and there the two men explored the possibilities of open revolt. It looks as if Buckingham could not decide whether to make a bid in his own right, as at first he probably intended, or whether to aim at the role once played by the earl of Warwick, and to set Henry Tudor up as king with himself as the power behind the throne. Indeed, he may well have suffered because his own bid for power coincided with the involved planning already in hand to see Henry Tudor established as king. By the autumn he was a marked man, and in mid-October he was proclaimed a rebel. In a crisis he proved himself a poor leader. Powerful and influential as he was, Buckingham could not muster and hold a convincing force, perhaps because he had been so deeply implicated in Richard III's activities after Edward IV had died. Buckingham had difficulty in moving from Brecon into Herefordshire: Morton abandoned him, and others held aloof, and in the end he abandoned his men and fled. He was taken prisoner and handed over to the sheriff of Shropshire. Trial and sentence were a formality, if not a mockery, and he was executed at Salisbury.

For Henry Tudor, an abortive attempt at a landing on the south coast of England in 1483 was a setback. In 1485, heavily subsidised by the king of France, Henry and Jasper sailed from Honfleur and made for Milford Haven. For nearly fifteen years, Wales had been under Yorkist control and as far as the Tudors were concerned it was, as it were, a neglected constituency. Their hope was that in the south Rhys ap Thomas would rally to their support while in the north they relied heavily on Henry's step-father, Lord Stanley, and his connections in Cheshire and Flintshire. Failing a quick response, it was difficult for them to decide on the route into England which would avoid premature confrontation with Richard III's supporters and which would enable them to link up with Stanley's forces. They decided in favour of a route which took them to Cardigan and northwards to Machynlleth; there they turned north-east and travelled towards Welshpool on their way to Shrewsbury. Minor reinforcements came to them at Cardigan, but the most important of their potential allies, Rhys ap Thomas, held back. Only when they were near Welshpool did he decide to back their venture. It was a gamble for the leading figure in a prosperous Welsh family to take and later propaganda put out by the Tudors and by Rhys' family may obscure the truth rather than reveal it. Perhaps Rhys had to decide at what point he might most profitably bargain for power if Henry's invasion was successful: to leave it too late might have seen him excluded from the spoils of victory.

If Welsh support was late in rallying to Henry, the support of Thomas, Lord Stanley, and his brother, Sir William, was delayed to the last possible moment. Sir William Stanley's forces and Henry's army were together briefly in Lichfield, but they did not form a single army, and Sir William retained a complete freedom of action by moving his troops to Tamworth. Lord Stanley, who had been lucky to escape from earlier intrigues by his wife without loss, was inhibited by the fact that Richard III held his heir, George, Lord

Strange, as a hostage. He manoeuvred his forces so that the king might interpret his movements as those of an army shadowing an enemy. As Richard's forces and Henry's troops drew up for battle near Bosworth, the Stanley contingent stood aloof capable of moving in either direction. Only with battle fully committed did Sir William Stanley show his hand and support Henry. Lord Stanley's support was tentative and ineffectual. It is trite but true to say that the success of Henry's venture depended upon the outcome of the battle of Bosworth; right to the last moment, experienced politicians could not read the signs of the times and assess which way to give their allegiance.

In the 1460s, Jasper Tudor had mobilised the efforts of a number of Welsh poets to strengthen the appeal of the Tudor family in Wales as leading supporters of the Tudor cause. He and his nephew knew the value of such propaganda as they were preparing to attack Richard III. Their choice of Wales for their initial landing, and as the area in which they hoped to see local forces rallying to them, was deliberately made. So was the use of the red dragon as Henry's standard. But their attempt to mobilise local forces met with very limited success. They cannot easily be presented as a dynasty, enthroned with strong Welsh support. Their primary target was the English kingdom, and once the dynasty was established, Wales and Welsh interests became subsidiary interests. Henry VII appointed Rhys ap Thomas to a position of power, though not of supreme authority. He was knighted after the battle of Bosworth, and given offices in the lordships of Brecknock and Builth; he was also made chamberlain of Carmarthen and Cardigan. He had to wait until 1496 before he could be appointed justiciar of south Wales; his appointment as a knight of the Garter in 1505 was the crowning achievement for him. Other Welshmen and men from the marches served the king loyally and were continued in office when Henry VIII succeeded. But already, from 1489–90, Henry VII was making use of a council in the marches made up, not of Welshmen, but of English magnates and officials, and the future would lie with the development of the powers of that council, notably when Henry VIII augmented the council of Princess Mary and gave it firm powers. Henry VII had to win his major political battles in England; it was left to his son to endorse Cromwell's view of the unity of the kingdom of England as an empire, and to incorporate Wales and the marches firmly into the English state through the Act of Union. It would be Henry VIII who would also endorse the view that a single kingdom required a single common language. Nowhere was that more obvious or more significant than in the sphere of religion; the use of an English Bible, and, at later stages, of an English Prayer Book contributed a great deal to the emergence of a common culture throughout England. It was intended to embrace a wider area of culture and tradition, and in Cornwall especially royal policy saw the eclipse of the old Celtic language and culture. The same was expected in Wales: the establishment of schools like Christ College at Brecon was seen as a means of educating boys of promise in English and the classics so that they could be useful servants of the state. In fact, those who wished to profit from such an approach had to migrate to England and seek careers there, and for the fortunate few, education at the Inns of Court and a career in the law was the means of finding wealth and status.

Yet, curiously, Henry VII retained a strong affection for Wales and things Welsh. He shared the Welsh passion for genealogy, and for Welsh history and romance; it is no accident that he revived the use of the name, Arthur, and linked his family with a legendary past. He patronised harpists, and with Welshmen at his court he observed the feast of St David as an important occasion. Historians, looking beyond his day, can identify one decision made by his grand-daughter, Elizabeth, and see it as a major element in the survival of Welsh consciousness and Welsh culture: the decision to authorise the use of a Welsh Prayer Book and a Welsh Bible. Outwardly, it ran counter to the whole trend of Tudor policy, and at a time when the queen was imposing a single religious pattern upon her people it allowed a division in this most sensitive area of Tudor policy. But it was a decision entirely in accord with the acumen and the emotional outlook of the first, and most Welsh, of the Tudor monarchs. Enshrined in language, Welsh culture could survive; that was by no means the least part of the legacy of the young earl of Richmond, born at Pembroke, who survived to establish himself and his dynasty in the English kingdom.

SELECT BIBLIOGRAPHY

This select bibliography has been compiled for English readers on two basic principles: it contains those studies which have formed my own understanding of Welsh history, and those studies to which readers may turn for more detailed analysis of individuals, periods and problems. Place of publication, unless otherwise indicated, is London.

Abbreviations

Arch. Camb.	*Archaeologia Cambrensis*
BBCS	*Bulletin of the Board of Celtic Studies: Bwletin y Bwrdd Gwybodau Celtaidd*
CMCS	*Cambridge Medieval Celtic Studies*
EHR	*English Historical Review*
JHSCW	*Journal of the Historical Society of the Church in Wales*
NLWJ	*National Library of Wales Journal: Cylchgrawn Llyfrgell Genedlaethol Cymru*
PBA	*Proceedings of the British Academy*
PBC	*Proceedings of the Battle Conference on Anglo-Norman Studies* (continued as *Anglo-Norman Studies*)
TRHist.S	*Transactions of the Royal Historical Society*
Trans. B&GAS	*Transactions of the Bristol and Gloucestershire Archaeological Society*
Trans. Cymmrodorion	*Transactions of the Honourable Society of Cymmrodorion*
WHR	*Welsh History Review*

Bibliographies

The principal bibliography, now much out of date, is *A Bibliography of the History of Wales* (2nd edn, Cardiff, 1962, with supplements in *BBCS*, 20 (1962–4), 22 (1966–8), 23 (1968–70), and 24 (1970–2); a new edition, prepared by P. H. Jones, has been published in microfiche (Cardiff, 1989). There are detailed bibliographies in recent studies: Wendy E. Davies, *Wales in the early Middle Ages* (Leicester, 1982); R. R. Davies, *Conquest Coexistence and Change: Wales 1063–1415* (Oxford and Cardiff, 1987); Glanmor Williams, *Recovery Reorientation and Reformation: Wales c. 1415–1642* (Oxford and Cardiff, 1987). R. I. Jack, *Medieval Wales* (1972) is a general survey of Welsh sources for the series The Sources of History, ed. G. Elton.

Maps

A basic series of maps illustrating the history of Wales, still indispensable, is William Rees, *An Historical Atlas of Wales from Early to Modern Times* (2nd edn, 1959). His older survey in four sheets for the Ordnance Survey, *South Wales and the Border in the Fourteenth Century* (Southampton, 1932), retains its value. Historical atlases for individual shires have also been published, either in English or Welsh: *Atlas Hanesyddol Ceredigion* (Aberystwyth, 1955); *Atlas Brycheiniog* (Llandysul, 1960); *An Atlas of Anglesey* (Llangefni, 1971); *Atlas Meirionydd* (Bala, 1975); and *Atlas of Caernarvonshire* (Caernarfon, 1977). The Ordnance Survey *Monastic Britain* (South Sheet) covers Welsh religious houses (Chessington, 1950). Professor H. Carter completed the production of the *National Atlas of Wales* in 1989.

Sources

The English kings' interest in Wales means that royal records and historical narratives are rich sources for many aspects of Welsh history. So, too, are collections of material relating to major baronial families: the earls of Gloucester and of Hereford in the twelfth century, the Clares, Marshals, Mortimers and fitz Alans, in later centuries, are cases in point.

There are two major series of record publications for Wales, the Cymmrodorion Record Series, published by the Honourable Society of Cymmrodorion, and the History and Law Series of the Board of Celtic Studies of the University of Wales. Local Societies have added valuable material to this stock.

The principal narrative sources are the *Brut y Tywysogyon*, *The Chronicle of the Princes*, a thirteenth-century compilation based on earlier material, which survives in more than one version. Like the *Anglo-Saxon Chronicle*, it is a multiple source. The early annals are the *Annales Cambriae*, ed. J. Williams ab Ithel (Rolls Series, 1860). J. E. Lloyd published the annals (in three separate versions) for the period 1039–93 as an appendix to 'Wales and the coming of the Normans' (*Trans. Cymmrodorion* (1899–1900), 165–79). The two versions of the *Brut y Tywysogyon* are identified from their manuscripts as Peniarth MS 20 and the Red Book of Hergest; they have been edited and translated in a series of volumes by Thomas Jones for the History and Law Series (Cardiff, 1952, 1955). The third version, the *Brenhinedd y Saeson, The Kings of the Saxons*, is a composite source which incorporates material from English annals; this was edited and translated by Thomas Jones for the same series (Cardiff, 1971). Professor Jones discussed textual problems at length in his introductions to these volumes and in 'Cronica de Wallia and other documents from Exeter Library MS. 3154', *BBCS*, 12 (1946–8), 17–44; so also did Kathleen Hughes, 'The Welsh Latin Chronicles: Annales Cambriae and related texts', *PBA*, 59 (1973), 233–58. In terms of political history, the biography of Gruffydd ap Cynan, who ruled Gwynedd until 1137, is a remarkable survival: *History of Gruffydd ap Cynan (1054–1137)*, ed. and trans. A. Jones (Manchester, 1910). D. Simon Evans, *Historia Gruffud vab Kenan* (Cardiff, 1971), is the most recent critical study in Welsh.

Gerald of Wales was the most prolific writer Wales produced in the middle ages. His *Opera* were edited for the Rolls Series by J. S. Brewer and G. F. Warner (8 vols., 1861–91); the *Speculum Duorum*, ed. M. Richter, Yves Lefèvre and R. B. C. Huygens, with a translation by Brian Dawson (Cardiff, 1974); the *De Invectionibus*, ed. W. S. Davies in *Y Cymmrodor*, 20 (1920); the *Topographia Hibernia*, ed. J. J. O'Meara (*Proceedings of the Royal Irish Academy*, 52, sect. c, 1949); *Expugnatio Hibernica*, ed. A. B. Scott and F. X. Martin (Dublin, 1978); these are the major additions in recent years. Gerald's studies of Wales and Ireland are easily available in translation: *The Itinerary through Wales: Description of Wales*, trans. R. C. Hoare (Everyman, London, 1908, reissued 1976); *The Journey through Wales and the Description of Wales*, trans. Lewis Thorpe (Penguin, Harmondsworth, 1978); *The History and Topography of Ireland*, trans, J. J. O'Meara (1951, reissued Penguin, Harmondsworth, 1982, reprint 1985).

For the thirteenth century, two volumes of the History and Law Series are invaluable: *Calendar of Ancient Correspondence concerning Wales* (Cardiff, 1935), and *Littere Wallie* (Cardiff, 1940), both edited by J. G. Edwards, whose introduction to *Littere Wallie* especially is the basis of much which has been written about Wales in the latter half of the thirteenth century in the last fifty years. A short selection of documents relating to 1282, published by the National Library of Wales, provides good photographs of fourteen records relating to the death of Llywelyn ap Gruffydd: *1282: Casgliad o Ddogfennau: A Collection of Documents*, ed. Rhiannon Griffiths (Aberystwyth, 1986). Of many sources relating to the Edwardian settlement in Wales, *The Welsh Assize Roll 1277–84*, ed. J. Conway Davies (Cardiff, 1940), is particularly rich.

Ecclesiastical records of particular Welsh interest are comparatively sparse. In the 1940s J. Conway Davies published his *Episcopal Acts and Cognate Documents relating to Welsh Dioceses 1066–1272* (Historical Society of the Church in Wales, Cardiff, 1948–53), a diffuse calendar of documents and entries in chronicles and histories relating to Wales. The two volumes which he produced covered the dioceses of St David's and Llandaff; his material for the two northern dioceses was not published. He was an avid collector, but his critical treatment of documents has been called into question. His account of 'The records of the Church in Wales' (*NLWJ*, 4 (1945–6), 1–34) remains a useful guide. There is a very small body of monastic cartularies from Wales: Aberconwy, 'Register of Aberconwy', ed. H. Ellis, *Camden Miscellany I* (1847), 1–23; Brecon priory, *Cartularium prioratus S. Johannis evangeliste de Brecon*, ed. R. W. Banks (*Arch. Camb.*, 4th series, 13 and 14 (1882–3), subsequently issued as a single volume); Carmarthen, *Cartularium S. Johannis Baptiste de Carmarthen*, ed. T. Philips (Cheltenham, 1865). The richest unpublished source is the archive of Llanthony (overshadowed by the foundation of Llanthony Secunda at Gloucester). The records of a number of monasteries, especially in the English border shires, have much to do with property and churches in Wales: St Peter's abbey, Gloucester, *Historia et Cartularium Monasterii S. Petri Gloucestriae*, ed. W. H. Hart, 3 vols. (Rolls Series, 1863–7), and 'A Register of the Churches of the Monastery of St Peter's Gloucester' (Gloucester, Register A, fols. 82–178), ed. D. Walker, in *An Ecclesiastical Miscellany*, ed. D. Walker, W. J. Sheils and J. Kent (*B&GAS*, Record Series, vol. 11 (1976), 1–58; Haughmond, *Cartulary of Haughmond Abbey*, ed. Una Rees (Cardiff, 1985); Shrewsbury, *Cartulary of Shrewsbury Abbey*, ed. Una Rees (Aberystwyth, 1975); Worcester, *The Cartulary of Worcester Cathedral Priory*, ed. R. R. Darlington, Pipe Roll Society, New Series, 38 (1968). For the secular church, the resources of Llandaff are very rich: the main collection is the *Liber Landavensis: The Text of the Book of Llan Dâv*, ed. J. G. Evans and J. Rhys (Oxford, 1893; reissued, Aberystwyth, 1979), which must be used in conjunction with the seminal studies by Wendy Davies (see under chapter 1). The *acta* of the bishops of Llandaff have been edited by David Crouch, *Llandaff Episcopal Acta 1140–1287*, South Wales Record Society (Cardiff, 1989). A great deal of material from ecclesiastical foundations is to be found in *Cartae et alia Munimenta quae ad Dominium de Glamorganica pertinent*, ed. G. T. Clark, 6 vols. (2nd edn, Cardiff, 1910), and *Earldom of Gloucester Charters: The Charters and Scribes of the Earls and Countesses of Gloucester to A.D. 1217*, ed. R. B. Patterson (Oxford, 1973), both of which make good use of material from Margam abbey; see 'Charters of the Earldom of Hereford, 1095–1201', ed. D. G. Walker, *Camden Miscellany XXII* (1964), for material from Brecon and Llanthony. *The Letters and Charters of Gilbert Foliot*, ed. A. Morey and C. N. L. Brooke (Cambridge, 1967), draws heavily on the resources of Gloucester and Hereford cathedral archives.

A number of printed sources have been included in the sections which follow.

Welsh literary and poetic sources are amongst the most difficult for English readers to master, or for an English historian to assess. For poetry, J. P. Clancy, *Medieval Welsh Lyrics* (1965), and *The Earliest Welsh Poetry* (1970) are helpful; so are *The Oxford Book of Welsh Verse in English*, ed.

G. Jones (Oxford, 1977), and *The Penguin Book of Welsh Verse* (Harmonds-
worth, 1967). T. Parry, *Hanes Llenyddiaeth Gymraeg hyd 1900* (3rd edn,
Cardiff, 1953), was translated by H. I. Bell, *A History of Welsh Literature*
(Oxford, 1955); *A Guide to Welsh Literature*, ed. A. O. H. Jarman and G. R.
Hughes, 2 vols. (Swansea, 1976–9), and J. E. Caerwyn Williams, *The Poets
of the Welsh Princes* (Cardiff, 1978), are both helpful guides.

General studies

The classic survey of medieval Wales is J. E. Lloyd, *A History of Wales from
the Earliest Times to the Edwardian Conquest* (first published in 1911; 3rd edn,
1939; with subsequent reprints). Two volumes in *History of Wales*, ed.
Glanmor Williams, cover the period: R. R. Davies, *Conquest Coexistence and
Change: Wales 1063–1415* (Oxford and Cardiff, 1987), and Glanmor
Williams, *Recovery Reorientation and Reformation: Wales c. 1415–1642* (Oxford
and Cardiff, 1987). Two surveys of the later middle ages are especially
important, William Rees, *South Wales and the March 1284–1415: A Social and
Agrarian Study* (Oxford, 1924), and R. R. Davies, *Lordship and Society in the
March of Wales 1282–1400* (Oxford, 1978). R. R. Davies, R. A. Griffiths, I. G.
Jones and K. O. Morgan, eds., *Welsh Society and Nationhood: Historical Essays
Presented to Glanmor Williams* (Cardiff, 1984), contains a number of import-
ant studies. There are many attempts to identify the peculiar elements which
make up the Welsh personality and shape Welsh history: W. Ll. Griffiths,
The Welsh (Penguin, Harmondsworth, 1950); D. Thomas, ed., *Wales: A
New Study* (Newton Abbot, 1977); G. A. Williams, *The Welsh in their
History* (1982), and *When Was Wales?* (1985); and, in a different format,
Glanmor Williams, *Religion, Language and Nationality in Wales* (Cardiff,
1979). The *Welsh History Review* includes annual reports on articles relating
to the history of medieval Wales, and occasional reports on theses written on
Welsh history (vols. 5, 7, 9, 11). Two short but popular presentations of the
theme are A. H. Williams, *An Introduction to the History of Wales*, 2 vols.
(Cardiff, 1969), and A. J. Roderick, ed., *Wales Through the Ages* (Llandybie,
1959–60). A number of distinguished Welsh medievalists contributed
articles to the *Dictionary of Welsh Biography down to 1940* (1959) (an English
version of the basic text *Y Bywgraffiadur Cymraeg hyd 1940* (1953), for which
a supplement for 1941–50 with additional material for the original volume
was published in 1970). For place-names, see G. M. Richards, *Welsh
Administrative and Territorial Units* (Cardiff, 1969); Elwyn Davies, ed., *A
Gazetteer of Welsh Place-Names: Rhestr o Enwau Lleoedd* (2nd edn, Cardiff,
1958); B. G. Charles, *Non-Celtic Place-Names in Wales* (1938), and 'The
Welsh, their language and place-names in Archenfield and Oswestry',
Angles and Britons (O'Donnell Lectures) (Cardiff, 1963). There are important
regional studies of the borders and of Wales: R. Millward and A. Robinson,
The Welsh Marches (1971); Dorothy Sylvester, *The Rural Landscape of the
Welsh Borderland: A Study in Historical Geography* (1969); A. D. Carr,
Medieval Anglesey (Anglesey Antiquarian Society, 1982); J. E. Lloyd, ed., *A

History of Carmarthenshire, 2 vols. (Cardiff, 1935–9); A. H. Dodd, *A History of Caernarvonshire 1284–1900* (Denbigh, 1968); J. E. Lloyd, *The Story of Ceredigion (400–1277)* (Cardiff, 1937); *Glamorgan County History*, vol. III: *The Middle Ages*, ed. T. B. Pugh (Cardiff, 1971), vol. IV: *Early Modern Glamorgan*, ed. Glanmor Williams (Cardiff, 1974); Dorothy Sylvester, *A History of Gwynedd* (Chichester, 1983). Three specialist studies are J. G. Edwards, *The Principality of Wales 1267–1961: A Study in Constitutional History* (Caernarfon, 1969); R. A. Griffiths, *The Principality of Wales in the Later Middle Ages: The Structure and Personnel of Government. I. South Wales, 1277–1536* (Cardiff, 1972); R. Somerville, *A History of the Duchy of Lancaster* (1953). For Welsh towns: R. A. Griffiths, ed., *Boroughs of Medieval Wales* (Cardiff, 1978); H. Carter, *The Towns of Wales: A Study in Historical Geography* (2nd edn, Cardiff, 1966); I. N. Soulsby, *The Towns of Medieval Wales: A Study in their History, Archaeology and Early Topography* (Chichester, 1983). For buildings: R. Haslam, *The Buildings of Wales: Powys* (Cardiff, 1979); J. B. Hilling, *The Historic Architecture of Wales* (Cardiff, 1976); E. Hubbard, *The Buildings of Wales: Clwyd* (1986). On castles, the indispensable works of A. J. Taylor and D. J. Cathcart King are noted in chapter 6. In general, see D. J. Cathcart King, *Castellarium Anglicanum: An Index and Bibliography of Castles in England, Wales and the Islands*, 2 vols. (1983). For general studies of the church in Wales, see D. G. Walker, ed., *A History of the Church in Wales* (Historical Society of the Church in Wales, Penarth, 1976; reprinted 1991); E. J. Newell, *A History of the Welsh Church to the Dissolution of the Monasteries* (1895); F. Jones, *The Holy Wells of Wales* (Cardiff, 1954); D. R. Thomas, *History of the Diocese of St. Asaph*, 3 vols. (Oswestry, 1908–13); E. T. Davies, *The Story of the Church in Glamorgan, 560–1960* (1962). 'The legal position of Wales in the middle ages', by J. B. Smith, is a useful analysis, in A. Harding, ed., *Law-Making and Law-Makers in British History* (1980), 21–53. The standard work on Welsh society is a volume of collected papers, T. Jones Pierce, *Medieval Welsh Society*, ed. J. B. Smith (Cardiff, 1972). A useful supplement is L. A. S. Butler, 'The study of deserted medieval settlements in Wales (to 1968)', in M. Beresford and J. G. Hurst, eds., *Deserted Medieval Villages* (1971), 249–76. An aspect of Welsh history which matches a once-famous range of English historical studies is examined by D. H. Williams, *Welsh History through Seals* (Cardiff, 1982), supplemented by catalogues of seals in articles in *Arch. Camb.*, 133 (1984), 100–35, and 134 (1985), 162–89.

I WALES IN THE DARK AGES

Angles and Britons (O'Donnell Lectures) (Cardiff, 1963)

Baring-Gould, S., and Fisher, J., *The Lives of the British Saints*, 4 vols. (1907–13)

Binchy, D. A., *Celtic and Anglo-Saxon Kingship* (Oxford, 1970)

Bowen, E. G., *Saints, Seaways and Settlements in the Celtic Lands* (2nd edn, Cardiff, 1977)

Bromwich, R., 'The character of the early Welsh tradition', in N. K. Chadwick, ed., *Studies in Early British History* (Cambridge, 1954, reissued 1959), 83–136
ed. and trans., *The Beginnings of Welsh Poetry* (Cardiff, 1972)
Chadwick, N. K., 'Intellectual life in west Wales in the last days of the Celtic Church', in N. K. Chadwick, ed., *Studies in the Early British Church* (Cambridge, 1958, reissued 1973), 121–82
ed., *Studies in Early British History* (Cambridge, 1954, reissued 1959)
ed., *Studies in the Early British Church* (Cambridge, 1958, reissued 1973)
ed., *Celt and Saxon: Studies in the Early British Border* (Cambridge, 1963, reissued 1964)
Coplestone-Crow, B., 'The dual nature of the Irish colonization of Dyfed in the Dark Ages', *Studia Celtica*, 16/17 (1981–2), 1–24
Davies, Wendy E., 'The consecration of the bishops of Llandaff in the tenth and eleventh centuries', *BBCS*, 26 (1974–6), 53–73
An Early Welsh Microcosm: Studies in the Llandaff Charters (1978)
'Land and power in early medieval Wales', *Past and Present*, 81 (1978), 3–23
The Llandaff Charters (Aberystwyth, 1979)
'Property rights and property claims in Welsh "Vitae" of the eleventh century', in E. Patlagean and P. Riché, eds., *Hagiographie cultures et sociétés, IV–XII siècles* (Paris, 1981), 515–33
Wales in the Early Middle Ages (Leicester, 1982)
Dumville, D. N., 'Kingship, genealogies and regnal lists', in P. Sawyer and I. N. Woods, eds., *Early Medieval Kingship* (Leeds, 1977), 72–104
'The "six" sons of Rhodri Mawr: a problem in Asser's Life of King Alfred', *CMCS*, 4 (1983), 5–18
Goetinck, Glenys, 'Lifris and the Italian connection', *BBCS*, 35 (1988), 10–13
Hughes, Kathleen, *Celtic Britain in the Early Middle Ages: Studies in Scottish and Welsh Sources* (Woodbridge, 1980)
'The Celtic Church: is this a valid concept?', *CMCS*, 1 (1981), 1–20
Johns, C. W., 'The Celtic monasteries of north Wales', *Trans. Caernarvonshire Historical Society*, 21 (1960), 14–43
Jones, G. R., 'Post-Roman Wales', in H. P. R. Finberg, ed., *Agrarian History of England and Wales*, vol. I, part 2 (Cambridge, 1982), 283–382
Kirby, D. P., 'Hywel Dda: anglophil?', *WHR*, 8 (1976–7), 1–13
'Welsh bards and the border', in A. Dornier, ed., *Mercian Studies* (Leicester, 1977), 31–42
Lapidge, M., 'The Welsh Latin poetry of Sulien's family', *Studia Celtica*, 8–9 (1973–4), 68–106
Loyn, H. R., *The Vikings in Wales* (1976)
'Wales and England in the tenth century: the context of the Athelstan charters', *WHR*, 10 (1980–1), 283–301
Manley, J., 'Cledemutha: a late Saxon burh in north Wales', *Medieval Archaeology*, 31 (1987), 13–46
Maund, K. L., 'Cynan ab Iago and the killing of Gruffydd ap Llywelyn', *CMCS*, 10 (1985), 57–65

Miller, Molly, 'The foundation legend of Gwynedd', *BBCS*, 27 (1976–8), 515–32

The Saints of Gwynedd (Woodbridge, 1979)

Peden, A., 'Science and philosophy in Wales at the time of the Norman conquest: a Macrobius manuscript from Llanbadarn', *CMCS*, 1 (1981), 21–46

Rhigyfarch, *Life of St David*, ed. J. W. James (Cardiff, 1967)

Rhigyfarch, *Life of St David*, trans. A. W. Wade-Evans, *Y Cymmrodor*, 24 (1913), 1–73

Richards, G. M., 'Places and persons of the early Welsh church', *WHR*, 5 (1970–1), 339–49

'The Irish settlements in south-west Wales', *Journal of the Royal Society of Antiquaries of Ireland*, 90 (1972), 110–18

Sawyer, P., and Woods, I. N., eds., *Early Medieval Kingship* (Leeds, 1977)

Stenton, F. M., *Anglo-Saxon England* (3rd edn, Oxford, 1971) (Indispensable for early contacts between Welsh and English, and for the developments of ideas of overlordship.)

Victory, Siân, *The Celtic Church in Wales* (1977)

Walker, D. G., 'A note on Gruffydd ap Llywelyn', *WHR*, 1 (1960–3), 83–98

White, R. B., *Early Christian Gwynedd* (Bangor, 1975)

'New light on the origins of the kingdom of Gwynedd', in R. Bromwich and R. B. Jones, eds., *Astudiaethau ar yr Hengerdd* (Cardiff, 1978), 350–5

2 THE NORMANS IN WALES

Alexander, J. W., 'New evidence on the palatinate of Chester', *EHR*, 85 (1970), 715–29

Barker, P. A., and Higham, R., *Hen Domen Montgomery: A Timber Castle on the English–Welsh Border*, vol. I (1982)

Barraclough, G., *The Earldom and the County Palatinate of Chester* (Oxford, 1953)

Chandler, V., 'The last of the Montgomeries: Roger the Poitevin and Arnulf', *Historical Research*, 62 (1989), 1–14

Coplestone-Crow, B., 'The Baskervilles of Herefordshire 1086–1300', *Trans. Woolhope Naturalists' Field Club*, 43 (1979), 18–39

'The fief of Alfred of Marlborough in Herefordshire in 1086 and its descent in the Norman period', *Trans. Woolhope Naturalists' Field Club*, 45, pt ii (1986), 376–414

Crouch, D., 'Oddities in the early history of the lordship of Gower, 1107–1166', *BBCS*, 31 (1984), 133–42

Davies, R. R., 'Kings, lords and liberties in the March of Wales, 1066–1272', *TRHist.S*, 5th series, 29 (1979), 41–61

'Henry I and Wales', in H. Mayr-Harting and R. I. Moore, eds., *Studies in Medieval History Presented to R. H. C. Davies* (1985), 132–47

Edwards, J. G., 'The Normans and the Welsh March', *PBA*, 42 (1956)

Hogg, A. H. A., and King, D. J. Cathcart, 'Early castles in Wales and the Marches', *Arch. Camb.*, 112 (1963), 77–144
  'Masonry castles in Wales and the Marches', *Arch. Camb.*, 116 (1967), 71–132; 119 (1970), 119–24
King, D. J. Cathcart, 'The castles of Breconshire', *Brycheiniog*, 7 (1961), 71–94
  'Pembroke castle', *Arch. Camb.*, 127 (1978), 75–121
King, D. J. Cathcart, and Spurgeon, C. J., 'The mottes in the vale of Montgomery', *Arch. Camb.*, 114 (1965), 69–87
Kissack, K. E., *Medieval Monmouth* (Monmouth, 1974)
Le Patourel, J., *The Norman Empire* (Oxford, 1976)
  Feudal Empires: Norman and Plantagenet (1984)
Lewis, C., 'The Norman settlement of Herefordshire under William I', *Anglo-Norman Studies*, 7 (1984), 195–213
Lloyd, J. E., 'Wales and the coming of the Normans', *Trans. Cymmrodorion* (1899–1900), 122–79
  'Carmarthen in early Norman times', *Arch. Camb.*, 6th series, 7 (1907), 281–92
Mason, J. F. A., 'Roger de Montgomery and his sons 1067–1102', *TRHist.S*, 5th series, 13 (1963), 1–28
Mein, A. G., *Norman Usk* (Usk, 1986)
Nelson, L. H., *The Normans in South Wales 1070–1171* (Austin, Texas, 1966)
Orderic Vitalis, *Ecclesiastical History*, ed. and trans. Marjorie Chibnall, 6 vols. (Oxford, 1969–80) (Orderic was an articulate and informed writer with a wide knowledge of many Anglo-Norman families and, because of his birth and early life in the earldom of Shrewsbury, with a particular interest in the history of the marches and Wales.)
Owen, H., 'The Flemings in Pembrokeshire', *Arch. Camb.*, 5th series, 12 (1895), 96–106
Patterson, R. B., ed., *Earldom of Gloucester Charters: The Charters and Scribes of the Earls and Countesses of Gloucester to A.D. 1217* (Oxford, 1973)
Rees, William, 'The medieval lordship of Brecon', *Trans. Cymmrodorion* (1915–16), 165–244
Renn, D. F., *Norman Castles* (2nd edn, 1973)
Robinson, W. R. B., 'The medieval charters of Cardiff: some neglected aspects', *BBCS*, 28 (1978–80), 615–22
Round, J. H., 'The family of Ballon and the conquest of south Wales', in J. H. Round, *Studies in Peerage and Family History* (Westminster, London, 1901), 181–215
  'Domesday Herefordshire', in W. Page, ed., *Victoria County History of England, Herefordshire*, vol. I (1908), 263–307
Rowlands, I. W., 'The making of the March: aspects of the Norman settlement of Dyfed', *PBC*, 3 (1981), 142–57
Tait, J., 'Introduction to the Shropshire Domesday', in W. Page, ed., *Victoria County History of England, Shropshire*, vol. I (1908), 279–308

'Flintshire in Domesday Book', *Flintshire Historical Society Journal*, 11 (1925), 1–37

Walker, D. G., 'Miles of Gloucester, earl of Hereford', *Trans. B&GAS*, 77 (1958– 9), 66–84

'The "Honours" of the earls of Hereford in the twelfth century', *Trans. B&GAS*, 79 (1960–1), 174–211

'Charters of the earldom of Hereford, 1095–1201', *Camden Miscellany XXII* (1964), 1–75

'William fitz Osbern and the Norman settlement of Herefordshire', *Trans. Woolhope Naturalists' Field Club*, 39 (1967–9), 402–12

The Norman Conquerors, A New History of Wales (Llandybie, 1977)

'Cardiff', in R. A. Griffiths, ed., *Boroughs of Medieval Wales* (Cardiff, 1978), 103–30

'The Norman settlement in Wales', *PBC*, 1 (1978), 131–43

'The lordship of Builth', *Brycheiniog*, 20 (1982–3), 23–33

'Cultural survival in an age of conquest', in R. R. Davies, R. A. Griffiths, I. G. Jones and K. O. Morgan, eds., *Welsh Society and Nationhood: Historical Essays Presented to Glanmor Williams* (Cardiff, 1984), 35–50

Great Domesday Book, Gloucestershire, County Edition, Alecto Historical Editions (1988), fols. 162–70v

Wightman, W. E., 'The palatine earldom of William fitz Osbern in Gloucestershire and Herefordshire', *EHR*, 77 (1962), 6–17

3 THE MARCHER LORDSHIPS

Many of the books and articles noted for chapter 2 cover part of chapter 3. In addition, the following studies are useful:

Davies, R. R., 'The law of the March', *WHR*, 5 (1970–1), 1–30

Edwards, J. G., 'The Normans and the Welsh March', *PBA*, 42 (1956), 155–77

'Henry II and the fight at Coleshill: some further reflections', *WHR*, 3 (1966–7), 251–65

Flanagan, M.-T., 'Strongbow, Henry II and Anglo-Norman intervention in Ireland', in J. B. Gillingham and J. C. Holt, eds., *War and Government in the Middle Ages: Essays in Honour of J. O. Prestwich* (Woodbridge, 1984), 62–78

Griffiths, M., 'Native society on the Anglo-Norman frontier: the evidence of the Margam charters', *WHR*, 14 (1988–9), 179–216

Hillaby, J., 'Hereford gold: Irish, Welsh and English land: the Jewish community at Hereford and its clients, 1179–1253', Parts I and II, *Trans. Woolhope Naturalists' Field Club*, 44 (1984), 358–419: 45 (1985), 193–270

Howell, M., '"Regalian right" in Wales and the March: the relation of theory to practice', *WHR*, 4 (1968–9), 269–88

King, D. J. Cathcart, 'Henry II and the fight at Coleshill', *WHR*, 2 (1964–5), 367–75

Otway-Ruthven, A. J., 'The constitutional position of the great lordships of south Wales', *TRHist.S*, 5th series, 8 (1958), 1–20

Owen, D. H., 'Tenurial and economic developments in north Wales in the twelfth and thirteenth centuries', *WHR*, 6 (1972–3), 117–42

Rees, William, *Cardiff: A History of the City* (2nd edn, Cardiff, 1969)

Roderick, A. J., 'Marriage and politics in Wales, 1066–1282', *WHR*, 4 (1968–9), 1–20

'The feudal relations between the English crown and the Welsh princes', *History*, 37 (1952), 201–12

Roderick, A. J., and Rees, William, eds., 'Accounts of the Ministers for the Lordships of Abergavenny and the Three Castles 1256–7', *South Wales and Monmouthshire Record Society*, 2 (1950), 67–125; 3 (1954), 21–47; 4 (1957), 5–29

Rowlands, I. W., 'William de Braose and the lordship of Brecon', *BBCS*, 30 (1982–3), 122–33

Smith, J. B., 'Owain Gwynedd', *Trans. Caernarvonshire Historical Society*, 32 (1971), 8–71

Taylor, A. J., 'Usk castle and the Pipe Roll of 1185', *Arch. Camb.*, 99 (1946–7), 249–56

Walter Map, *De Nugis Curialium: Courtiers' Trifles*, ed. M. R. James, with J. E. Lloyd and E. S. Hartland, Cymmrodorion Record Series, no. IX (1923) (This text was revised and reissued under the editorship of M. R. James, C. N. L. Brooke and R. A. B. Mynors (Oxford, 1983).)

Warren, W. L., *Henry II* (1973) (Valuable for the interplay between Henry II's policies in England, Wales and Scotland in the setting of his continental interests.)

King John (1961) (Places John's interest in Wales and the earldom of Gloucester in the setting of Anglo-Norman politics.)

4 THE CHURCH IN WALES

Bartlett, R., *Gerald of Wales 1146–1223* (Oxford, 1982)

Birch, W. de G., *A History of Margam Abbey* (1897)

A History of Neath Abbey (1902)

Bowen, E. G., 'The monastic economy of the Cistercians at Strata Florida', *Ceredigion*, 1 (1950), 34–7

Butler, L. A. S., 'The Augustinian priory of St. Kinmark near Chepstow', *JHSCW*, 15 (1965), 9–19

'Medieval ecclesiastical architecture in Glamorgan and Gower', *Glamorgan County History*, 3 (1971), 379–415

'Neath abbey: the twelfth-century church', *Arch. Camb.*, 133 (1984), 147–51

Brooke, C. N. L., *The Church and the Welsh Border in the Central Middle Ages* (Woodbridge, 1986)

Clarke, M. L., *Bangor Cathedral* (Cardiff, 1969)

Clover, H., and Gibson, M., eds., *The Letters of Lanfranc, Archbishop of Canterbury* (Oxford, 1979)

Cowley, F. G., 'The church in Glamorgan from the Norman conquest to the beginning of the fourteenth century', *Glamorgan County History*, 3 (1971), 87–135

    The Monastic Order in South Wales 1066–1349 (Cardiff, 1977)

    'Historical Introduction', in G. R. Orrin, *Medieval Churches of the Vale of Glamorgan* (Cowbridge, 1988), 3–36

Crouch, D., ed., *Llandaff Episcopal Acta 1140–1287*, South Wales Record Society (Cardiff, 1988)

Davies, J. Conway, 'Ewenny priory: some recently found records', *NLWJ*, 3 (1944), 107–37

    'Giraldus Cambrensis', *Arch. Camb.*, 99 (1946–7), 85–108, 256–80

Davies, Wendy E., 'St Mary's Worcester and the Liber Landavensis', *Journal of the Society of Archivists*, 4 (1972), 459–85

    '*Liber Landavensis*: its construction and credibility', *EHR*, 88 (1973), 335–51

    An Early Welsh Microcosm: Studies in the Llandaff Charters (1978)

Donkin, R. A., *The Cistercians: Studies in the Geography of Medieval England and Wales* (Toronto, 1978)

Donnelly, J. S., 'Changes in the grange economy of English and Welsh Cistercian abbeys', *Traditio*, 10 (1954), 399–458

Easterling, R. C., 'The friars in Wales', *Arch. Camb.*, 6th series, 14 (1914), 323–56

Gresham, C. A., 'Archbishop Baldwin's journey through Merioneth in 1188', *Journal Merioneth Historical Society*, 10 (1985–8), 186–204

Hays, R. W., *The History of the Abbey of Aberconway 1186–1537* (Cardiff, 1963)

Jones, A., 'Basingwerk abbey', in J. G. Edwards, V. H. Galbraith and E. F. Jacob, eds., *Essays Presented to James Tait* (Manchester, 1933), 169–78

Jones, O. W., and Walker, D. G., eds., *Links with the Past: Swansea and Brecon Historical Essays* (Llandybie, 1974)

Jones, W. B., and Freeman, E. A., *The History and Antiquities of St. David's* (1856)

Knowles, D., *The Monastic Order in England* (Cambridge, 1940)

    The Religious Orders in England, 3 vols. (Cambridge, 1948–59)

Knowles, D., Brooke, C. N. L., and London, Vera, *The Heads of Religious Houses: England and Wales 940–1216* (Cambridge, 1972)

Knowles, D., and Hadcock, R. N., *Medieval Religious Houses: England and Wales* (2nd edn, 1971)

Le Neve, J., *Fasti Ecclesiae Anglicanae 1300–1541*, XI. The Welsh Dioceses, ed. B. Jones (1965)

Lewis, F. R., 'Racial sympathies of Welsh Cistercians', *Trans. Cymmrodorion* (1938), 103–18

North, F. J., *The Stones of Llandaff Cathedral* (Cardiff, 1957)

Orrin, G. R., *Medieval Churches of the Vale of Glamorgan* (Cowbridge, 1988)

O'Sullivan, J. F., *Cistercian Settlement in Wales and Monmouthshire, 1140–1540* (New York, 1947)

Pierce, T. Jones, 'Einion ab Ynyr (Anian II), Bishop of St. Asaph', *Flintshire Historical Society*, 17 (1957), 1–14

Radford, C. A. Ralegh, 'The Cistercian abbey of Cwmhir, Radnorshire', *Arch. Camb.*, 131 (1982), 58–76

Rees, William, *A History of the Order of St. John of Jerusalem in Wales and on the Welsh Border* (Cardiff, 1947)

'The priory of Cardiff and the possessions of the abbey of Tewkesbury in Glamorgan', *South Wales and Monmouthshire Record Society*, 2 (1950), 129–86

'The friars at Cardiff and Newport', *South Wales and Monmouthshire Record Society*, 4 (1958), 51–6

Richter, M., 'Professions of obedience and the metropolitical claims of St. David's', *NLWJ*, 15 (1967–8), 197–214

'Canterbury's primacy in Wales and the first stage of Bishop Bernard's opposition', *Journal of Ecclesiastical History*, 22 (1971), 177–89

'Gerald of Wales: a reassessment on the 750th anniversary of his death', *Traditio*, 29 (1973), 379–90

Giraldus Cambrensis: The Growth of the Welsh Nation (2nd edn, Aberystwyth, 1976)

'The political and institutional background to national consciousness in medieval Wales', in T. W. Moody, ed., *Nationality and the Pursuit of National Independence, Historical Studies*, 12 (Belfast, 1978), 37–55

ed., *Canterbury Professions*, Canterbury and York Society, 57 (1973)

Smith, D. M., 'The episcopate of Richard, bishop of St. Asaph: a problem of twelfth-century chronology', *JHSCW*, 24 (1974), 9–12

Walker, D. G., 'The medieval bishops of Llandaff', *Morgannwg*, 6 (1962), 5–32

'Brecon priory in the middle ages', in O. W. Jones and D. G. Walker, eds., *Links with the Past: Swansea and Brecon Historical Essays* (Llandybie, 1974), 37–65

'Gerald of Wales, archdeacon of Brecon', in O. W. Jones and D. G. Walker, eds., *Links with the Past: Swansea and Brecon Historical Essays* (Llandybie, 1974), 67–88

'Gerald of Wales. A review of recent work', *JHSCW*, 24 (1974), 13–26

'Gerald of Wales', *Brycheiniog*, 18 (1978–9), 60–70

Ward, J. C., 'Fashions in monastic endowment: the foundations of the Clare family 1066–1314', *Journal of Ecclesiastical History*, 32 (1981), 427–51

Williams, D. H., *The Welsh Cistercians: Aspects of their Economic History* (Pontypool, 1969)

White Monks in Gwent and the Border (Pontypool, 1976)

The Welsh Cistercians, 2 vols. (Caldy Island, Tenby, 1983–4)

Williams, Glanmor, *The Welsh Church from Conquest to Reformation* (Cardiff, 1962, and subsequent reissues)

'Neath abbey', in E. Jenkins, ed., *Neath and District: A Symposium* (Neath, 1974), 73–91

Williams-Jones, K., 'Thomas Becket and Wales', *WHR*, 5 (1970–1), 35–65

Williamson, E. A., 'The inimitable chancellor Bogo de Clare', *JHSCW*, 1 (1947), 15–25

Willis, Browne, *A Survey of the Cathedral Church of Llandaff* (1719)

A Survey of the Cathedral Church of Bangor (1721)

A Survey of the Cathedral Church of St. Asaph, 2 vols. (Wrexham, 1801)

Willis-Bund, J. W., ed., *Black Book of St. David's*, Cymmrodorion Record Series, 5 (1902)

5 THE CRISIS OF IDENTITY: TOWARDS A PRINCIPALITY OF WALES

Altschul, M., *A Baronial Family in Medieval England: The Clares 1217–1314* (Baltimore, 1965)

Arnold, C. J., and Huggett, J. W., 'Mathrafal, Powys: a reassessment', *BBCS*, 33 (1986), 436–51

Davies, R. R., 'Law and national identity in thirteenth-century Wales', in R. R. Davies, R. A. Griffiths, I. G. Jones and K. O. Morgan, eds., *Welsh Society and Nationhood: Historical Essays Presented to Glanmor Williams* (Cardiff, 1984), 51–69

Edwards, J. G., ed., *Calendar of Ancient Correspondence concerning Wales* (Cardiff, 1935)

ed., *Littere Wallie* (Cardiff, 1940)

Jenkins, Dafydd, 'Kings, lords and princes: the nomenclature of authority in thirteenth-century Wales', *BBCS*, 26 (1974–6), 451–62

'*Cynghellor* and Chancellor', *NLWJ*, 27 (1976), 115–18

Lewis, C. W., 'The treaty of Woodstock: its background and significance', *WHR*, 2 (1964–5), 37–65

Morgan, R., 'The foundation of the borough of Welshpool', *Montgomeryshire Collections*, 65 (1977), 7–24

Powicke, F. M., *Henry III and the Lord Edward*, 2 vols. (Oxford, 1947)

The Thirteenth Century (2nd edn, Oxford, 1962)

(Powicke's studies are perhaps the most successful attempt by an English historian to integrate Welsh affairs into his text, and certainly the most sympathetic analysis of Welsh personalities and problems by an English historian working in the classical tradition of English historical studies from the 1920s to the 1950s.)

Richter, M., 'David ap Llywelyn, the first prince of Wales', *WHR*, 5 (1970–1), 205–19

Roderick, A. J., 'The four cantreds: a study in administration', *BBCS*, 10 (1939–41), 246–55

Smith, J. B., 'The middle march in the thirteenth century', *BBCS*, 24 (1970–2), 77–93

Stephenson, D., 'The politics of Powys Wenwynwyn in the thirteenth century', *CMCS*, 7 (1984), 39–61

The Governance of Gwynedd (Cardiff, 1984)

Walker, R. F., 'Hubert de Burgh and Wales 1218–32', *EHR*, 87 (1972), 465–94

Williams, G. A., 'The succession to Gwynedd 1238–47', *BBCS*, 20 (1962–4), 393–413

6 THE EDWARDIAN CONQUEST

Arnold, C. J., 'Powis castle: recent excavations and observations', *Montgomeryshire Collections*, 73 (1985), 30–7

Avent, R., *Cestyll Tywysogion Gwynedd: Castles of the Princes of Gwynedd* (Cardiff, 1983)

Beresford, M. W., *New Towns of the Middle Ages: Town Plantation in England, Wales and Gascony* (1967; reprinted Gloucester, 1988)

Butler, L. A. S., 'The boundaries of the abbey of Aberconwy at Maenen, Gwynedd', *Arch. Camb.*, 130 (1981), 19–35

Butler, L. A. S., and Evans, D. H., 'The old vicarage, Conway: excavations, 1963–64', *Arch. Camb.*, 128 (1979), 40–103

Carr, A. D., 'The last days of Gwynedd', *Trans. Caernarvonshire Historical Society*, 43 (1982), 7–22

Llywelyn ap Gruffydd (Cardiff, 1982)

'Crown and communities: collaboration and conflict', in T. Herbert and G. E. Jones, eds., *Edward I and Wales* (Cardiff, 1988), 123–44

Chrimes, S. B., *King Edward I's Policy in Wales* (Cardiff, 1969)

Colvin, H. M., Brown, R. A., and Taylor, A. J., *The History of the King's Works: The Middle Ages*, 2 vols. (1963)

Coss, P. R., 'Sir Geoffrey de Langley and the crisis of the knightly class in thirteenth-century England', *Past and Present*, 68 (1975), 3–37

Davies, R. R., 'Llywelyn ap Gruffydd, prince of Wales', *Journal of Merioneth Historical Society*, 9 (1981–3), 264–77

'Edward I in Wales', in T. Herbert and G. E. Jones, eds., *Edward I and Wales* (Cardiff, 1988), 1–10

Dodd, A. H., ed., *A History of Wrexham* (Wrexham, 1957)

Douie, Decima, *Archbishop Pecham* (Oxford, 1952)

Edwards, J. G., 'Edward I's castle-building in Wales', *PBA*, 32 (1950), 15–81

Greenway, W., 'Archbishop Pecham, Thomas Bek and St David's 1293–6', *JHSCW*, 10 (1960), 9–16

Griffiths, J., 'The revolt of Madog ap Llywelyn in 1294–95', *Trans. Caernarvonshire Historical Society* (1955), 12–24

Griffiths, R. A., 'Aberystwyth' and 'Carmarthen', in R. A. Griffiths, ed., *Boroughs of Medieval Wales* (Cardiff, 1978), 19–46, 131–64

Herbert, T., and Jones, G. E., eds., *Edward I and Wales* (Cardiff, 1988)

Higounet, C., 'Bastides et Frontières', *Le Moyen Age*, 54 (1948), 113–31

Jack, R. I., 'Welsh and English in the medieval lordship of Ruthin', *Trans. Denbighshire Historical Society*, 18 (1969), 23–49

'Ruthin', in R. A. Griffiths, ed., *Boroughs of Medieval Wales* (Cardiff, 1978), 245–62

Kaeuper, R. W., 'The role of Italian financiers in the Edwardian conquest of Wales', *WHR*, 6 (1972–3), 387–403

King, D. J. Cathcart, 'Two castles in northern Powys: Dinas Bran and Caergwrle', *Arch. Camb.*, 123 (1974), 113–39

King, D. J. Cathcart, and Cheshire, M., 'The town walls of Pembroke', *Arch. Camb.*, 131 (1982), 58–76

Lewis, E. A., *The Medieval Boroughs of Snowdonia* (1912)

Lloyd, J. E., 'The death of Llywelyn ap Gruffydd', *BBCS*, 5 (1929–31), 349–53

Maud, R., 'David, the last prince of Wales', *Trans. Cymmrodorion* (1968), 43–62

Morris, J. E., *The Welsh Wars of Edward I: A Contribution to Medieval Military History* (Oxford, 1901)

Owen, D. H., 'The Englishry of Denbigh: an English colony in medieval Wales', *Trans. Cymmrodorion* (1974–5), 57–76

Pratt, D., 'The medieval borough of Holt', *Trans. Denbighshire Historical Society*, 14 (1965), 9–74

Prestwich, M. C., *War, Politics and Finance under Edward I* (1972)

'A new account of the Welsh campaign of 1294–5', *WHR*, 6 (1972–3), 89–94

The Three Edwards: War and State in England 1272–1377 (1980)

Edward I (1988)

Rowlands, I. W., 'The Edwardian conquest and its military consolidation', in T. Herbert and G. E. Jones, eds., *Edward I and Wales* (Cardiff, 1988), 41–72

Shirley, H. W., ed., *Royal and Other Historical Letters Illustrative of the Reign of Henry III*, 2 vols., Rolls Series (1862–6)

Simpson, W. D., 'Harlech castle and Edwardian castle plan', *Arch. Camb.*, 95 (1940), 153–69

Smith, J. B., 'The origins of the revolt of Rhys ap Maredudd', *BBCS*, 21 (1964–6), 15–63

'Llywelyn ap Gruffydd and the March of Wales', *Brycheiniog*, 20 (1982), 9–22

'Dynastic succession in medieval Wales', *BBCS*, 33 (1986), 199–232

'Welsh society and native power before the conquest', in T. Herbert and G. E. Jones, eds., *Edward I and Wales* (Cardiff, 1988), 41–72

Smith, Llinos B., 'The death of Llywelyn ap Gruffydd: the narratives reconsidered', *WHR*, 11 (1982–3), 200–14

'The gravamina of the community of Gwynedd against Llywelyn ap Gruffydd', *BBCS*, 31 (1984), 158–76

'Llywelyn ap Gruffydd and the Welsh historical consciousness', *WHR*, 12 (1984–5), 1–28

Spurgeon, C. J., 'Builth castle', *Brycheiniog*, 18 (1978–9), 47–59

Stephenson, D., *The Last Prince of Wales* (Buckingham, 1983)

'Llywelyn ap Gruffydd and the struggle for the principality of Wales 1258–82', *Trans. Cymmrodorion* (1983), 39–61

Studd, J. R., 'The Lord Edward's lordship of Chester', *Trans. Historical Society of Lancashire and Cheshire*, 128 (1979), 1–25

Taylor, A. J., 'Master James of St George', *EHR*, 65 (1950), 433–57

'Castle building in Wales in the thirteenth century: the prelude to construction', in E. M. Jope, ed., *Studies in Building History* (1961), 104–33

The History of the King's Works in Wales 1277–1330 (1973). Reprinted from H. M. Colvin, R. A. Brown, and A. J. Taylor, eds., *The History of the King's Works*, 2 vols. (1963), vol. I, 293–408

'Castle building in thirteenth-century Wales and Savoy', *PBA*, 63 (1977), 104–33

Studies in Castles and Castle-Building (1985)

Williams, Glanmor, 'The church and monasticism in the age of Conquest', in T. Herbert and G. E. Jones, eds., *Edward I and Wales* (Cardiff, 1988), 97–122

Williams-Jones, K., 'Caernarfon', in R. A. Griffiths, ed., *Boroughs of Medieval Wales* (Cardiff, 1978), 73–102

7 UNDER THE HEEL: WALES IN THE FOURTEENTH CENTURY

Davies, R. R., 'Richard II and the principality of Chester, 1397–9', in F. R. H. DuBoulay and C. M. Barron, eds., *The Reign of Richard II: Essays in Honour of May McKisack* (1971), 256–79

'Colonial Wales', *Past and Present*, 65 (1974), 3–23

'Race relations in post-conquest Wales', *Trans. Cymmrodorion* (1974–5), 32–56

Lordship and Society in the March of Wales 1282–1400 (Oxford, 1978)

Dodd, A. H., 'Welsh and English in east Denbighshire: a historical retrospect', *Trans. Cymmrodorion* (1940), 34–65

Edwards, J. G., 'Sir Gruffydd Llwyd', *EHR*, 30 (1915), 589–601

'The battle of Maes Madog and the Welsh war of 1294–5', *EHR*, 39 (1924), 1–12

'Madog ap Llywelyn, the Welsh leader in 1294–5', *BBCS*, 13 (1948–50), 207–10

Fryde, N. M., *List of the Welsh Entries in the Memoranda Rolls, 1282–1343* (Cardiff, 1974)

Greenway, W., 'Archdeacons of Carmarthen in the fourteenth century', *Carmarthenshire Antiquary*, 3 (1959–61), 63–71

'The election of John of Monmouth, bishop of Llandaff, 1287–97', *Morgannwg*, 5 (1961), 3–22

Griffiths, M., 'The manor in medieval Glamorgan: the estates of the Raleigh family in the 14th and 15th centuries', *BBCS*, 32 (1985), 173–201

Griffiths, R. A., 'The revolt of Llywelyn Bren', *Glamorgan Historian*, ed. S. Williams, 2 (1965), 186–96

'The revolt of Rhys ap Maredudd, 1287–8', *WHR*, 3 (1966–7), 121–43

'Medieval Severnside: the Welsh connection', in R. R. Davies, R. A. Griffiths, I. G. Jones and K. O. Morgan, eds., *Welsh Society and Nationhood: Historical Essays Presented to Glanmor Williams* (Cardiff, 1984), 70–89

Holmes, G. A., *The Estates of the Higher Nobility in Fourteenth-Century England* (Cambridge, 1957)

Jack, R. I., 'The cloth industry in medieval Ruthin', *Trans. Denbighshire Historical Society*, 12 (1963), 10–25

'The cloth industry in medieval Wales', *WHR*, 10 (1980–1), 443–60

Johnstone, Hilda, *Edward of Caernarvon 1284–1307* (Manchester, 1946)

Lloyd-Jones, J., 'The court poets of the Welsh princes', *PBA*, 34 (1948), 167–97

Morgan, R., 'The barony of Powys, 1275–1360', *WHR*, 10 (1980–1), 1–42

'The territorial divisions of medieval Montgomeryshire', *Montgomeryshire Collections*, 69 (1981), 9–44; 70 (1982), 11–32

Philips, J. R. S., *Aymer de Valence, Earl of Pembroke 1307–24: Baronial Politics in the Reign of Edward II* (Oxford, 1972)

Pratt, D., 'Fourteenth-Century Bromfield and Yale; a gazetteer of lay and ecclesiastical territorial units', *Trans. Denbighshire Historical Society*, 27 (1978), 89–149

'Bromfield and Yale in English politics 1387–99', *Trans. Denbighshire Historical Society*, 30 (1981), 109–47

Prestwich, M. C., 'A new account of the Welsh campaign of 1294–5', *WHR*, 6 (1973–4), 89–92

Rees, William, *South Wales and the March 1284–1415: A Social and Agrarian Study* (Oxford, 1924)

Smith, J. B., 'Edward II and the allegiance of Wales', *WHR*, 8 (1976–7), 139–71

Smith, Llinos B., 'The Arundel charters of the lordship of Chirk in the fourteenth century', *BBCS*, 23 (1968–70), 153–66

'The gage and land market in late medieval Wales', *Economic History Review*, 2nd series, 29 (1976), 537–50

'Seignorial income in the fourteenth century: the Arundels in Chirk', *BBCS*, 28 (1978–80), 443–57

'The statute of Wales, 1284', *WHR*, 10 (1980–1), 127–54

'The governance of Edwardian Wales', in T. Herbert and G. E. Jones, eds., *Edward I and Wales* (Cardiff, 1988), 73–96

Sylvester, Dorothy, 'From tribalism to landed gentry of Flintshire', *Flintshire Historical Society Journal*, 31 (1983), 29–56

Waters, W. H., 'The first draft of the statute of Rhuddlan', *BBCS*, 4 (1927–9), 344–8

The Edwardian Settlement of Wales in its Administrative and Legal Aspects (Cardiff, 1935)

Williams-Jones, K., *The Merioneth Lay Subsidy Roll, 1292–93* (Cardiff, 1976)

Welsh law

For convenience, studies in Welsh law have been grouped together in this section of the bibliography.

Butler, L. A. S., 'Domestic building in Wales and evidence of the Welsh law', *Medieval Archaeology*, 31 (1987), 47–58

Celtic Law Papers Introductory to Welsh Medieval Law and Governance (Studies Presented to the International Commission for the History of Representative and Parliamentary Institutions), 42 (Brussels, 1973)

Charles-Edwards, T. M., 'The heir-apparent in Irish and Welsh law', *Celtica*, 9 (1971), 180–90

Davies, R. R., 'The twilight of Welsh law', *History*, 51 (1966), 143–64
'The survival of the blood-feud in medieval Wales', *History*, 54 (1969), 338–57
'The law of the March', *WHR*, 5 (1970–1), 1–30

Edwards, J. G., *Hywel Dda and the Welsh Lawbooks* (Bangor, 1929)
'The historical study of the Welsh lawbooks', *TRHist.S*, 5th series, 12 (1961), 141–55
'The royal household and the Welsh lawbooks', *TRHist.S*, 5th series, 13 (1962), 163–76
'Studies in the Welsh laws since 1928', *The Welsh Laws* (*WHR*, Special Number, 1963), 1–18

Ellis, T. P., *Welsh Tribal Law and Custom in the Middle Ages*, 2 vols. (Oxford, 1926)

Emmanuel, H. D., 'The Latin texts of the Welsh laws', *The Welsh Laws* (*WHR*, Special Number, 1963), 25–32
'Studies in the Welsh laws', in Elwyn Davies, ed., *Celtic Studies in Wales* (Cardiff, 1963), 71–100
The Latin Texts of the Welsh Laws (Cardiff, 1967)

Huws, D., 'Leges Howelda at Canterbury', *NLWJ*, 19 (1976), 340–4; 20 (1977), 95
The Medieval Codex with Reference to the Welsh Law Books (Aberystwyth, 1980)

Jenkins, Dafydd, 'Legal and comparative aspects of the Welsh laws', *The Welsh Laws* (*WHR*, Special Number, 1963), 51–60
'A lawyer looks at Welsh land law', *Trans. Cymmrodorion* (1967), 220–48
'The significance of the law of Hywel Dda', *Trans. Cymmrodorion* (1977), 54–76

Jenkins, Dafydd, and Owen, Morfydd E., 'Welsh laws in Carmarthenshire', *Carmarthenshire Antiquary*, 18 (1982), 17–28
eds., *The Welsh Law of Women* (Cardiff, 1980)

Pierce, T. Jones, 'Social and historical aspects of the Welsh laws', *The Welsh Laws* (*WHR*, Special Number, 1963), 33–50
'The laws of Wales: the kindred and the bloodfeud', in J. B. Smith, ed., *Medieval Welsh Society* (Cardiff, 1972), 289–307
'The law of Wales. The last phase', in J. B. Smith, ed., *Medieval Welsh Society* (Cardiff, 1972), 369–89
Richards, G. M., ed. and trans., *The Laws of Hywel Dda* (Liverpool, 1954)
Stephenson, D., *Thirteenth-Century Welsh Law Courts* (Aberystwyth, 1980)
Wade-Evans, A. W., ed., *Medieval Welsh Law* (Oxford, 1909)
Waters, D. B., *The Comparative Legal Method: Marriage, Divorce and the Spouses' Property Rights in Early Medieval European Law and Cyfraith Hywel* (Aberystwyth, 1982)
Wiliam, Aled Rhys, 'The Welsh texts of the laws', *The Welsh Laws* (*WHR*, Special Number, 1963), 19–24

8 RESURGENCE AND DECLINE: THE FIFTEENTH CENTURY

Allmand, C. T., 'A bishop of Bangor during the Glyn Dŵr revolt', *JHSCW*, 18 (1968), 47–56
Bradley, A. G., *Owen Glyndwr and the Last Struggle for Welsh Independence* (1901)
Carr, A. D., 'The barons of Edeyrnion 1282–1485', *Journal Merioneth Historical Society*, 4 (1961), 187–93, 289–301
'The making of the Mostyns: the genesis of a landed family', *Trans. Cymmrodorion*, 31 (1982), 5–27
Chotzen, T. M., 'Yvain de Galles in Alsace-Lorraine', *BBCS*, 4 (1927–9), 231–40
Coward, B., *The Stanleys: Lords Stanley and Earls of Derby, 1385–1672* (Manchester, 1983)
Davies, R. R., 'Owain Glyn Dŵr and the Welsh squirearchy', *Trans. Cymmrodorion* (1968), 150–69
Gabriel, J. R., 'Wales and the Avignon papacy', *Arch. Camb.*, 7 (1923), 70–86
Griffiths, R. A., 'Some partisans of Owain Glyn Dŵr at Oxford', *BBCS*, 20 (1962–4), 282–92
'The rise of the Stradlings of St Donats', *Morgannwg*, 7 (1963), 15–47
'Gruffydd ap Nicholas and the rise of the house of Dinefwr', *NLWJ*, 13 (1964), 256–68
'Some secret supporters of Owain Glyn Dŵr', *Bulletin of the Institute of Historical Research*, 37 (1964), 77–100
'Gruffydd ap Nicholas and the fall of the house of Lancaster', *WHR*, 2 (1964–5), 213–31
'Gentlemen and rebels in later medieval Cardiganshire', *Ceredigion*, 5 (1964–7), 143–67
'Wales and the Marches', in S. B. Chrimes, ed., *Fifteenth-Century England 1399–1509* (Manchester, 1972), 145–72

Griffiths, Rhidian, 'Prince Henry, Wales, and the royal exchequer, 1400–13', *BBCS*, 32 (1985), 202–15
   'Prince Henry's war: armies, garrisons and supply during the Glyndŵr rising', *BBCS*, 34 (1987), 165–73
Isaacson, R. F., ed., *The Episcopal Registers of St David's 1397–1518*, 3 vols. (1917–20)
Jack, R. I., 'Owain Glyn Dŵr and the lordship of Ruthin', *WHR*, 2 (1964–5), 303–22
Jones, D. C., 'The Bulkeleys of Beaumaris 1440–1547', *Trans. Anglesey Antiquarian Society* (1961), 1–20
Jones, E. J., 'Bishop John Trevor (II) of St Asaph', *JHSCW*, 23 (1968), 36–46
Jones, T., 'Pre-Reformation Welsh versions of the Scriptures', *NLWJ*, 4 (1946), 97–114
Lewis, F. R., 'The rectors of Llanbadarn Fawr from 1246–1360', *Arch. Camb.*, 92 (1937), 133–46
   'The history of Llanbadarn Fawr, Cardiganshire, in the later middle ages', *Trans. Cardiganshire Antiquarian Society*, 12 (1938), 16–41
Lewis, H. E., 'Welsh Catholic poetry of the fifteenth century', *Trans. Cymmrodorion* (1911–12), 23–41
Lloyd, J. E., *Owen Glendower* (Oxford, 1931)
McFarlane, K. B., *The Nobility of Medieval England* (Oxford, 1973)
Morgan, C. L., 'Prophecy and Welsh nationhood in the fifteenth century', *Trans. Cymmrodorion* (1985), 9–25
Owen, E., 'Owen Lawgoch: Yvain de Galles', *Trans Cymmrodorion* (1899–1900), 6–18
Philips, J. R. S., 'When did Owain Glyn Dŵr die?', *BBCS*, 24 (1970–2), 59–70
Pugh, T. B., *The Marcher Lordships of South Wales 1415–1536* (Cardiff, 1963)
Rawcliffe, C., *The Staffords, Earls of Stafford and Dukes of Buckingham* (Cambridge, 1978)
Rosenthal, J., *The Estates and Finances of Richard Duke of York, 1441–60* (Lincoln, Nebraska, 1968)
Skeel, C. A. J., *The Council in the Marches of Wales* (1903)
Slack, W. J., *The Lordship of Oswestry, 1393–1607* (Shrewsbury, 1951)
Smith, J. B., 'The regulation of the frontier of Meirionydd in the fifteenth century', *Journal Merioneth Historical Society*, 5 (1965–6), 105–11
   'The last phase of the Glyn Dŵr rebellion', *BBCS*, 22 (1966–8), 250–60
Thomson, D., 'Cistercians and schools in late medieval Wales', *CMCS*, 3 (1982), 76–80
Williams, Glanmor, *Owen Glendower* (Oxford, 1966)
   'The church in Glamorgan from the fourteenth century to the Reformation', *Glamorgan County History*, 3 (1971), 135–66
Williams, J. E. Caerwyn, 'Medieval Welsh Prose', *Proceedings of the Second International Congress of Celtic Studies 1963* (Cardiff, 1966), 65–97

Williams-Jones, K., 'The taking of Conwy castle, 1401', *Trans. Caernarvon-shire Historical Society*, 39 (1978), 7–43

9 A NEW DAWN? THE COMING OF THE TUDORS

Griffiths, R. A., and Thomas, R. S., *The Making of the Tudor Dynasty* (Gloucester, 1985)

Gunn, S. J., 'The regime of Charles, duke of Suffolk, in north Wales and the reform of Welsh government 1509–25', *WHR*, 12 (1984–5), 461–94

Jones, E. G., ed., *Exchequer Proceedings concerning Wales* (Cardiff, 1939)

Lewis, E. A., ed., *Early Chancery Proceedings concerning Wales* (Cardiff, 1937)

Pryce, A. I., *The Diocese of Bangor in the Sixteenth Century* (Bangor, 1923)

Pugh, T. B., 'The indenture for the Marches between Henry VII and Edward Stafford, duke of Buckingham', *EHR*, 71 (1956), 436–9

Rees, William, ed., *Calendar of Ancient Petitions relating to Wales* (Cardiff, 1975)

Robinson, W. R. B., 'Knighted Welsh landowners 1485–1558: a provisional list', *WHR*, 13 (1986–7), 282–98

'The marriages of knighted Welsh landowners 1485–1558', *NLWJ*, 25 (1987–8), 387–98

Smith, J. B., 'Crown and community in the principality of north Wales in the reign of Henry Tudor', *WHR*, 3 (1966–7), 145–71

Williams, Glanmor, *Harri Tudur a Chymru: Henry Tudor and Wales* (Cardiff, 1985)

'Henry Tudor: Mab Darogan (Son of Prophecy)', *Carmarthenshire Antiquary*, 21 (1985), 3–9

The following material has been published since this book was written:

Crouch, David, 'The earliest original charter of a Welsh king', *BBCS*, 36 (1989), 125–31

Davies, R. R., *Domination and Conquest: the experience of Ireland, Scotland and Wales, 1100–1300* (Cambridge, 1990)

Siddons, Michael, 'Welshmen in the service of France', *BBCS*, 36 (1989), 161–84

Turvey, R. K., 'The marcher shire of Pembroke and the Glyndŵr rebellion', *WHR*, 15 (1990), 151–68

INDEX

Place-names have been identified by modern counties: Clwyd; Dyfed; Mid, South and West Glamorgan; Gwent; Gwynedd; and Powys. Dyfed, Gwynedd and Powys do not cover the same areas as the medieval principalities. For convenience, Anglesey has been retained as a separate entity, though it is part of Gwynedd.

Where a member of a Welsh dynasty has been mentioned in the text, a reference in italic type has been given to the genealogy in which the name is to be found.